# MANAGING COST IN TODAY'S MANUFACTURING ENVIRONMENT

# MANAGING COST IN TODAY'S MANUFACTURING ENVIRONMENT

**Peter Chalos**

Dept. of Accounting
University of Illinois at Chicago

Prentice Hall, Englewood Cliffs, New Jersey 07632

Library of Congress Cataloging-in-Publication Data

Chalos, Peter.
    Managing cost in today's manufacturing environment / Peter
  Chalos.
       p.    cm.
    Includes bibliographical references and index.
    ISBN 0-13-616277-0
    1. Managing product cost.    I. Title
  HF5R97.13.C95  1991
  65R.8'02--dc20                                    92-10591
                                                      CIP

Acquisition Editor    Garret White
Production Editor    Maureen Wilson
Cover Designer    Franklyn Graphics
Prepress Buyer    Trudy Pisciotti
Manufacturing Buyer    Bob Anderson

© 1992 by Prentice-Hall, Inc.
A Simon & Schuster Company
Englewood Cliffs, New Jersey 07632

Printed in the United States of America
10  9  8  7  6  5  4  3  2  1

ISBN 0-13-616277-0

Prentice-Hall International (UK) Limited, *London*
Prentice-Hall of Australia Pty. Limited, *Sydney*
Prentice-Hall Canada Inc., *Toronto*
Prentice-Hall Hispanoamericana, S.A., *Mexico*
Prentice-Hall of India Private Limited, *New Delhi*
Prentice-Hall of Japan, Inc., *Tokyo*
Simon & Schuster Asia Pte. Ltd., *Singapore*
Editora Prentice-Hall do Brasil, Ltda., *Rio de Janeiro*

To Jacqueline and Sarah,
with affection

# CONTENTS

**PART TWO:** <u>New Cost Management Practices</u>

# PREFACE

This book is about cost - specifically how to optimally manage product cost in an increasingly competitive business environment. Many of today's middle and upper level managers rely on accounting information that is simply not designed for their decision making needs. Managerial accounting systems often reflect yesterday's rather than today's production technology, and are more concerned with external reporting requirements than strategic cost information.

The purpose of this text is to evaluate the dramatic changes occurring in today's manufacturing environment and to assess their impact upon extant cost systems. Alternative costing and control paradigms are suggested for remedying deficiencies of extant cost systems.

First, the exponentially increasing literature that has recently appeared in conference proceedings, periodicals, cases and monographs is summarized and integrated into a cohesive whole. A critical assessment is made of this literature. Second, alternative cost systems are proposed. Finally, actual corporate cases are included that exemplify these alternative systems.

The reader should recognize potential cost practices in his/her own manufacturing environment that are deficient with respect to product costing, control and strategic cost management. Hopefully, some of the proposed cost systems may be helpful in both motivating and instituting needed cost management change.

Any book draws its inspiration from many sources. In particular, I would like to recognize the seminal thoughts of Bob Kaplan in this area. The corporate contributions of Duke Dahmen at Tellabs; Chris Schena at Caterpillar; Glen Neidermann at Hughes Aircraft; Bryan Ahlborn at Deloitte & Touche; Ian McKillop and Howard Armitage at the University of Waterloo; and Frank Gonsalves and Ashish Pradhan at Price Waterhouse are particularly appreciated. Editorial review and assistance was thoughtfully provided by Mian Asif at the University of Illinois at Chicago and John Willig at Prentice Hall. Additional helpful comments were provided by anonymous reviewers and colleagues at the University of Illinois at Chicago. All limitations of course remain my own.

Peter Chalos

# MANAGING COST IN TODAY'S MANUFACTURING ENVIRONMENT

# Part One

# COST CHALLENGES FACING TODAY'S MANUFACTURERS

# Chapter One

# INTRODUCTION

In order to successfully compete in today's manufacturing environment, astute cost management is essential. Unfortunately, too many firms are not deriving the maximum benefit from their cost accounting systems necessary for informed product costing, control and long term strategic planning.

The purpose of this book is threefold. One objective is to summarize for the uninitiated reader the revolutionary changes occurring on the factory floor, and as a result, the attendant costing challenges faced by today's cost and production managers. A second objective is proactive. New cost and control paradigms are discussed and illustrated. A final objective is to illustrate, via actual corporate cases, how these new paradigms are being implemented.

At the conclusion of this book, perhaps what the thoughtful reader will appreciate is how costing and control, taken in historical perspective, has not fundamentally changed. What has occurred, however, over the past twenty years has been a succession of environmental factors which managerial accounting has largely ignored. The prominence accorded external financial reporting requirements, the emphasis on short term accounting returns, poorly designed incentive plans, burgeoning overhead costs, inefficient production systems, and inexact product costing are all a reflection of mediocre costing and control systems. It is in this sense that the new cost paradigms discussed in this book are not revolutionary. Rather they serve as a reminder that the fundamental dictates of sound economic practice should not be forgotten.

**Part One** of the book provides background on why there is a need for managerial accounting to revamp its current practices. This is accomplished by first describing the technology that characterizes today's manufacturing environment, and then demonstrating how today's accounting systems have failed to adapt to this environment.

Among the manufacturing technologies discussed are Numerically Controlled Machinery, Computer-Aided Design and Manufacturing, Robotic Equipment, Flexible Manufacturing Systems, and Computer Integrated Manufacturing Systems. Many of the technologies attempt to increase the manufacturing flexibility of the firm without affecting the mass production benefits being derived. Standalone technologies significantly outnumber the more fully integrated technologies which require a more long term commitment for success as well as a complete revamping of the production operation.

Changes in plant configuration through the implementation of Just-in-Time production is also discussed. Significant improvements in production can be derived on the shop floor without costly investment in the above technologies. The "pull-through" concept of production, combined with the simplification of all aspects of production that underlie JIT philosophy, lead to significant improvements in productivity.

The evolution of production technology has resulted in fundamental changes in cost behavior and product cost mix. Decreasing lead times, shorter product life cycles, and inventory reduction and elimination all affect product costing, control and strategic planning. The increasing shift from variable to semi-fixed and fixed costs, along with new types of indirect costs, raises

4

issues of cost traceability to product and expense recognition. Current management accounting systems have come under fire for their inability to report product cost with any significant degree of accuracy.

Concerns about the ability of existing control systems to monitor and signal inefficiencies related to new manufacturing technologies also arise. Many traditional standard control systems monitor signals that do not economically maximize the firm resource allocations. In addition, accounting information often tends to be too dated for proactive utilization.

A final shortcoming of extant cost systems is their inability to address long term structural investment and strategic planning decisions. To the extent that the costs and benefits of new manufacturing investments are incorrectly estimated, synergistic effects of equipment configuration ignored, and short term performance emphasized, structural investments may be suboptimal. The firm must understand its long term competitive advantage in the market place. Cost information can and should be integrated into strategic planning, but rarely is.

Cost accounting is too often defined in terms of short term costing and control, while neglecting long term strategic implications. A thorough understanding of competitive cost structure is essential strategic information. A full value chain analysis of the firm's own cost structure, from supplier to customer, is also of vital strategic importance.

**Part Two** of the text is divided into three fundamental areas where new management techniques can improve firm performance: Operational Costing and Control; Structural Decision Making; and Strategic Cost Management.

A new method for improving operational costing, Activity Based Costing, is discussed. The Activity Costing model attempts to minimize arbitrary allocation of cost, by focusing on transactions that are the causes of cost. These transactions are then related to product lines. Specific applications of Activity Based Costing are provided in Cellular Manufacturing and Flexible Manufacturing environments.

On the control side, the primary focus is on how to reduce non-value added costs and improve quality. A non-value added cost is one that adds no value to the product from the customer's perspective. All non-value added costs from pre- through post-production are discussed. New real time control measures and statistical process control are proposed as alternatives to traditional standard costing. Included are many non-financial performance measures.

Improvements in operational costing and control are only one means of making the firm more efficient. Structural decision making is concerned with determining optimal economies of scale and technology. Without an ability to precisely measure cost-benefit considerations of capital investment, the firm will be laboring at a competitive disadvantage. How to marshall state of the art capital resources and optimally deploy them are additional cost management issues.

Strategic investment considerations are discussed both in terms of qualitative as well as quantitative indicators. Optimal asset deployment is explained through the Just-in-Time paradigm. While many firms invest in new technologies, empirical evidence indicates that return on inventory and plant and equipment assets could be increased. Improvements in inventory management and production processes are outlined.

Finally, strategic aspects of cost analysis are discussed. Too few firms consider the long term strategic implications of cost analysis. Several emerging paradigms are provided, outlining how a firm might improve its strategic costing. Greater attention to life cycle costing and the recognition of product costs is important. Value engineering in terms of target costing to market and decomposition of the value chain of production costs improves long term strategic planning. Strategic cost analysis also reveals the firm's long term market prospects relative to its competitors. All of these approaches are designed to improve the competitive posture and strategic planning of the firm.

**Part Three** of the text focuses on actual corporate implementations of new cost methods. Innovative Operational Costing and Control are illustrated through Activity Based Costing and Non-Valued Added case descriptions. An example of implementing Cost of Quality is provided. In the structural cost arena, cases are included on new Just-in-Time production systems and innovative Capital Budgeting methods.

Throughout the book, the assumption is made that the uninitiated reader has at least a conversational knowledge and familiarity with cost management. Beyond this, no expertise is presumed. Rather, the ideas proposed are intended to serve as a catalyst for concerted managerial action across all functional areas of management.

# Chapter Two

# MANUFACTURING TODAY

To remain internationally competitive, U.S. industries are undergoing radical transformation in production technology. One of Kodak's highly automated disc film manufacturing plants employs only 100 people, yet produces in excess of $120 million of business. Allen Bradley's contactor plant in Milwaukee has sales exceeding $50 million, yet is run by a skeletal production staff of only five operators. Increasingly, such dramatic changes in labor are not uncommon. Not only is the mix of human and investment capital shifting, the manufacturing process itself is undergoing radical transformation. For instance, Ford reduced inventories by $750 million through better supplier coordination. Over an eight year period, a Matsushita plant in the U.S. increased production volume by 40% while reducing defects from 150 to only 3 per 100 sets produced.

Some of these impressive achievements have come about through revolutionary technological means; others have been accomplished through simple redirection of management practices and production processes. Frequently one entails the other. Instituting technological change requires attentive forethought to production processes. This often enables significant economies and efficiencies to be realized prior to the implementation of the actual production change. Regardless of how productivity improvements are realized, U.S. factories are in the throes of significant change.

Typically, manufacturers may be classified as either mass or batch producers. The former include producers of high volume standardized products that involve continuous and sequential production. Batch manufacturers, on the other hand, produce fewer standardized products in lower volumes. The latter production process is relatively sporadic with more work-in-process, and is usually less automated. Industry practice reveals that the sectors most prone to technological change involve such mass production products as machinery tools, automotive parts and industrial electronics. Capital investment in these sectors has been increasing exponentially and the equipment itself has undergone radical changes with the advent of computerization (see Exhibit 2-1).

## Exhibit 2-1

TYPES OF ADVANCED MANUFACTURING
(Percentage of Respondents)

**Advanced Manufacturing Hardware**

Standalone Technology:

| | |
|---|---|
| Computer Aided Design | 50 |
| Computer Aided Engineering | 42 |
| Robotics Equipment | 22 |
| Numerically Controlled Machines | 45 |
| Automated Operating Systems | 33 |
| Computer Aided Inspection | 32 |
| Flexible Manufacturing Systems | 10 |
| Computer Integrated Manufacturing | 13 |

**Physical Arrangement**

| | |
|---|---|
| Group Similar Machinery | 47 |
| Cellular Manufacturing | 21 |
| Synchronous Flow | 39 |

Source: Howell, R.A., J.D. Brown, S.S. Soucy and A.H. Seed, Management Accounting in the New Manufacturing Environment. Montvale, N.J.: National Association of Accountants, 1987, p. 13.

9

As can be seen in Exhibit 2-1, standalone technologies significantly outnumber Flexible Manufacturing Systems (FMS) or Computer Integrated Manufacturing (CIM) systems. New production technologies also frequently lead to reconfigured plant layouts. Traditional manufacturing, in which similar machinery is clustered together, is giving way to cellular and synchronous manufacturing. This involves sequential production operations, joined by a single piece of equipment or alternatively configured pieces of equipment that perform a series of operations.

In addition, the above technologies, as illustrated in Exhibit 2-2, have varying degrees of computerization and mechanization sophistication. While Numerically Controlled Machinery (NCM) involves little computerization and medium mechanization, the converse holds true for Computer-aided Design and Computer-aided Manufacturing (CAD/CAM) systems.

**Exhibit 2-2**

DEGREES OF COMPUTERIZATION/MECHANIZATION

| Production Technology | Computerization | Mechanization |
|---|---|---|
| Numerically Controlled Machinery | LOW | MEDIUM |
| Direct Numerically Controlled Machinery | HIGH | MEDIUM |
| CAD/CAM Systems | HIGH | LOW |
| Robotic Equipment | HIGH | MEDIUM |
| Cellular Manufacturing | HIGH | HIGH |
| Computer Integrated Manufacturing | VERY HIGH | VERY HIGH |
| Flexible Manufacturing Systems | HIGH | HIGH |

This chapter will provide an overview of the various manufacturing technologies that characterize today's manufacturing systems. Production aspects of Numerically Controlled Machines and Robotic Equipment, Computer Aided Design and Manufacturing,

Cellular Manufacturing, Computer Integrated Manufacturing, and Flexible Manufacturing Systems will be discussed in that order. New production characteristics of Just-in-Time and Materials Requirement Planning will also discussed.

## NUMERICALLY CONTROLLED
## AND ROBOTIC MACHINERY

Numerically Controlled Machines (NCMs) are usually stand-alone computerized machines that perform a variety of raw material manufacturing operations such as milling, drilling and boring. The machines may be linked to each other via a central computer (direct NCMs). The technological capabilities of these machines vary significantly. For example, the more advanced numerically controlled machines have the ability to perform many different types of manufacturing operations, while the simpler ones are limited to a handful of processes.

The need for direct labor to accompany the machine also varies by machine type. Less sophisticated NCMs require more direct labor intervention in the loading and handling of raw material and physical inspection of the units produced. More advanced machinery may have robotic loading, automated materials handling and electronic sensors for quality inspection. Not only is direct labor reduced with advanced machinery, but physical output is also increased. Older machinery frequently requires a person for each machine, whereas more recent technology enables a single operator to simultaneously attend to several machines.

Other production characteristics of NCMs include the ability of more advanced machinery to record actual or "real" time worked on a particular job. This enables manufacturing time devoted to a particular product to be recorded, improving overhead allocations for subsequent costing and control of the manufacturing process itself. Some machines have multiple loading stations that allow a set up for the next job to be performed on a station while the current job proceeds uninterrupted on another station.

**Exhibit 2-3**

NUMERICALLY CONTROLLED MACHINERY

| Low Tech | High Tech |
|---|---|
| Manually Loaded | Robotically Loaded |
| Single Tool | Multi-Tool |
| Absence of Time Measures | Real Machine Time |
| Manual Handling | Automated Materials Handling |
| Single Operator-Single Machine | Single Operator-Multi Machines |
| Physical Inspection | Electronic Sensors |
| Low Output | High Output |
| Few Operations | Many Operations |

The production characteristics of first and second generation NCMs are summarized in Exhibit 2-3. As can be seen, the evolution of machine flexibility; degree of direct and indirect labor intervention; and amount of robotic and automated materials handling has been significant.

## COMPUTER-AIDED DESIGN AND MANUFACTURING

Computer-aided Design and Manufacturing (CAD/CAM) has evolved significantly over the past ten years. There are presently in excess of 6000 CAD/CAM systems in operation and their growth is forecasted to be in excess of 30% during the 1990's.[1] CAD/CAM applications are found primarily in aerospace, automotive and electronic industries. What exactly does a CAD/CAM system entail?

A typical turnkey operation includes a database to retrieve drawings and manufactured components; design prototypes for electronic or mechanical computer simulation; and numerically

12

controlled programs for robotics and production processes. Ancillary packages might include production scheduling, such as a Materials Requirement Planning (MRP) system, or a computerized supplier link. While both the design and the manufacturing components of CAD/CAM may exist independently, databases should ideally be integrated. For example, the design database might generate a bill of materials for manufacturing. Alternatively, simulated designs of various prototypes might be used for estimating product costs.

Key elements of computerized design and manufacturing are shown in Figure 2-1. As can be seen, CAD/CAM elements are linked to an integrated database of manufacturing data. This allows

**Figure 2-1**

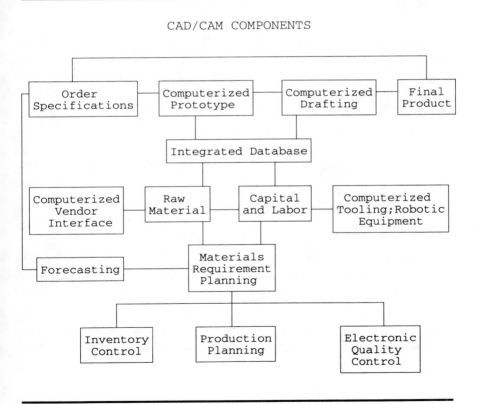

CAD/CAM COMPONENTS

the firm to more accurately design to customer specifications, while simultaneously being aware of the full costing implications of order changes. Other CAD benefits include improved drawing quality and increased design productivity.

Although the average manufacturer allocates approximately 4% of its resources to product design and engineering, these early decisions have tremendous implications for subsequent product costs. It is estimated that upon design completion, some 80% of product cost has already been built into the production process. **A key benefit of CAD therefore is not to reduce the actual 4% design cost; rather it is to decrease built-in manufacturing cost**. Another simultaneous benefit is that product quality is improved. For example, reducing parts in a product design does not merely decrease raw material cost. More importantly, it decreases quality problems and reduces overhead associated with raw material handling.

CAM involves production process planning and scheduling, robotic equipment, automated materials handling and computer-aided quality control. These computerized enhancements to traditional manufacturing have several advantages. As indicated in Figure 2-1, customer orders may be "exploded" into detailed materials requirement planning for sub-component product processing. This computerized scheduling minimizes inventory buildups and reduces cycle times. Computerized tooling, robotic equipment and quality sensors further improve productivity by decreasing direct labor involvement in the production process.

Productivity improvements in the order of 3:1 to 10:1 have been reported with CAM equipment. Design costs have decreased and human error has been significantly reduced as direct labor intervention is minimized. Shorter lead times, due to better materials requirement planning, and reduced set ups are also reported. 50% reductions in cycle time have been noted and reconfigured plant layouts have resulted in two- and threefold decreases in space.

While the potential benefits of CAD/CAM systems are significant, pitfalls also exist.   Primary among these are the numerous system linkages required between design, manufacturing and accounting systems, and between internal and external databases.  Integrated databases require standardized software and hardware.  The software must not only be helpful in deciding what to build; it must also be able to tell the machine how to build it. Another problem involves investment justification for the purchase. Many of the costs and benefits of CAD/CAM systems are very uncertain, making appropriation decisions difficult to quantitatively justify.


## CELLULAR MANUFACTURING

Manufacturing cells represent another step in the evolution of production change.   Cells reflect changes in the production configuration rather than in hardware.  These so called "islands of automation" represent an extension of process manufacturing and assembly to individual product cells.  Machines are configured in U-shaped proximity, eliminating the need for extensive transportation and inventory. Instead, simple transportation devices are used to move products from one machine to another.  Different parts may be manufactured within a cell, and products may be worked on by all machinery or a subset of the machinery.  The parts have similar set up and cycle times, tooling and fixture requirements and quality control measures.

Production of the same parts "family" is repetitive and an operator typically runs one or more machines within a cell.  A typical manufacturing cell is shown in Figure 2-2.  Relatively homogeneous incoming raw material is subjected to various drilling, boring, grinding and finishing production operations.  As shown, one or two operators maybe responsible for the various activities in the cell, such as set ups, re-tooling, preventative maintenance, loading and inspection.

**Figure 2-2**

## MANUFACTURING CELL

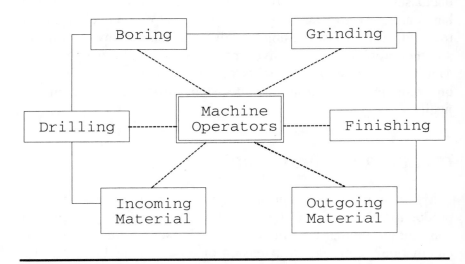

## COMPUTER INTEGRATED MANUFACTURING

Production has rapidly evolved from clustered to cellular manufacturing with the eventual goal being computer integrated manufacturing (CIM). It may generally be stated that cost accounting has not evolved in a parallel fashion. Clustered production places similar machining operations together. This leads to semi-finished material criss-crossing the plant, depending on the location of the next production operation, as depicted in Figure 2-3. The result is extended production cycle time, excessive materials handling, and increased rework and work-in-process inventory.

As production evolves from clustered to cellular manufacturing, different work stations as previously described are grouped into a cell to produce a product family. While the products are different, they employ common raw material, tooling, set up, labor, cycle times and work flow. Essentially, heterogeneous low volume production is differentially grouped and treated as a product family under more homogeneous cell process costing.

A complete CIM installation ties together several manufacturing cells or islands of automation as shown in Figure 2-3. A fully integrated CIM factory would have automated design cells feeding automated boring, in turn feeding automated finishing and so on through automated inspection and outbound freight. A centralized computer system would oversee the entire operation. In such an environment, throughput would be maximized and labor input minimized. Tooling and materials handling would be completely automated and integrated with production scheduling. Planning and

## Figure 2-3

CLUSTERED vs. CIM MANUFACTURING

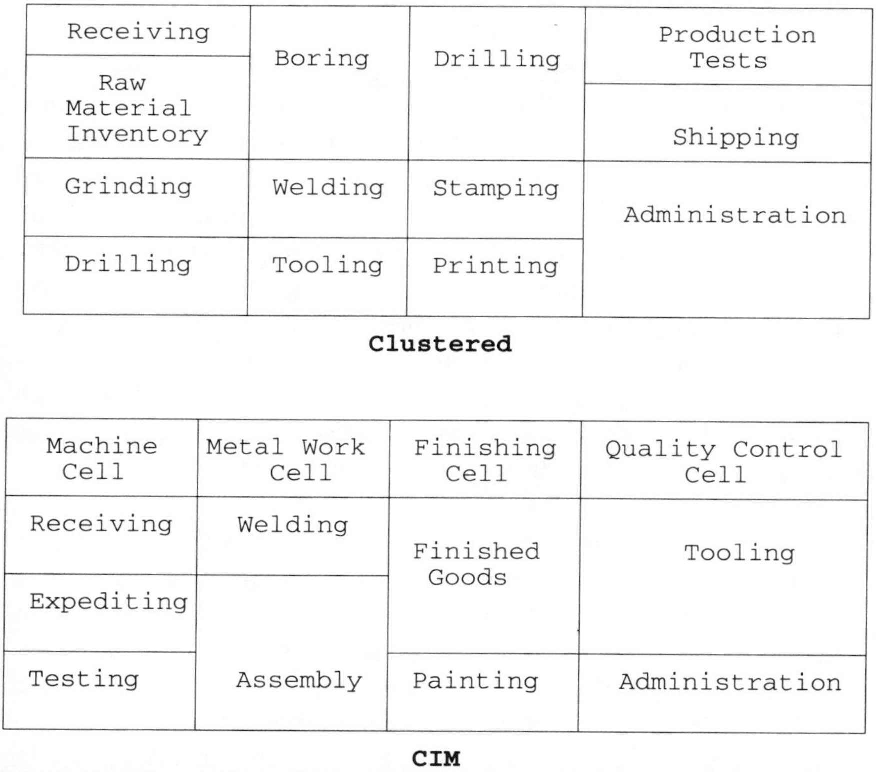

| Receiving | Boring | Drilling | Production Tests |
| --- | --- | --- | --- |
| Raw Material Inventory | | | Shipping |
| Grinding | Welding | Stamping | Administration |
| Drilling | Tooling | Printing | |

**Clustered**

| Machine Cell | Metal Work Cell | Finishing Cell | Quality Control Cell |
| --- | --- | --- | --- |
| Receiving | Welding | Finished Goods | Tooling |
| Expediting | | | |
| Testing | Assembly | Painting | Administration |

**CIM**

production databases would also be fully integrated. Vendor requisitions and production would be triggered by demand with no buffer stocks between machine operations.

There are relatively few fully integrated CIM installations. The General Electric dishwasher plant in Louisville, Kentucky, is one such example. Another is the $300 million I.B.M. photocopier plant in Charlotte, North Carolina. One of the most impressive CIM installations is found at Nippon Steel. Nippon Kokan's highly integrated steel plant required some $3.5 billion of investment. The result is an extensive network of computers and automated materials handling equipment. Continuous steel casting and recycling exists and production workers are few and far between.

## FLEXIBLE MANUFACTURING SYSTEMS

FMS were initially implemented in the mid 1960's when Molins Ltd., a British manufacturer of cigarette making machinery, designed an FMS to machine, transport and store parts and tools. The first U.S. installation at Caterpillar Tractor was done by Kearney and Trecker, which is still the largest U.S. supplier of FMS. Today's dominant suppliers of FMS are based in the U.S., Europe and Japan. Several large firms such as Renault, General Motors and British Leland have elected to develop their own in-house FMS technology. The first firms to utilize FMS in the U.S. were in the truck, farm and construction industry. Today, primary U.S. users include automotive, aerospace, defense and construction industries. Automobile users are significant in Europe, while the machine tool industry is a primary user in Japan.

European applications tend to involve shop floor automation such as machine tools, materials handling and robotic equipment to a higher degree. U.S. firms focus more on software such as CAD/CAM components and MRP applications. A typical user is Yamazaki Machine Works, which has a practically unmanned plant where 14 FMS produce machine tool components. Another is Vought aerospace, an LTV subsidiary, which purchased a $10 million FMS to produce parts for the B1 bomber. Of the plane's

2000 parts, 500 are machined on the FMS, reducing an estimated 200,000 conventional machine hours to about 70,000.

General Electric's much discussed locomotive plant in Erie, Pennsylvania, has 9 FMS that perform set ups, transportation and chip removal. Milling, machining and boring machines are equipped with robotic tool changers. An automated transportation system moves material between the 21 work stations in the system. This has led to a twofold productivity increase, significant quality improvement, decrease in cycle time from 16 days to 16 hours, a 38% increase in capacity utilization and a 25% reduction in floor space. Scaled down FMS's also exist. An FM cell is distinguished from a system more in terms of magnitude than definition. Usually a cell includes only some of the above mentioned components. It may also involve a small subset of plant activities, for instance 5% or 10% of floor space.

In 1985, there were approximately 50 completely automated FMS in the U.S. and 200 worldwide. By 1990, the number of U.S. systems had reached an estimated 300 operating systems. The average system investment in 1985 was some $3.5 million, a not insignificant amount. Cost components of these systems are machinery (50%), materials handling (10%), tools and fixtures (25%) and miscellaneous items (15%). FMS cells, which are considered to be less integrated and smaller in scope than full systems, were estimated at 250 in 1985, and are currently estimated to number some 2000. These figures indicate that despite a significant investment outlay, more and more firms are opting for FMS.

What are the technological changes involved in FMS? An FMS is an agglomeration of two or more programmable machines that can readily switch production operations from one product to another. This machine flexibility is what distinguishes an FMS from other standalone machinery. A cluster of machine tools and an inter-machine transportation system exists that shuttles tools from one machine to another. Typical machine operations include milling, boring and drilling. Welding and assembly systems are also possible. The transportation machinery, or so called materials

19

handling system, shuttles parts between work stations. While old transportation lines previously used in mass production had this capability, they could not accommodate heterogeneous products.

An example of a typical FMS is depicted in Figure 2-4. The production configuration is physically similar to cellular manufacturing. However the machining flexibility and inter-machine linkages differ, as do the degree of automated handling and inspection. Also, all operations are centrally controlled by computer.

An FMS employs robotic equipment and computer controlled handling systems to link the various programmable machinery. The system is generally used in low to medium volume production situations involving heterogeneous but related products. The result is a family of parts, varying from one to several hundred, which may be produced in quantities ranging from one to several

**Figure 2-4**

FLEXIBLE MANUFACTURING SYSTEM

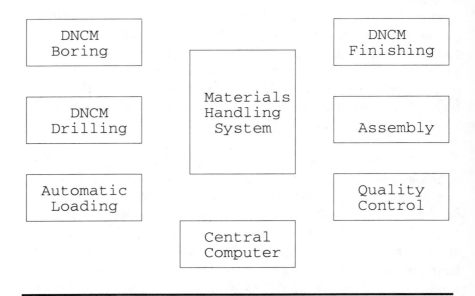

thousand. For example, the Ingersoll-Rand plant in Roanoke, Virginia, can handle 500 different machine tool parts and 16 different part designs. These systems are sometimes complemented by Automated Storage and Retrieval Systems for raw material and parts, plus automated washing and inspection stations. Labor for systems is generally engineering, maintenance and quality control labor. Loading and unloading and set ups may or may not be required, depending on the degree of automation.

Increasingly, orders are being relayed directly to the plant with exact customer specifications. Japanese manufacturers are on the cutting edge of this technology in cars, semiconducters, steel and bicycles. At the National Bicycle Industry, buyers can choose 18 models of bicycles with over 200 color combinations. Individual specifications of frames, tires and pedals are possible. Carrying inventory for so many combinations would be virtually impossible. Instead, orders are faxed directly to the factory when received, whereupon a computer determines a production bar code. Machine tools and Robotic Equipment that form part of the FMS read the bar code and fabricate the bicycle according to exact customer specifications. Customized production is clearly the industrial challenge of the future.

The advent of a computerized NCM is the first step towards a Flexible Manufacturing System. To be successful, the implementation of the FMS should be evolutionary rather than revolutionary. Efficient process manufacturing and cost system implementation must precede costly investment in an FMS that presumes efficient plant configuration. Simply reconfiguring the plant may eliminate the need for costly investment. John Deere for example, which has extensive experience with FMS, has found that improved production processes may eliminate the need for costly automated production systems. Given this cautionary note, it is worth examining when such systems reap tangible dividends for the firm.

## Costs and Benefits of FMS

The production benefits of FMS are many. Primary among

these is the increasing variability of product output available because of machine flexibility. This in turn leads to more economically viable low production volumes. Production quality also increases as responsibility increases within the cell, leading to less scrap and rework. Computerization decreases set up costs, and direct labor and reduces lead times. This in turn decreases work-in-process between work stations and therefore reduces space requirements. As product heterogeneity increases, demand is less prone to cyclical swings, increasing machine utilization rates. Response time also decreases as flexible machining and assembly can accommodate changes in customer specifications. This also leads to faster market reaction times for new products.

While these benefits may appear to be significant, they are not always realized. Investment costs are often underestimated. Labor problems may arise with unions and machine problems may be unanticipated. A recent study found that U.S. firms trailed badly behind Japanese companies in successful FMS implementation.[2] As shown in Exhibit 2-4, the average number of parts produced per U.S. system was only 10 compared to nearly 100 for the Japanese firms. Conversly, U.S. volume per part was much higher, 1727 versus 258, suggesting that the U.S. systems were being used in a counter-productive fashion. High volumes were coupled with fewer parts, defeating the purpose of the FMS. Capacity utilization was also lower and significantly fewer new parts were introduced per year by U.S. firms. Finally, virtually no U.S. systems were reported to be unattended, raising the question of how significant the direct labor savings of FMS actually were. These rather sobering findings suggest that FMS have excellent production potential which may not always be realized.

## JUST-IN-TIME SYSTEMS

Just in Time, or JIT, is a manufacturing philosophy that has significant implications for cost management. Although pioneered by the Japanese over 20 years ago, it is only now beginning to make significant inroads into U.S. manufacturing practices. What are the characteristics of a JIT environment? Essentially, JIT

**Exhibit 2-4**

### FLEXIBLE MANUFACTURING SYSTEMS
### in the UNITED STATES & JAPAN

|  | United States | Japan |
|---|---|---|
| Years to Develop | 2.5-3.0 | 1.25-1.75 |
| Machines per System | 7 | 6 |
| Different Parts per System | 10 | 93 |
| Annual Part Volume | 1,727 | 258 |
| Number of Parts per Day | 88 | 120 |
| Number of New Parts per Year | 1 | 22 |
| Unattended Systems | 0 | 18 |
| Rate Utilization | 52% | 84% |

Source: R. Jaikumar, "Postindustrial Manufacturing," Harvard Business Review, Nov.-Dec. 1986, p. 70.

implies that the firm produces only to demand, without the benefit and cost of buffer inventories. Production is dictated by demand and "pulled" through the system rather than "pushed," suggesting that JIT is not feasible for firms whose demand is highly unpredictable.

Traditional manufacturing involves one or more sequential production processes. Raw material inventory exists as well as buffer stocks of work-in-process and finished goods. An acceptable predetermined rate of defects is budgeted and feedback regarding these defective products is provided only at the end of the production period. Plant support services such as quality control or maintenance are usually centrally located within the plant.

A typical plant layout is shown in Figure 2-5. Raw material enters the plant via receiving, where it is stored prior to production. Various work-in-process departments sequentially perform manufacturing operations, at the termination of which the product is inspected and packaged for finished goods prior to customer shipment. In reality, the sequential production process may involve additional inter-departmental flows, as production is reworked.

The JIT manufacturing layout is radically different. Materials are delivered directly to the production area, reducing materials handling. Production is grouped into homogeneous product families. A manufacturing cell is responsible for performing all operations on a particular product. While the production cell may appear to be no more than a variant of the sequential production encountered in the traditional plant layout, significant differences exist. First, raw material is received for production only when required, eliminating raw material storage.

Second, each cell has its own machinery required for all manufacturing operations. An operator is responsible for several

**Figure 2-5**

## TRADITIONAL PLANT LAYOUT

| Receiving | | | |
|---|---|---|---|
| Raw Material Storage | Department X | Department Y | Department Z |
| Department A | Repair and Maintenance | Quality Control | Finished Goods Inventory |
| Department B | | | |
| Department C | Scheduling | | Plant Support |
| Finished Goods Shipping | | Accounting | Personnel |

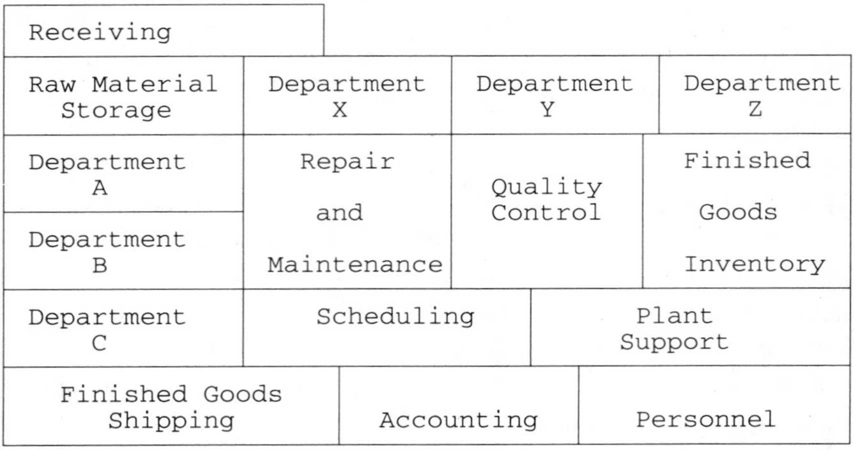

**Figure 2-6**

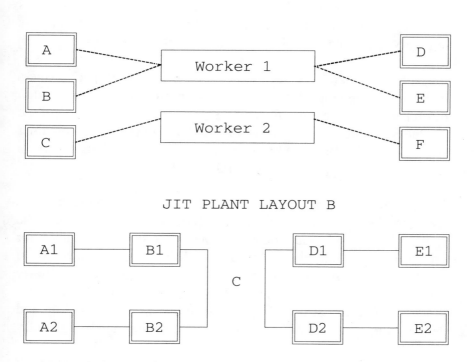

JIT PLANT LAYOUT A

JIT PLANT LAYOUT B

machines, as shown in Figure 2-6. This has several advantages. First workers are more flexible, enabling them to work on many operations rather than only one, which is the case in the traditional plant layout. This means that various sub-operations of the production process are interdependent. The operator of machine A is the same as that of machine B. If a production problem arises at a particular point in the process, the operator will slow down or stop the process until the problem is rectified. In this way, work-in-process inventory is not built up between production operations.

Quality is also improved under JIT production. Previously, operation A might have been done in such a way as to cause problems for operator B. Because each operation was independent, there was no incentive for A to be cognizant of B's subsequent manufacturing problems. This problem is alleviated under group technology, as operators are now interdependent. Also, many of the support services previously necessary under traditional layouts are now localized. For example, raw material and work-in-process handling is minimized or eliminated. Preventative maintenance is regularly performed within the cell, as is quality control.

Kanban is a Japanese term for cards attached to parts containers in JIT environments. Kanban are used to pull production through the JIT system. Demand for parts is pulled backwards through the production system, as shown in Figure 2-7. As parts in a container are used for final assembly, withdrawal Kanban is detached from the container and placed in a withdrawal box.

When the withdrawal box reaches a predetermined level, it is taken to the store of the preceding production process. At the store, the Kanban production requirements are signalled to the prior production process via a production Kanban so that work on another lot of units might begin. Vendor Kanban are similarly used for raw material requirements. A small buffer work-in-process equal to that used in final assembly is then picked up and delivered to the assembly station to replace what has been used.

The advantage of the Kanban method is that inventory is not built

**Figure 2-7**

---

### KANBAN PROCESS

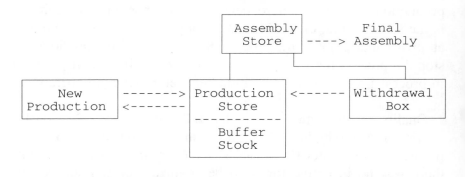

up at prior production stages until used. A delay in one part of the system stops the entire production process. The virtual absence of work-in-process between assembly stations makes all system components interdependent. Not only does this prevent raw material or work-in-process from being stockpiled, but it also signals quality and production problems along the line and encourages team problem solving. Kanban is best utilized when production is level. If there is much variation in external demand, buffer stocks would be required, as in an MRP environment. The pull system is not a panacea in a highly variable production environment.

## MATERIALS REQUIREMENT PLANNING

Like JIT, Materials Requirement Planning, or MRP, is demand driven by finished product. Product demand explodes a master production schedule into sub-schedules of sequenced part runs for individual sub-components. MRP proceeds through the bill of materials and releases parts only according to the predetermined production schedule. Different lead times and buffer work-in-process are used to balance production. The goal is to balance production in such a way as to minimize lead times and decrease buffer stock amounts. Unlike JIT, optimal lot sizes are the result. Theoretically, if MRP could reduce the optimal lot sizes to one, then the two systems would be similar.

MRP is particularly valuable in production environments where demand is unpredictable and lead times are highly variable. Unfortunately, MRP systems frequently have difficulty estimating lead times accurately. Although only one lead time is permitted in MRP optimization, variance in actual lead times exists. Thus, "worst case" lead times are built into MRP planning, increasing inventory buffer stocks. Because production scheduling is completely predetermined and relatively inflexible, no behavioral incentives exist for production workers to decrease lead times. These MRP limitations suggest that, when demand is relatively stable and predictable, a simpler, more flexible, and less centralized production scheduling system is more efficacious.

## SUMMARY

In the past decade, manufacturing changes have been occurring at an exponential rate. Technology has evolved from simple standalone NCM to RE, CAD/CAM and CIM. In tandem with technological change, production improvements have taken place within the plant. Cellular Manufacturing and Just-in-Time processes have had a profound impact upon production.

Numerous benefits have ensued from technological and production changes. Product heterogeneity has increased; labor productivity has risen; quality has improved; and inventories have been reduced. Several problems remain, however. U.S. manufacturers must continue to make appreciable investments in capital equipment in order to remain internationally competitive. Comparative data from Western Europe and Japan suggest that the U.S. is lagging in capital expenditure investment. Furthermore, U.S. manufacturers do not always derive maximum productivity from their existing investments. Again empirical evidence suggests that room for further productivity improvements exists.

A question central to this book is whether or not the revolutionary changes taking place on the production floor are being reflected in cost control and in the accounting systems. New production processes entail fundamental changes in existing cost pools and cost behavior. If cost information is deficient, it is virtually impossible to assess whether or not a firm is operating in the most economically efficient manner.

Subsequent chapters will provide a conceptual framework that characterizes efficient cost and control systems in the new manufacturing environment. This framework will be illustrated with both numerical examples as well as state of the art cost system descriptions of firms that are on the forefront of new cost system design.

# REFERENCES

1. E. Teicholz, <u>CAD/CAM Handbook</u>, McGraw-Hill: New York, 1985.

2. R. Jaikumar, "Postindustrial Manufacturing," <u>Harvard Business Review</u>, Nov.-Dec. 1986.

# BIBLIOGRAPHY

Bennett, R.E., J.A. Hendricks, D.E. Keys, and E. J. Rudnicki. <u>Cost Accounting For Factory Automation</u>. Montvale, N.J.: National Association of Accountants, 1987.

Cooper, R. <u>The Ingersoll Milling Machine Company</u>. Case #9 186-189. Boston, Mass: Harvard Business School Press, 1988.

Dilts, D.M. and G.W. Russell. "Accounting For the Factory of the Future." <u>Management Accounting</u> (April, 1985): 34-42.

Engwall, R.L. "CIM/JIT Investment Justification." <u>Journal of Cost Management</u> (Fall, 1989): 35-39.

Foster, G. and C.T. Horngren. "Flexible Manufacturing Systems: Cost Management and Cost Accounting Implications." <u>Journal of Cost Management</u> (Fall, 1988): 16-24.

Frescoln, L. "The CAM-I Cost Accounting Model and Cost Accounting at Williams International." In R. Capettini and D.K. Clancy, eds., <u>Cost Accounting, Robotics and The New Manufacturing Environment</u>: 6.1-6.20. Sarasota, FL: American Accounting Association, 1987.

Hayes, R.H. and R. Jaikumar. "Manufacturing's Crisis: New Technologies, Obsolete Organizations." <u>Harvard Business Review</u> (Sept. - Oct. 1988): 77-85.

Howell, R.A., J.D. Brown, S.R. Soucy and A.H. Seed. <u>Management Accounting in the New Manufacturing Environment</u>. Movtvale, N.J.: National Association of Accountants, 1987.

Jaikumar, R. "Postindustrial Manufacturing." <u>Harvard Business Review</u> (Nov.-Dec. 1986): 70-76.

Marks, P.A. "Understanding CAD/CAM's Strategic Importance." <u>Journal of Cost Management</u> (Winter, 1988): 33-38.

Schonberger, R.J. "Frugal Manufacturing." <u>Harvard Business Review</u> (Sept. - Oct. 1987): 95-101.

_____. <u>World Class Manufacturing</u>. New York: Free Press, 1986.

_____. <u>Japanese Manufacturing Techniques</u>. New York: Free Press, 1982.

Schubert, J.K. "The Pitfalls of Product Costing." <u>Journal of Cost Management</u> (Summer, 1988): 16-26.

Wells, J. "Selecting Cost Management Practices: A Decision Model." In A.M. King and N.E. Hadad, eds., <u>Cost Accounting For the '90's: Responding to Technological Change</u>: 229-240. Montvale, N.J.: National Association of Accountants, 1988.

Young, C. and A. Greene. <u>Flexible Manufacturing Systems</u>. New York: American Management Association, 1986.

# Chapter Three

# EXTANT COST SYSTEMS

This chapter discusses the inability of today's accounting systems to meet current cost management needs. First, characteristics and trends that distinguish today's manufacturing from that of the past are outlined. This is followed by a detailed discussion and numerous illustrations of how today's accounting systems do not account for today's manufacturing cost.

## CURRENT PRODUCTION TRENDS

Chapter Two's review of new manufacturing technologies suggests that these technologies have at least three things in common. First, is the exponential increase in **automation.** Second there is the fundamental change in **production flow**. Lastly, each of the technologies is accompanied by an increase and improvement in the availability of **data on the production process**.

What are the results of the above characteristics on cost in a manufacturing environment? The effects may briefly be summarized as follows:

### Shift in Cost Behavior

With the increased use of automation and advanced technology on the factory shop floor, more and more of manufacturing cost is becoming fixed in nature. This is occurring because increasingly capital is being substituted for labor. As a consequence, cost which was originally *directly traceable* to products is now being *allocated* to product instead.

## Reduced Inventories

New production technologies, with their emphasis on flexibility and speed, have resulted in a drastic reduction in the level of inventory present on the shop floor at any given moment. The disappearance of much Raw Material and Work-in-Process inventory has significant implications as to the level of importance today's accounting systems should attach to inventory valuation.

## Shorter Production Lead Times

The reconfiguration of the factory floor has reduced, by several fold, the time it takes to convert raw material into finished product. The flow of product across various "departments" has in many cases been entirely eliminated, with product now manufactured in a matter of hours rather than weeks. Such reconfiguration of the manufacturing floor has significant implications in terms of the definition of cost centers used in the design of existing cost systems.

## Shorter Product Lifecycles

With the rapid increase in technology and competitive forces, products are facing much shorter lifecycles. This leaves little room for "on-the-factory-floor" improvements in product cost and quality. As a result, increasing emphasis is being placed on perfecting the product from the beginning, at the design phase. The reduced time frame also makes it necessary to consider all costs, from designing and testing, to manufacturing and selling the product, in determining the profitability of the product.

## Emphasis on Product Quality

With advanced technology and automation has come the promise of high levels of quality without correspondingly high cost. Attempts to manufacture higher quality products have been a driving force in the shift towards advanced technology on the factory floor. As a result, it has become imperative for today's cost systems to be able to derive the cost of producing a low quality product and match it against the additional investment needed to raise the quality level of the product.

## SHORTCOMINGS OF EXTANT COST SYSTEMS

To what extent do the above production trends portend a shift in the nature of cost systems? Limitations of current cost systems can be defined in terms of five principle areas that together comprise the umbrella of cost management in a manufacturing environment: Product Costing; Cost Control; Inventory Management; Capital Investment; and Strategic Costing.

## Product Costing

Product Costing systems have simply not adapted to the changes occurring in manufacturing. This is reflected by a general disatisfaction with existing cost systems. A recent survey indicated that some 54% of managers felt "dissatisfied" with product costs and indicated that "they needed improvement".[1] This percentage increased to 76% in high technology environments.

Calculation of product cost in a manufacturing environment involves three basic steps:

* Classifying cost by behavior (**Product vs Period Costs**).
* Segregating it into distinct cost pools (**Cost Center Definition**).
* Assigning the cost to products (**Overhead Allocation**).

**Product vs Period Costs**: Traditional product costing first distinguishes between product and period costs. The former include raw material, direct labor and overhead required to manufacture a product. The latter typically involve selling and administrative costs not directly related to production. This distinction has been drawn for financial reporting purposes to better match expenses to revenue under GAAP. Costs that can theoretically be traced to products are capitalized. Other costs are considered to expire as a function of time. Changes in manufacturing technology have occured that directly affect this traditional distinction.

One of these changes involves the traceability of cost to individual products. Technologies such as FMS permit heterogeneous production in low volumes heretofore unimagined. In such a production environment, allocating certain cost components, such as variable overhead and direct labor, to an individual product becomes much more difficult.

Classification of fixed and variable cost behavior is also changing. Traditionally, raw material and direct labor is considered to be a variable cost, while overhead is divided between fixed and variable components. In some FMS environments, direct labor no longer exists, as the system is able to function unmanned. When direct labor does exist, it has more of the characteristics of a fixed cost. Typically, it is spread over many products and does not vary directly with production volume. Labor is usually loading and unloading material, or mounting tools. Production scheduling becomes another function of direct labor. These activities are more akin to fixed costs, yet traditional cost systems continue to treat labor as a variable cost. Furthermore, these same systems do not allocate increasing fixed overhead costs to products, but instead continue to treat them as period costs. Yet these fixed costs are in essence substitutes to shrinking labor costs and should be part of the product cost.

**Cost Center Definitions**: How costs are accumulated plays an important role in the eventual accuracy of the derived product costs. With the enormous production changes that have taken place, in terms of reorganization, on the factory floor, the question remains as to the whether extant cost systems have adapted their cost center structures to match these changes. With few exceptions, the response of extant cost systems, at least in the area of cost centers, has been positive. Part of the reason is simply that introduction of automation to a labor intensive production floor does not create too much difficulty in terms of segregating the new cost centers from existing ones.

Still, care needs to be exercised in choosing the most obvious solution as to the cost center structure. For instance, treating a production cell as a single cost center can result in a number of discrepancies, including diproportionate allocation of overhead to parts using significantly different machine time.

**Overhead Allocation**: A charge historically levelled at managerial accounting is that it is subsumed by the dictates of financial reporting requirements. Because of the concern with matching aggregate periodic overhead expenses to revenue, financial reporting is typically concerned with absorbing total overhead rather than tracking it to specific products. This is because auditors are concerned with matching aggregate periodic Cost of Goods Sold to Revenue. Accurate product costing however requires much finer disaggregated product cost data. Which overhead costs add value to the product, and which can be reduced or eliminated? Is cycle time a truer reflection of depreciation expense than calendar period? To the extent that financial reporting is emphasized at the expense of managerial accounting, such issues are downplayed.

The burden rate used to absorb overhead may be adequate for financial reporting, as overhead is eventually picked up one way or another. Managerially speaking however, the more overhead cost pools are disaggregated and related to appropriate cost drivers, the more accurate product costing becomes. Financial reporting may also inventory only traditional product costs of labor, material and overhead while treating equally important logistical or distribution product costs as period expenses.

Typically, variable overhead is presumed to change with volume of output. In reality, many variable overhead items increase in a stepwise or semi-variable fashion relative to output. This occurs because many of the cost drivers related to various variable overhead cost pools do not vary linearly with volume. Figure 3-1 illustrates the relative mix of variable, semi-variable and fixed overhead costs typically found in new production environments. As can be seen, semi-variable costs represent a significant portion of overhead. To the extent that these costs are considered directly variable with volume of output, product costing will be inaccurate.

Not only do many cost systems not distinguish types of overhead cost behavior, they frequently use either an insufficient number of cost pools and/or incorrect allocation bases for the cost pools in question. In fact, empirical evidence suggests that as many as one third of firms use a single overhead rate. The result is that overhead costs are not accurately tracked to the product that generates the cost. This problem is compounded when product diversity exists. Although each product makes different demands upon overhead components, this is not recognized when an average rate is used. The problem is further accentuated by large volume differences between products. Because volume is typically used to allocate overhead costs, many of which do not vary directly with volume, this results in high volume items being overcosted and low volume items being undercosted.

**Case Example:** Several of the above issues are summarized in the following actual case. Firm XYZ is a large manufacturer. The company recently introduced 6 NCMs and an Automated Handling System to transport products between each machine. The machines are able to work several different products, each requiring different amounts of production time. Only one technician supports the manufacturing operation, performing preventative maintenance and making minor adjustments and repairs as necessary. The firm continues to classify the technician as direct labor and uses this basis to absorb overhead. Absorption is on a plant wide basis and the firm uses a normalized rate based on estimated costs and volume for subsequent overhead allocation purposes.

**Figure 3-1**

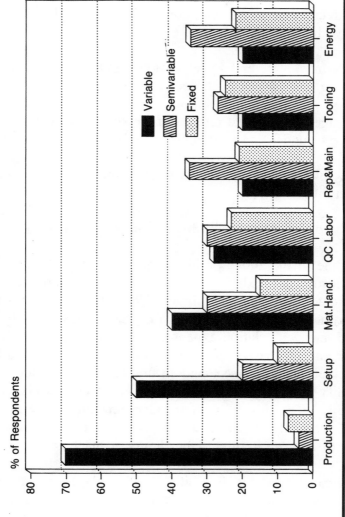

OVERHEAD COST BEHAVIOR

% of Respondents

■ Variable
▨ Semivariable
░ Fixed

Production  Setup  Mat.Hand.  QC Labor  Rep&Main  Tooling  Energy

Source: R.A. Howell, J.D. Brown, S.R. Soucy, and A.H. Seed,
Management Accounting in the New Manufacturing Environment,
Montvale, NJ: Nat'l. Assoc. of Accountants, 1987, p. 42.

37

This procedure raises several interesting problems:

* As the direct labor hours decrease, the ratio of dollars of overhead to direct labor hours increases, resulting in increased volatility of under and overapplied overhead.

* Direct labor hours will not equal machine hours because of possible set ups, idle time etc.

* All machines, and by extension products, do not require the same amount of direct labor time.

* Usage of an annual rate results in significant volume variances due to under and overapplied overhead.

* A plant-wide rate obscures differences in departmental activities.

* The direct labor has an indirect labor component.

Some of the above problems resulting from the use of NCMs are illustrated in Exhibits 3-1 through 3-3. Two products requiring different machine and direct labor time are produced by departments 1 and 2 of Firm XYZ. Each department has its own NCM and depreciation expense. Indirect departmental costs also differ and are based upon such items as square foot allocations, machinery maintenance, and insurance and tax allocations. To simplify the illustration, direct labor is presumed to be completely variable. Two issues bear consideration: one is the denominator level of activity, departmental or plant wide; the other involves the basis of allocation, direct labor hours or machine hours.

As can be seen in Exhibit 3-2, when departmental allocations using direct labor are compared to plant wide allocations, product A becomes relatively more expensive and product B relatively less so. This occurs because department 2 overhead allocations are higher and product A requires more department 2 labor hours, the cost allocation basis. Product B requires relatively more labor hours in department 1, where overhead costs are proportionately lower.

38

# Exhibit 3-1

## PRODUCT COSTING DATA

|  | Product A | Product B |
|---|---|---|
| Units Produced | 5,000 | 25,000 |
| **Machine Hours:** | | |
| Department 1 | 8,000 | 2,000 |
| Department 2 | 16,000 | 4,000 |
| **Labor Hours:** | | |
| Department 1 | 2,000 | 12,000 |
| Department 2 | 8,000 | 4,000 |

**Machinery Depreciation:**
Department 1 - $80,000
Department 2 - $120,000

**Indirect Costs:**
Department 1 - $20,000
Department 2 - $40,000

Using an average plant wide rate obscures these departmental cost differences. When machine hours are used to allocate costs, product A becomes even more costly because of the number of machine hours required for its production. There is no difference between plant wide and departmental machine hour allocations however because the ratio of machine hours for the two products is the same between the two departments, leaving the overall average unchanged.

Two lessons emerge from this simple illustration. One is that departmental rates need only be calculated when a significant difference exists in the departmental bases of allocation. The other is that a mis-specified allocation basis completely masks true product cost. In all cases, the same total overhead is absorbed but the overhead absorbed by the individual products differs noticeably according to the allocation basis. While this problem may not be significant when overhead is relatively low, it becomes a major

**Exhibit 3-2**

## DIRECT LABOR COST ALLOCATIONS

Plant Wide Direct Labor Allocation

Overhead Rate per Labor Hour:
($80,000 + 120,000 + 20,000 + 40,000) /
(8,000 + 2,000 + 12,000 + 4,000)          $10.00

Unit Allocation to Product A:
$10 x (2,000 + 8,000) / 5,000          $20.00

Unit Allocation to Product B:
$10 x (12,000 + 4,000) / 5,000          $6.40

Departmental Direct Labor Allocation

Overhead Rate for Department 1:
($80,000 + 20,000) / (2,000 + 12,000)          $7.14

Overhead Rate for Department 2:
($120,000 + 40,000) / (8,000 + 4,000)          $13.33

Unit Allocation to Product A:
{($7.14 x 2,000) + ($13.13 x 8,000)} / 5,000          $24.19

Unit Allocation to Product B:
{($7.14 x 12,000) + ($13.13 x 4,000)} / 5,000          $5.56

---

consideration as the proportion of overhead cost to total cost increases.

To return to the original case of the six NCMs, the above problems suggest several possible solutions:

* Track overhead at the departmental rather than the plant level.

* Divide direct labor into a direct component for such items as materials handling and machine maintenance, and an indirect component for items such as idle time, set ups and overtime.

# Exhibit 3-3

## MACHINE HOUR COST ALLOCATIONS

### Plant Wide Machine Hour Allocation

Overhead Rate per Machine Hour:
($80,000 + 120,000 + 20,000 + 40,000) /          $8.67
(8,000 + 16,000 + 2,000 + 4,000)

Unit Allocation to Product A:
$8.67 x (8,000 + 16,000) / 5,000                 $41.60

Unit Allocation to Product B:
$8.67 x (2,000 + 4,000) / 25,000                 $2.08

### Departmental Machine Hour Allocation

Overhead Rate for Department 1:
($80,000 + 20,000) / (8,000 + 2,000)             $10.00

Overhead Rate for Department 2:
($120,000 + 40,000) / (16,000 + 4,000)           $8.00

Unit Allocation to Product A:
{$10 (8,000) + $8 (16,000)} / 5,000              $41.60

Unit Allocation to Product B:
{$10 (2,000) + $8 (4,000)} / 25,000              $2.08

---

* Use machine time, either actual or the engineered time, to allocate the indirect portion of direct labor.

* Alternatively, use production cycle time by product, which may or may not include wait time between machine operations.

* Record new productivity measures such as rejects, inventory levels and cycle time rather than labor and overhead variances, which have little productivity significance.

These alternatives will be developed at length in subsequent chapters.

## Cost Control

There has been a significant slowdown in U.S. manufacturing productivity in recent years, particularly relative to other industrialized nations such as Japan and West Germany. At least part of the problem is attributable to the productivity measures themselves. A recent survey indicated generally widespread disatisfaction with manufacturing performance measurement systems.[2] Over one half of respondents surveyed indicated that performance measures in their organizations needed improvement. This applied to both users and preparers of performance measurement data. There appears to be generally widespread consensus that reported measures of performance are not reflective of true manufacturing productivity. The result is that sub-optimal productivity measures are being emphasized, while other more economically significant measures go unreported.

Productivity is generally defined in terms of input-output ratios of performance. Emphasizing the wrong ratios, ignoring other important ratios, or simply mismeasuring the numbers themselves can lead to errors in productivity judgment. For example, the National Bureau of Labor Statistics focuses on output per labor hour. Given the relatively low degree of labor in many plants, this is not a very meaningful index. Today, capital and raw material are more significant investment components than direct labor. Furthermore, other factors of production may be substituted for direct labor, increasing labor productivity but decreasing actual overall firm productivity. This labor measurement focus is often reflected in a firm's control system, to the extent that labor standards and variances are emphasized to the exclusion of other cost components. In fact, direct labor productivity measures continue to be the most commonly reported measures of performance.

Standard costs are usually the foundation of many firms' control systems. Unfortunately, standard cost systems frequently obstruct rather than strengthen cost control. This occurs for several reasons. First, standard costs may have slack built into them because of initial budget biasing. Second, standard costs are not immutable.

Even annual standard cost revisions may be inadequate. There should be continual efforts to decrease total standard cost over a product's life cycle.

Another standard cost problem is that each component of total product cost is often treated as though it were independent of other value-added activities, when in fact interdependencies frequently exist between cost components. Attempting to define a standard cost for an activity in isolation from other cost components is not very meaningful. Raw material quantity, for example, often impacts labor productivity; capital and labor intensity intereact; and acceptable quality levels dictate initial raw material and labor standards. Because of these interdependencies, a product's full standard cost assumes more importance than any sub-component of cost. Maximizing cost component efficiency, a tenet of traditional standard costing decomposition analysis, inevitably leads to overall costing and quality inefficiencies.

Standard costing facilitates inventory valuation but does little for controlling actual cost variances from standard. Variance reports are frequently too aggregated across product lines and too dated to be of immediate costing and control value. Monthly control reports at the managerial level do little to encourage corrective action on the plant floor. Immediate, hourly and daily production feedback to line personnel is of more control value than monthly labor and overhead variance reporting. Finally, standard costing traditionally reports raw material, direct labor and overhead variances but overlooks other pre and post production cost components, as well as productivity measures.

Exhibit 3-4 indicates some of the dysfunctional consequences of actual standard cost reporting systems. For example, reporting material price variances may lead to increased inventory as volume discounts are taken. Important quality measures, reflected in yield, scrap and rework variances are typically reported less frequently than raw material price variances. Although direct labor is frequently less than 10% of total cost, it is usually the most frequently reported variance, to the exclusion of other raw material and capital investment measures of productivity. Firms may also

## Exhibit 3-4

### STANDARD COST MEASURES

| Reported Measures | Consequences |
|---|---|
| Raw Material Variance | Volume discounts may lead to excess inventories |
| Direct Labor Variance | Excess focus on relatively small cost |
| Volume Variance | Excessive inventory to absorb overhead |
| Variable Overhead Variance (based on direct labor) | Incorrect allocation basis leads to wrong control signal |
| Cost Center Reports | Overhead activities are not controlled |
| Monthly Reports | Too tardy and aggregated |
| Historical Cost Basis | Current Costs are Ignored |
| Fixed Overhead Variance | Product cost is increased when based on estimated rather than theoretical capacity |
| Slack Built into Standard | No incentive to reduce cost |
| Material, Labor & Overhead Variances | Other productivity measures are ignored |

produce to fully absorb fixed overhead in inventory, so that unfavorable periodic volume variances are not reported. If inventory turnover is not measured, this leads to increased inventory holding costs.

Both the locus of cost control, that is the department or cost center, and the reporting time period, either weekly or monthly, may lead to dysfunctional control consequences. The department may simply be passing costs along to products for absorption because overhead activities are not under its jurisdiction. The department is not a very worthwhile control locus for overhead activities. The activity centers themselves are in a better position to control overhead costs. More frequent monitoring of overhead activities, in addition to direct labor and material measures would also improve control.

Another problem associated with traditional standard cost measures is that variances report outcomes, but not explanations of the underlying cause of a production problem. No information regarding corrective action is provided. Furthermore, focusing only on a subset of performance measures can lead to optimization of the subset at the expense of overall efficiency. For example, if direct labor usage is measured, and maximum utilization is sought, then operations that are on an off bottleneck production path will produce for inventory. Slack time may be necessary for non-critical path activities. Standards often presume a "push" rather than "pull" strategy. If Just-in-Time production is instituted, overall efficiency is best measured at the product and plant level, rather than by department specific cost components.

Incentive systems under standard costing focus on narrowly defined measures of product cost control determined by top level management. Increasingly however, production is being defined in terms of product families where responsibility is interdepartmental. This bottom up approach is more participative and requires different incentive scheme designs than local departmental incentives, which are counter-productive to overall production efficiency.

## Inventory Management

Inventory Management in the U.S. has historically been based upon erroneous paradigms. Economic Order Quantity models, for example, minimize total ordering and carrying costs. These models pre-suppose that such costs are unavoidable. The net result is that inventory optimization occurs based upon inflated costs. Likewise, Statistical Quality Control investigation models place a mis-directed emphasis on optimal investigation strategies, rather than on the outright elimination of defective units. Incentive plans often reward excessive production by focusing on departmental or divisonal performance, not on the true cost of inventory and quality. Accounting Systems frequently fail to charge back to products the full costs of overhead and finance charges related to their production, understating the true cost of holding inventory.

Extant cost systems are deficient with respect to all three areas of inventory management - raw material, work-in-process, and finished goods. Raw material is frequently excessive and of sub-standard quality. Numerous studies have shown U.S. suppliers to deliver components with higher defect rates relative to European and Japanese suppliers. U.S. firms also deal with significantly more suppliers and generally have shorter term contracts.

Materials handling, inspection and rework is much more prevalent in U.S. production floors. Amounts of raw material on hand is often excessive, increasing storage, insurance and interest costs. In short, many non-value added overhead costs exist that should be traced by the accounting system to inventory, and thus highlighted for reduction and elimination.

Work-in-process is a deficient area of cost systems as well. Most accounting systems focus more upon the equivalent-unit valuation of end-of-period work-in-process rather than on the managing of the cost itself. As production technology has evolved, cellular manufacturing has resulted in less work-in-process between departments, increased quality, more worker flexibility, and faster throughput. These manufacturing changes have important implications for work-in-process inventory valuation and control.

One important change is that the tedious equivalent-unit calculations for product families may not be necessary. As cycle times increase, work-in-process is minimized. Rather than tracking work-in-process inventory costs, it may be more efficient to allocate unit costs once in finished goods. Much of the costly record-keeping that is associated with physical production flow would become unnecessary. Instead more emphasis would be placed upon "real time" control measures associated with the production process. Traditional standard costs concentrate on labor and raw material variances that bear little relationship to controllable and material work-in-process production costs.

Because carrying and holding costs are under-estimated and not accurately traced to product lines, levels of finished goods are often excessive. As product lifecycles have dramatically decreased, obsolescence costs have increased. These, along with warranty service costs for sub-standard production, are not often traced to product lines in extant cost systems. As a result, accounting systems are deficient in reporting the true cost of finished goods.

## Capital Investment

Advanced technology capital investment proposals and project analyses entail large expenditures in the initial stages of project development. Depending upon the product life cycle, revenues generated from these expenditures are usually not realized until a significant time period has elapsed. Since traditional incentive systems are customarily based upon accounting numbers, managers are motivated to maximize reported income. The net result of the above is that quick payback projects are encouraged. These are the projects where revenues most quickly recover heavy initial expenditures. Possibly more lucrative projects with longer term revenue horizons are thus discouraged in extant cost system environments.

**Limitations of Traditional Capital Budgeting**: Capital budgeting techniques project net after tax cash inflows related to an investment. These inflows are then used to assess the time or payback period required for recovery of the investment. Frequently, in order to determine if the net present value of the project is positive, these cash flows are also discounted over the life of the project at the firm's cost of capital. Alternatively, the internal rate of return, that is the present value rate needed to equate the inflows with the investment, may be calculated and compared to a required rate of return. While theoretically defensible, many problems arise when implementing these cash flow techniques in highly automated environments. This is reflected by a general disatisfaction with existing capital budgeting techniques.

The first problem involves the interdependent nature of sequentially discrete automation projects. Because high technology investments are often substantial, comprehensive projects may have to be implemented sequentially, and therefore justified on a piecemeal basis. The technology itself might not yet be fully developed or some of the interrelated investments may already have been made. In all of these scenarios, partial investments, independently valued, may look unpromising based upon a discounted cash flow analysis. When jointly evaluated however, synergistic benefits often result.

For example, a Flexible Manufacturing System might be less successful without an Automated Materials Handling System. Computerized Numerically Controlled Machinery in one part of the plant may not realize its full potential without additional machinery investment elsewhere in the production process. A total systems approach recognizes synergistic effects while eliminating the possibility of double counting costs and benefits between projects.

A problem often encountered when adopting a more integrated project systems approach however is that the total investment may well exceed firm capital budgeting authorization guidelines. Frequently, investments are done on a piecemeal basis precisely because they fall within the bounds of company dictated capital authorization limits. This procedure may actually encourage smaller less economically viable projects. The result is that the sum of the disparate investment cash flows are less than the total cash flow of a more comprehensive investment.

Another problem arises when firms consider the rapidity of payback as a criterion in investment selection, in addition to the more conceptually accurate discounted cash flow method. This analysis tends to work against acceptance of highly automated investments, which generally have much longer payback periods, as well as greater initial start up costs and technical learning. This is particularly true of larger scale projects such as FMS. In these cases, the uncertainty is greater than for more short lived investments. Carried to its logical extreme, investing in a series of smaller scale quick return projects can lead to a lack of strategic positioning for the firm. Over the years, the quick return payback from these projects may fall significantly short of more comprehensive investments.

Incremental quick payback projects generally do not favor technical learning and product evolution essential to the firm's survival. Investing in a new replacement piece of equipment which stresses cost reduction is not as radical as investing in a new technical process or product. Although more attendant risks may exist, in the latter case, the investment has significantly greater long term revenue opportunities. Inevitably with high technology investments, the greater the potential return, the more uncertain are cost and revenue projections.

A closely related problem is choosing the base case against which to compare the automation investment. Many firms use the status quo as the most viable base case yardstick. Ideally, one should have some idea of the product's life cycle. The future cash flows should be projected as a function of where the firm is in its product life cycle. A mature product for example suggests declining cash flows. Thus the base case should be the firm's most realistic projection of future cash flows with and without the capital expenditure. Of course, the mere availability of the technology suggests that the marketplace itself has changed and that all firms are facing similar decisions. This may also affect the base case projections.

Suppose for example Firm XYZ, a competitor, decides to invest in new production technology. The changed nature of its cost structure, typically a higher capital to labor ratio, suggests that this firm may price aggressively in the hopes of significant volume increases. This may well be possible with faster throughput on the new machinery. This could change the base rate cash projections of Firm ABC, as its projected market share declines. Once lost, market share recapture may require even more investment than that foregone by the disinvestment.

High hurdle rates are another problem that bedevil discounted cash flow analyses of factory automation. Figure 3-2 indicates the

**Figure 3-2**

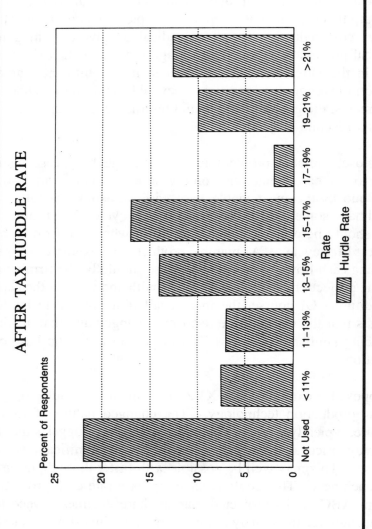

AFTER TAX HURDLE RATE

Percent of Respondents

Rate

Hurdle Rate

Source: R.A. Howell, J.D. Brown, S.R. Soucy, and A.H. Seed,
Management Accounting in the New Manufacturing Environment.
Montvale, NJ: Nat'l. Assoc. of Accountants, 1987, p. 32.

50

proportion of some recently surveyed firms using different hurdle rates in capital budgeting decisions. As can be seen, the modal rate used was approximately 15-17%. Kaplan, in a recent article, argues that the true historical equity cost for the firm is close to 8%[3]. Net of inflation, real annual stock returns from 1950-1984 were approximately 8.4%, while long term bond yields, it is claimed, yielded less than 1% after inflation. To the extent that the firm uses non inflation adjusted inflows in its discounted cash flow analysis, to be consistent "real" cost of capital rates should be used. In this case, 15% to 17% hurdle rates would appear to be very high, unless they were offset with very generous inflation adjusted cash flow projections.

Many firms use a high cost of capital when evaluating automation requisitions in order to offset perceived risk. Given the lengthy time horizon of many projects, this compounds the problem and precludes many viable projects from acceptance. Higher discount rates used in conjunction with longer time horizons accentuate projected return differences. Many U.S. firms argue that Japanese competitors have a significantly lower cost of capital than they do, when in fact high hurdle rates are artificially imposed by top management as a means of counteracting risk and increasing managerial motivation. In reality, they appear to serve neither purpose.

Another capital budgeting problem is that firms frequently ignore indirect cost savings that are not immediately quantifiable. Residual values of new machinery for example are often excluded from investment analyses because such numbers are difficult to quantify. Customer satisfaction and product quality are other intangibles that clearly affect market share. They impact future revenues in more indirect ways. Greater production flexibility opens up new markets. Faster throughput time and increased response time lead to lower inventory level requirements, which in turn lead to less floor space. The difficulty of quantifying indirect benefits is not a reason to exclude them from investment analyses.

Finally, there may be behavioral impediments to adopting new technologies. A sunk cost mentality of seeking to justify outdated equipment may prevail. Another behavioral problem may be the existant performance measurement system. If the control system does not report additional benefits such as cycle time or improved quality that will ensue from new technologies, then little managerial motivation will exist to replace outdated technology.

**Consistency of Accounting Measurements**: Not only do pitfalls exist when analyzing high technology investments with traditional capital budgeting techniques, accounting measures also frequently distort post purchase measures of production performance. Several logical inconsistencies exist between ROI based accounting measures of performance and discounted cash flow investment measures, which are exacerbated in high technology environments. In particular, the original investment is justified at least in part based upon discounted cash flows over the life of the project. Periodic accounting rates of return however measure accounting profit, not cash flow, based on historical cost allocation of depreciation. These depreciation charges generally are based on financial reporting considerations. As such, they frequently bear little or no relationship to the stream of revenue flows against which they are matched.

A logical solution to the above problem is to more closely match depreciation expense to economic expense. This requires choosing a depreciation method that reflects the underlying economic phenomena such as process or machine time. Such a measure better reflects machine utilization and revenue flows rather than showing a constant expense as a function of time.

Another inconsistency arises when historical cost depreciation is matched against current cost revenue for periodic reporting. Discounted cash flow analysis measures inflows and outflows in equivalent present value dollars. Periodic historical cost depreciation expense should therefore be converted into a present value equivalent in such a way that the "real" not nominal depreciation expense is constant over time. These annualized present value depreciation equivalents can then be written off using a basis that best matches the time adjusted expenses to revenues.

The cost basis used for depreciation should also be adjusted to include all related capital costs, which might otherwise be expensed. Normally, all historical asset costs and related preparation and installation charges are capitalized for financial reporting. Significant additional start-up costs however arise in high technology environments. These include investments in software, industrial engineering and training. If these costs are expensed rather than capitalized, they will be mismatched against the revenues which they generate. These costs are really project costs, not initial period costs, to be amortized over the economic life of the investment.

A related problem is the learning inherent in adoption of a sophisticated automated production system. Cost behavior in such an environment often follows a traditional learning curve as depicted in Figure 3-3. These start up costs include installation and learning associated with new software and hardware; indirect labor learning related to control and machinery maintenance; and scheduling and optimal utilization of available machinery.

As workers gain experience with new production techniques, the indirect support costs for a given level of activity begin to decline

**Figure 3-3**

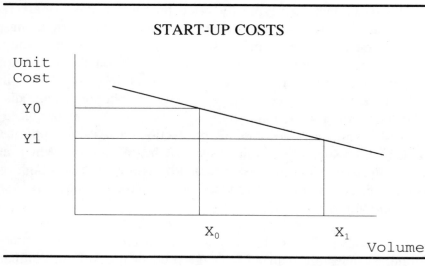

START-UP COSTS

Again, mismatching of expenses to revenues can occur if actual support costs are expensed as incurred. A preferable treatment is to project the rate of decline, be it linear or logarithmic, using a few production points over a suitable range of activity. These different unit costs must then be reflected in the accounting measurement system

A final accounting precaution involves the allocation of all costs to the project. Ancillary costs should not be ignored in the measurement of investment returns. For example, all indirect investment and operating costs, such as materials handling, space and software should be traceable to the investment, and not be treated as general overhead. Otherwise, both investment and operating costs of the project will be underestimated.

Summarizing, the accounting measurements used to evaluate high technology investments must be consistent with the assumptions behind the initial investment analysis. While this may appear intuitively obvious, firms frequently allow the requirements of external reporting to dictate accounting measurements that are inconsistent with measures used to evaluate capital budgeting.

**Strategic Costing**

U.S. manufacturers typically price products using a mark-up over average full-cost. Due to accounting system shortcomings, several conceptual problems exist with this pricing methodology. One is that all relevant cost pools and allocation bases are not properly accounted for. Another is that costs, in reality, occur in a curvilinear fashion over a range of activity. Economies and diseconomies of production occur as more units are produced. Typically unit costs decrease as production increases to optimal capacity, at which point unit costs then begin to rise. When an economically optimal level of production is not used, too high or low a unit cost is chosen, product cost is misstated and over- or under-pricing occurs.

Unit costs are also often misstated unless projected across time. While revenues are realized over the product lifecycle in familiar bell-shaped fashion, costs are disproportionately incurred at the onset of the cycle. These costs include such items as research and development, design, prototype, and computer start-up costs, and are usually expensed for product costing purposes because of external financial reporting requirements. For internal reporting purposes, however, failure to capture and match these expenses to the inflows of revenue results in management incentives to recoup costs as quickly as possible. This leads to overpricing and maximization of short-term profit at the expense of long-term profit.

Empirical evidence strongly suggests that U.S. accounting practices, incentive contracts and stock market considerations of quarterly earnings reports drive firms to maximize short-term profits at the expense of long-term market share. Rather than using strategic lifecycle costing and target costing to capture the maximum market at the minimum price, accounting systems often encourage the opposite behavior.

## SUMMARY

Frequently encountered characteristics of extant cost systems are summarized in Exhibit 3-5. Extant systems are not meeting the cost accounting needs of today's manufacturing environment. The reason for the "outdatedness" of these systems can be attributed in part to the trends that have accompanied new manufacturing technologies. This has led to fundamental problems in costing and control, inventory management, capital investment decisions and strategic costing.

As indicated in the exhibit, numerous product costing and control problems arise when a firm's managerial cost system has any or all of the indicated characteristics. Managerial system weaknesses may be indicated in other ways. External market signals as well as internal production changes may be an indication that all is not well with the firm's costing system. Generally, new production technologies, unexplainably high margins or lack of product competition are all signals of suspect cost margins.

# Exhibit 3-5

## CHARACTERISTICS OF MANAGERIAL COST SYSTEMS

Characteristic:    * **Primary emphasis is on Financial Reporting**

Results:    * Outdated Managerial information
* Aggregated costs do not permit product line profitability analysis
* Poor performance monitoring
* Pre and post-production costs are treated as period, not product, costs
* Two different operating systems

Characteristic:    * **Utilization of aggregate overhead burden rates based on output**

Results:    * Individual overhead cost drivers are ignored
* High volume products subsidize low volume products
* With product hetrogeneity, misallocations arise

Characteristic:    * **Semi-variable costs are treated as either variable or fixed**

Results:    * Flexible budgeting and variable cost estimates are inaccurate
* Overhead allocations are inaccurate

Characteristic:    * **Monthly financial performance feedback**

Results:    * No monitoring of physical perfromance measures
* Feedback is too dated and aggregated

Characteristic:    * **Cost Control Emphasis**

Results:    * Inadequate focus on non-value added charges
* No accounting involvement in ex ante standard cost development
* Cost control rather than cost reduction is emphasized

Characteristic:    * **Incentives are based on Financial Accounting measures**

Results:    * Short term accounting measures are emphasized to the detriment of real economic returns

# REFERENCES

1. R.A. Howell, J.D. Brown, S.R. Soucy and A.H. Seed, Management Accounting in the New Manufacturing Environment. Montvale,N.J.: National Association of Accountants, 1987, 41.

2. R.A. Howell, J.D. Brown, S.R. Soucy and A.H. Seed, Management Accounting in the New Manufacturing Environment. Montvale,N.J.: National Association of Accountants, 1987, 63.

3. R. Kaplan, "Must CIM Be Justified by Faith Alone?" Harvard Business Review (March-April 1986): 87-95.

# BIBLIOGRAPHY

Bennett, R.E., J.A. Hendricks, D.E. Keys, and E. J. Rudnicki. Cost Accounting For Factory Automation. Montvale, N.J.: National Association of Accountants, 1987.

Berliner, C. and J.A. Brimson. Cost Management For Today's Advanced Manufacturing. Boston, Mass.: Harvard Business School Press, 1988.

Bruns, W.J. and R.S. Kaplan. Accounting and Management Field Study Perspectives. Boston : Harvard Business School Press, 1987.

Cooper, R. "You Need a New Cost System When..." Harvard Business Review (Jan.-Feb. 1989): 77-82.

Hayes, R.H. and R. Jaikumar. "Manufacturing's Crisis: New Technologies, Obsolete Organizations." Harvard Business Review (Sept.-Oct. 1988): 77-85.

Howell, R.A. and S.R. Soucy. "Cost Accounting in the New Manufacturing Environment." Management Accounting (August, 1987): 42-49.

Kaplan, R. "The Four Stage Model of Cost Systems Design." Management Accounting (Feb. 1990): 22-26.

_____ "Must CIM be Justified by Faith Alone?" Harvard Business Review (March-April 1986) : 87-95.

_____ "One Cost System Isn't Enough." Harvard Business Review (Jan.-Feb. 1988): 61-66.

Miller, J. and T.E. Vollman. "The Hidden Factory." Harvard Business Review (Sept.-Oct. 1985) : 142-150.

Shank, J.K. and V. Govindarajan. "The Perils of Cost Allocation Based on Production Volumes." Accounting Horizons (Dec.1988): 71-79.

Schubert, J.K. "The Pitfalls of Product Costing." Journal of Cost Management. (Summer, 1988): 16-26.

Steedle, L. "Has Productivity Measurement Outgrown Infancy?" Management Accounting (Aug. 1988): 15-16.

# Part Two

# NEW COST MANAGEMENT PRACTICES

# Chapter Four

# ACTIVITY-BASED PRODUCT COSTING

A paramount concern in business is costing products in today's manufacturing environment. Product cost provides information that is used in a variety of settings ranging from decisions on the design of product, to decisions on pricing, to eventually decisions on product discontinuance. The focus of this chapter is on Activity-Based Costing (ABC) techniques which are designed to overcome many of the mis-allocation problems associated with extant cost systems. Discussion of ABC will be supplemented with detailed examples of its use in CAD/CAM, Cellular, and FMS manufacturing environments.

## THE ACTIVITY ACCOUNTING MODEL

ABC is a subset of a much larger Activity Accounting Model, which in itself is a much broader cost management tool. For instance, Activity Accounting can provide information for capital budgeting decisions, lifecycle costing, and performance measurement aspects. The Activity Accounting Model presumes that every action of an organization can be attributed to a larger activity of the firm. The operation of a firm can therefore be described as the performance of a number of distinct **activities** or processes. Examples of activities include, for instance, the process of making an 'engineering change' to a product, scheduling of production, or assembly of a product. It should be noted that while the assembly of a product may be a very complex process, involving numerous steps and consuming a large proportion of total business cost, it is but only one of many activities performed by a firm.

Costs are the result of the performance of an activity. Thus, if an activity is eliminated, so should the cost of performing the activity. Central to the model of Activity Accounting is the concept of the **Cost Driver**. The cost driver is that action or transaction that results in cost being incurred. Conversely, every cost in the business has a cost driver. Examples of cost drivers include direct labor, purchase orders, and customer billings. In most instances, a significant amount of a firm's total cost can be traced to a dozen or so cost drivers. The Activity Accounting model thus accumulates costs on an activity basis as opposed to the traditional practice of accumulating costs on a functional basis. This chapter will focus only on the product costing aspects, i.e. ABC, of the Activity Accounting Model.


## ACTIVITY-BASED COSTING

The basic premise of Activity-based Costing is that **activities consume resources** and **products consume activities**. This means that costs in a business must be first accumulated at the activity level, and from there traced to the product. The costs accumulated under an activity are traced to the product using cost drivers, depending upon how much of the cost driver the product consumes. Once again, as detailed earlier in the previous chapter, product costing involves three basic steps:

1. Determination of which costs will be part of product cost.
2. Definition of cost pools used to accumulate cost.
3. Allocation of indirect costs to product

## Cost Inclusion

As discussed previously, the issue of which costs to include as part of product cost in traditional cost systems is dictated by financial accounting. Activity-based Costing on the other hand stresses that product costs include most production and support costs incurred by a business. As a result, fixed production and support department costs that were previously expensed every period are now traced to products. Research and development, design, advertising, transportation and indirect selling and administrative support costs are now part of product cost. Since GAAP does not allow such costs to be inventoried, use of the financial accounting system to cost products for both financial as well as managerial purposes is no longer possible, and additional record keeping is necessitated for the latter purpose.

Inclusion of period costs in the calculation of product costs is justified because of structural changes to traditional cost systems.[1] Previously, variable cost of direct labor, material and factory overhead made-up a large proportion of total cost. Expensing of the fixed portion of cost on a periodic basis did not cause much distortion. Today, however, variable cost is nowhere as high a proportion of total factory cost as was previously the case. As variable labor has decreased, fixed overhead has increased proportionately. Depreciation on new machinery, computerization and most support departments exemplify new fixed overhead. These costs are material and in most cases, at least indirectly attributable to products.

The new manufacturing environment is in certain cases reversing the very definition of what constitutes the product/period cost. For example, direct labor, typically a product cost, is a very small proportion of total cost in an FMS environment, usually in the order of 2% to 5%. The result is that several companies such as I.B.M. and Hewlett-Packard do not bother inventorying direct labor cost, but instead simply expense it as a period cost. Conversely, both developmental period costs incurred prior to production as well as distribution and support costs incurred subsequent to production have more of the characteristics of product costs. Research and development, design, advertising, transportation and indirect selling and administrative support costs can all be traced back to individual product or product lines.

Another structural change is that in the past reasonably equal demand was placed by products on services of support departments. This is not the case today. New manufacturing allows firms to produce increasingly complex variations of product lines. Products make varying demands on time resources, equipment and support personnel involved with production. As a result, support costs have to be included into the product cost to arrive at an accurate estimate of the product's resource consumption.

**Cost Center Structure**

Before costs can be traced to products, they must be accumulated in cost pools or cost centers. The determination of what constitutes a cost center is a crucial step in the product costing process. A cost center in Activity-based Costing is simply an activity. Thus, any costs associated with the new product development activity should be accumulated in the New Product Development cost center.

Traditional cost systems attempt to mirror the firm's organizational structure in their definition of cost centers. Three distinct levels in a firm's organizational structure can be identified that vary in their degree of conformance with ABC's definition of a cost center. The first level comprises **support manufacturing departments**, such as quality control, material handling, shipping etc. These departments are already organized around a central activity and are currently treated as cost centers in existing cost systems. They require little change in terms of accumulation of cost in an ABC system.

The second organizational level is the **factory floor** itself. While it would appear that the cost center structure of the factory floor would vary little between traditional and ABC systems, that is not always the case, for example:

"A large NC line (eight machines with an automated material handling system for each machine and between machines) was installed in a very large machine shop.....this NC line was included with all other direct labor machines to develop a composite machining overhead rate based on direct labor hours involved. Obviously, the parts produced on the NC machines were undercosted and all other parts were overcosted. To correct this, the NC machine center was broken out as a separate cost center."[2]

Progression towards Cellular and FMS technologies can simplify the identification of cost centers on the factory floor. The subdivision of the manufacturing floor into cost centers should be performed using the following criteria:[3]

* Process Cost Differentials: Material differences in the cost of performing the same task (e.g. using labor vs using automated machinery to build a component) should result in separate cost centers.

* Specialized or Dedicated Equipment: If equipment is used for specific product lines, it should be made into a cost center with the associated cost traced directly to those product lines.

* Multiple Cost Drivers Within a Single Process: Costs incurred by a process on the floor may be driven by more than a single driver, necessitating division of the process into multiple cost centers.

* Product Flow: If the same products pass through the entire process, the process itself can constitute a cost center.

The third organizational level involves **non-manufacturing support departments** such as engineering and marketing. As

**Figure 4-1**

---

TRADITIONAL vs ACTIVITY COST ACCUMULATION

| Marketing Dept. | | Marketing Dept. | |
|---|---|---|---|
| Salaries | $ 800,000 | Pricing | $ 200,000 |
| Supplies | $ 20,000 | After-sales Service | $ 420,000 |
| Travel Expenses | $ 650,000 | New Product Sales | $ 500,000 |
| Sales Commissions | $ 600,000 | Advertising | $ 350,000 |
| Miscellaneous | $ 180,000 | ECN Processing | $ 200,000 |
| | ------------ | Forecasting | $ 180,000 |
| | | Old Product Sales | $ 400,000 |
| | | | ----------- |
| Total | $2,250,000 | Total | $2,250,000 |

---

shown in Figure 4-1, costs in such departments are frequently those which are the least traced to products in today's cost systems. Part of the problem is that costs incurred in these departments are accumulated in very superficial accounts that provide little information on their own as to the traceability of the cost.


**Cost Allocation**

Traditional cost allocation is depicted in Figure 4-2a. General manufacturing overhead support costs are allocated on a usage basis to cost centers through which products pass. These cost centers add labor and possibly raw material, and reallocate the total overhead to products passing through their department. The point at which the allocation procedure becomes suspect is in the allocation of the overhead to products. Customarily, the basis chosen, machine hours for example, is common to all cost centers. This implies that the overhead attached to the product in each cost center is a function of the machine time spent on the product. Labor and machine hours are the most frequently mentioned bases of overhead allocation both in the United States and Japan.

**Figure 4-2a**

## TRADITIONAL ALLOCATION SCHEME

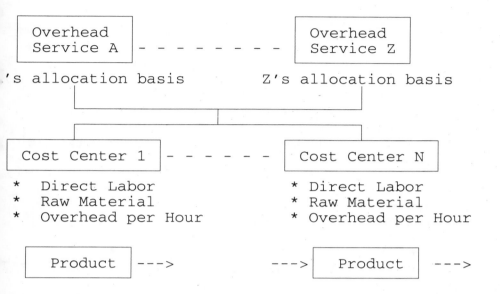

There are several problems with this logic. The first is that all manufacturing overhead costs, so carefully allocated to each cost center as a function of usage, are now allocated on an average basis, purely as a function of machine time. Thus, the product that requires twice the machine time, but "causes" very little variable or semi-variable overhead is overcosted and vice versa. To the extent that different products require significantly different amounts of overhead, this results in cost misallocation. This is compounded to the degree that the amount in the overhead pool is significant.

Another problem arises because overhead components will not vary directly, except by chance, with the chosen basis of allocation. The result is that two products that share the same overhead cost will be costed disproportionately. Although within a relevant range of production, a high volume product causes no incremental stepwise overhead costs relative to a lower volume product, it is allocated more overhead because the allocation basis is linear

**Figure 4-2b**

## ACTIVITY ALLOCATION BASES

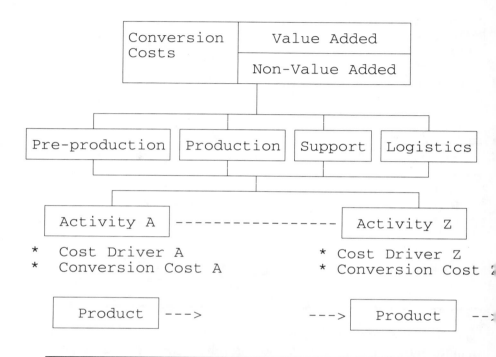

relative to output. Another way of saying this is that low volume units create more transactions per unit than high volume units, but are costed identically on a per unit transaction basis.

An Activity-based Costing allocation scheme is depicted in Figure 4-2b. Conversion costs include all production and pre- and post-production costs that can be directly or indirectly traced to theproduct. Non-value added elements of conversion where possible should be eliminated or reduced as previously discussed. At this point, activities now effectively replace what were once cost centers. Individual cost drivers that best reflect changes in each cost activity are then used to allocate the activity costs directly to products. Prior to this allocation, the only product cost is raw material.

In implementing such an allocation scheme, the question arises whether standard or actual costing is preferred. Several arguments can be made in favor of standard costing. The first is that cycle time is so short that invariably the product will be completed and shipped before actual costs are compiled. The second is that the sheer number of activities makes actual tracking of costs to products in real time very cumbersome. A predetermined aggregate standard conversion cost simplifies record keeping. It also makes one product's predetermined conversion cost independent of mix and volume variances caused by forecasting errors of another product. A product is charged only for its budgeted share of overhead transactions. On the other hand, constant technological changes and shorter product life cycles necessitate more frequent revisions of standard cost.


**Example of ABC**

The following example involves four products that are to be allocated overhead, for expository purposes, based on only three support activities, Machining, Material Receiving and Machine Set Ups. The cost driver of the Receiving activity is the number of component parts per finished unit of product. These parts naturally vary depending on the product. The percentage of total receiving activity cost allocated to each product line is based on this cost driver. Set up activity costs are allocated based on the number of set ups which vary by product line relative to volume. For instance, products A and C were produced in the same volume and coincidentally have the same number of set ups per unit produced. However, product B, which was produced in the same volume as product D, has six times as many set ups per unit of production. Exhibit 4-1 details the example.

Assuming, that overhead is allocated based on machine hours under traditional methods, total overhead is divided by machine hours. The resulting hourly rate is then used to assign overhead to each product based on the number of machine hours used in its production. Under ABC, overhead is allocated by using each activity's cost driver(s). Only machine costs are allocated based on

# Exhibit 4-1

## OVERHEAD VOLUME AND ACTIVITY
## EFFECTS ON PRODUCT COST

**Data**:

| Products | Finished Units | Machine Hours | Receiving* | Set Ups | Total Overhead |
|----------|---------------|---------------|-----------|---------|----------------|
| A | 1,000 | 10 | .25 | 6 | |
| B | 2,000 | 50 | .40 | 12 | |
| C | 1,000 | 120 | .25 | 6 | |
| D | 2,000 | 50 | .10 | 2 | |
| Total Activity: | 230 | | 1.00 | 26 | |
| Total Dollars: | 1,200 | 3,000 | 1,800 | 6,000 | |

**Traditional Allocation to Products**:

Overhead Rate = $6,000/230 hours = $26.09/hour

| | | |
|---|---|---|
| A | (10 hrs. X $26.09)/1,000 units = | **$ 0.2609/unit** |
| B | (50 hrs. X $26.09)/2,000 units = | **$ 0.6522/unit** |
| C | (120 hrs. X $26.09)/1,000 units = | **$ 3.1308/unit** |
| D | (50 hrs. X $26.09)/2,000 units = | **$ 0.6522/unit** |

**Activity Allocation to Products**:

| | Machinery | Receiving | Set Ups | Total / Units = Cost | | |
|---|-----------|-----------|---------|-------|--------|------|
| A | (10/230)1200 | .25(3000) | 6/26(1800) | 1217.55 / 1000 | = | **$ 1.2175/unit** |
| B | (50/230)1200 | .40(3000) | 12/26(1800) | 2291.64 / 2000 | = | **$ 1.1458/unit** |
| C | (120/230)1200 | .25(3000) | 6/26(1800) | 1791.47 / 1000 | = | **$ 1.7915/unit** |
| D | (50/230)1200 | .10(3000) | 2/26(1800) | 699.33 / 2000 | = | **$ 0.3497/unit** |

* Based on Component Parts Per Finished Unit.

machine time, which is viewed as the cost driver of tying up the machine. Receiving, as previously discussed, is allocated based on the percentage of each product line's component parts to total component parts handled. Set ups are allocated in proportion to the number of set ups by product line relative to total set ups.

The difference in cost allocation under the two schemes is striking. First, examining the effect of volume on allocations, products B and D have the same number of machine hours per unit and therefore unit cost under traditional allocation methods. Similarly, product A bears very little overhead, while product C picks up a substantial amount. If products B and D are now compared under the activity allocation procedure, their unit costs are significantly different. Product B approximately doubles in cost, while product D's unit cost is cut in half. Product A now has a sixfold unit cost increase, while product C's cost is reduced by 50%.

The effect of product diversity can also be examined by comparing products A and C with products B and D. A and C consume identical receiving and set up activity per unit produced, while products B and D, which have identical machine hours per unit, consume significantly different amounts of receiving and set up cost. Traditional schemes result in product C costing twelve times as much as product A. Under activity costing, the ratio is only one and one half times, due to the difference in machine hours. In contrast, products B and D, which have identical unit costs under traditional schemes, now have a fourfold cost difference under activity costing. This is because product heterogeneity results in significantly different demands on overhead, as reflected and reported in product B's overhead consumption.

Summarizing, total overhead absorbed is the same under either allocation scheme. However, different allocation methods result in significantly different product line profitability reporting. These differences are attributable to volume differences in production when an average allocation basis is used. They are also due to product diversity. This results in different consumption patterns of variable and semi-variable overhead, not recognized under traditional allocation schemes. Finally, although not manipulated in the numerical example, the materiality of the dollars involved in the activity pool would further accentuate the direction of the cost bias.

When overhead activities of a product line are significant and production volume is relatively low, then products will always be undercosted. Conversely, when overhead activities are relatively low and production volume is high, then products will always be overcosted. When volume is high but transactions are relatively low, then products may be over or undercosted, depending on the dominance of the ratio of product volume differences to the ratio of product diversity differences.[4] This is summarized in Figure 4-3.

**Figure 4-3**

### COSTING IMPLICATIONS OF VOLUME/OVERHEAD LEVELS

|  | High Overhead Activities | Low Overhead Activities |
|---|---|---|
| High Volume | overcosted or undercosted | overcosted |
| Low Volume | undercosted | overcosted or undercosted |

In light of the above, a logical conclusion for the firm is to focus on large dollar items of activity, where:

1. the production volume is high and overhead activities are not diverse

2. the production volume is low and overhead activities are diverse

3. the ratio of product production volume to product activity consumption differs significantly from unity, in either direction. In practice, volume diversity often exceeds product activity diversity.

## Cost Driver Selection

An unresolved issue in the above discussion of ABC is how to realistically limit the number of cost drivers being derived. For a firm with hundreds of products and numerous overhead activities, the procedure of allocating activity costs can become cumbersome indeed. Once cost drivers have been derived for all the costs in the systems, a first step is to perform a judgmental analysis of the data in an effort to reduce product and cost driver redundancy. For example, if design changes double, do engineering orders increase correspondingly? If component parts increase, does materials handling rise proportionately, and if so, over which products? In other words, which overhead activities share the same cost drivers? A judgmental analysis may be performed by categorizing activities in a matrix relative to the cost driver or drivers that generate each activity. In this way, some measure of the most frequent cost drivers may be determined.

Another solution is to obtain data on all cost drivers over different levels of production activity. A correlation matrix of cost drivers over a range of volume can be constructed. The covariation of cost drivers can be measured and those that are highly correlated reduced to a few drivers that best explain several others. This is a more formal statistical approach than the judgmental method.

This leaves unresolved the issue of how the drivers should be traced back to individual products. One way is to group "families" of products or product lines by seeing which categories consume similar amounts of overhead for a particular level of output. This can be done judgmentally or statistically by examining input to output ratios of various cost drivers and products. Those products having similar consumption ratios of overhead activities can be grouped together for product costing purposes.

A highly simplified illustration is provided in Exhibit 4-2. Overhead activities are presumed to involve only four cost pools. Judgmental inspection of the data indicates that components are nearly perfectly collinear with shipping orders, engineering orders

**Exhibit 4-2**

## PRODUCT AND ACTIVITY COST ANALYSIS

**Data**:

| Products | Finished Units | Components | Shipping Orders | Engineering Orders | Design Changes | Total |
|---|---|---|---|---|---|---|
| A | 500 | 250 | 5 | 4 | 8 | |
| B | 1,000 | 250 | 6 | 4 | 8 | |
| C | 200 | 100 | 2 | 2 | 4 | |
| D | 2,000 | 500 | 10 | 9 | 16 | |
| Total Activity: | 1,100 | | 23 | 19 | 36 | |
| Total Dollars: | 2,220 | | 2,300 | 3,800 | 5,400 | 13,700 |

**Complete Activity Allocation to Individual Products**:

| | Components | Shipping Orders | Engineering Orders | Design Changes | Total/Units | = | Unit Cost |
|---|---|---|---|---|---|---|---|
| A | (250/1100)2200 | (5/23)2300 | (4/19)3800 | (8/36)5400 | 3000 /500 | | **6.0** |
| B | (250/1100)2200 | (6/23)2300 | (4/19)3800 | (8/36)5400 | 3100 /1000 | | **3.1** |
| C | (100/1100)2200 | (2/23)2300 | (2/19)3800 | (4/36)5400 | 1400 /200 | | **7.0** |
| D | (500/ 100)2200 | (10/23)2300 | (9/19)3800 | (16/36)5400 | 6200 /2000 | | **3.1** |

**Consolidated Activity Allocation to Product Families**:

| | Components divided by Units | | Unit Cost |
|---|---|---|---|
| A and C | {(250+100)/1100}13700 | 700 = | **6.22** |
| B and D | {(250+500)/1100}13700 | 3000 = | **3.11** |

---

and design changes over different levels of volume. Further statistical analysis is not required, as the number of components is considered to be a good surrogate cost driver for other overhead activities. Additional analysis reveals that products A and C have the same input-output ratio of production as do products B and D.

A not very surprising result therefore is that unit costing done with four activity drivers and four products yields nearly identical results to one non-redundant driver and two product families. In this case, products A and C have actual costs of $6.07 and $7.00 versus an averaged cost of $6.22. Products B and D have a unit cost of approximately $3.10 in all cases. This admittedly overly simplified version of actual activity and product cost behavior serves to illustrate the basic point of trading off immaterial product costing inaccuracies in return for reduced pricing complexity.

Should a judgmental or statistical analysis of different cost drivers prove unwieldy and result in too many cost drivers, the increased complexity may lead to non acceptance by managers. In this case, an alternative approach is to focus on a few activities that account for an inordinate amount of total cost. A good example of this is the 80:20 rule, which states that on average a high percentage of overhead (approximately 80%) can be explained by very few cost drivers (approximately 20%). Implementing such a rule requires arraying various cost pools by magnitude and establishing some judgmental cutoff point. Only activities above a certain amount are the focus of additional cost driver analysis. This procedure reduces the number of activity cost drivers under consideration relative to a statistical correlation approach of all cost drivers. For example, a cost driver that does not correlate highly with other drivers using statistical analysis would be included in the allocation scheme regardless of magnitude. Under the 80:20 rule, such a cost driver would be excluded from the allocation basis unless sufficiently material in monetary amount. Regardless of the method used to determine appropriate cost drivers, it goes without saying that the data must be readily electronically accessible.

## COSTING ISSUES IN CAD/CAM

When implementing CAD/CAM, the firm is faced with the challenge of how to reorganize its cost centers to better reflect new automation costs. For example, traditional design, drafting and scheduling departments should be replaced with CAD/CAM cost centers. New issues of overhead allocation arise in CAD/CAM environments. Overhead costs now have to be accumulated by newly defined cost centers and suitable allocation bases found.

Computerized design departments for example may use actual engineering time per drawing and charge these costs to the job or customer rather than using an average predetermined rate over all jobs. The latter method would be unsuitable if different engineering grades existed within the department, or if different types of departments were averaged together. Empirical evidence suggests that many firms in fact do not bother to use actual time or departmental cost centers, but rather use an allocation procedure more reflective of an averaging allocation scheme.

Indirect labor pertaining to CAM cost centers must be accumulated and allocated. This includes raw material handling and expediting; inventory control; and production planning labor. Once such overhead activity costs are compiled, the problem of how to best allocate these costs needs to be addressed. A common denominator such as cycle or machine time may be an inappropriate basis of allocation if the costs are not causally related to the allocation basis. A preferable basis might be the transactions that cause the raw material expediting or production planning costs, such as orders processed or time per order.

Essentially, the goal is to account for these overhead costs as opportunity costs rather than arbitrarily trying to "absorb" them. This notion of opportunity costing can also be applied to the absorption of sunk fixed costs of machinery. In this case, current cost allocations might be preferred to historical costs, and allocations could be based upon technological rather than financial accounting service life. An illustration of pre and post CAD/CAM cost pools is summarized in Figure 4-4. As apparent, the basis of allocation is changed from a common denominator averaged over all products to unique allocation bases for the new cost pools.

Production changes are evolutionary. NCM are the simplest initial form of standalone technology. CAD/CAM is a more advanced production technology. Fully integrated CAD/CAM systems from initial design to finished product involve software and hardware enhancements to basic manufacturing technology. Each of these production changes requires a parallel evolution in the firm's cost accounting system.

**Figure 4-4**

## COST POOLS AND ALLOCATION BASES

### PRE CAD\CAM

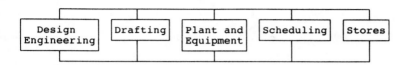

Allocation: Direct Labor Hours
{Predetermined Rate Averaged over Products}

### POST CAD\CAM

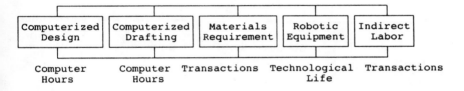

Various Allocation Bases
{Actual Rate by Product}

## COSTING IN CELLULAR MANUFACTURING

In a Cellular Manufacturing environment, production costs can be aggregated at three different levels of activity, as shown in Figure 4-5. At the most general level, plant costs are shared by all production departments. These include such items as factory depreciation, property taxes and insurance. At the sub-plant level, many service costs not directly traceable to the individual manufacturing cells also exist. These costs include such items as electrical utilities, computer and engineering support services, raw material storage and factory administration. Finally, micro-cell level costs are also incurred. These costs are the most directly related to products. Direct and indirect labor and machinery and

**Figure 4-5**

## COST AGGREGATION BY LEVEL

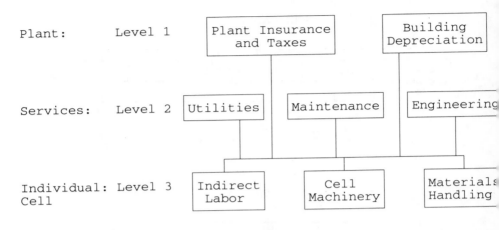

---

materials handling costs are clearly traceable to the individual production cell.

In a manufacturing cell environment, the most logical cost center basis is the cell itself. Machinery and indirect labor costs within the cell can be accumulated and allocated by product line. For example, if a product is machined by one or more pieces of equipment and its various machine times are significantly above or below that of another product, then an average cell rate over products misrepresents the overhead costs that should be attached to the product. In this case, individual rates should be derived. This assumes of course that the cell machinery is dissimilar, as is usually the case. Similar machinery eliminates the problem.

Another cell costing problem arise when two products are parallel processed through the cell. This double allocation of overhead to both products over-absorbs overhead and penalizes each product. As in CAD/CAM environments, indirect labor may be difficult to trace to individual products. Some activity basis of allocation should be used in accurately assigning costs to products as a function of the overhead activity cost generated by each product. Finally, machine depreciation should be based on the updated technological life of the machinery, not service life as defined for financial reporting purposes. The full current cost should also be used inclusive of start-up and financing costs, less forecast residual values. The pricing markup should not of course duplicate the financial component of the full cost. The assignment of the depreciation charge can be based on engineered standards or actual machine time. Alternatively, if cycle time is used, inventory turnover is a good basis of allocation.

At the second and third levels of activity, the sub-plant and plant levels, many service costs are generated that indirectly support the product. To correctly allocate these costs requires painstaking analysis of the users of the services. The nature of the support services defines the cost center and the allocation basis. For example, building maintenance can be assigned based on square footage of occupancy of each manufacturing cell. Equipment repair can be allocated based on work orders by cell and so on. General equipment such as computer services can charge a user fee directly to the manufacturing cell. Ideally, inter-service allocations should be made using a reciprocal algebraic method prior to manufacturing cell allocation. The above analysis requires a detailed study of all direct and indirect cost interrelationships that affect the manufacturing cell and the individual products passing through the cell. An updated costing system will involve greater record keeping as the number of cost centers increases in a cellular manufacturing environment. The additional effort however, should be more than offset by the resultant improvement in product cost accuracy.

An example of the effect of a revised cost pool structure and related allocation bases is provided in Exhibits 4-3 through 4-5. Initially, as shown in Exhibit 4-4, all direct labor is pooled and spread in proportion across units of products A and B based on total labor hours. Computerized drafting and design is similarly allocated. That is, total cost is allocated based on the number of pre-production prototype designs made for products A and B. Shared AMH equipment is depreciated based on financial accounting schedules, historical cost and units of production.

**Exhibit 4-3**

## COST ALLOCATION DATA

|  | Product A | Product B |
|---|---|---|
| Direct Labor Cost: | | |
| Set Up ($6,000) Frequency | 9 | 3 |
| Raw Material Handling | | |
| ($5,000) Transactions | 60 | 40 |
| Maintenance ($4,000) Hours | 70 | 30 |
| | | |
| Indirect Labor Cost: | | |
| Scheduling ($2,000) | | |
| Quality Control ($3,000) | | |
| Total Labor Hours | 6,000 | 8,000 |
| Units Produced | 4,000 | 5,000 |
| Design ($20,000) Computer Hours | 6,000 | 2,000 |
| Drafting ($10,000) Computer Hours | 2,000 | 1,000 |
| Number of Pre-Production Prototypes | 12 | 18 |

Design Computer Hours for Drafting: 2,000
Drafting Computer Hours for Design: 2,000

Cost of Automated Materials Handling Equipment:
$2,400,000 (120 Month Depreciation Schedule)

Current Cost: $3,000,000
(96 Month Revised Technological Life)

| | | |
|---|---|---|
| Automated Materials Handling Time | 5 | 15 |
| (Minutes) | | |

Exhibit 4-5 reveals striking allocation differences. First, at the cell level, the indirect component of direct labor, scheduling and quality control work that cannot directly be traced to individual products, is evenly allocated to products A and B. Variable labor however, is decomposed into setup, raw material handling and maintenance work which is all traced back to product. In this case, various bases of allocation such as set up frequency or number of raw material handling transactions are used to provide a more direct cause and effect relationship between the cost driver and allocation to the product. The result is an increase in product A's

**Exhibit 4-4**

## ORIGINAL COST POOLS AND ALLOCATION BASES

| Unit Cost:* | Product A | Product B |
|---|---|---|
| | | |
| **Labor:** | | |
| $20,000 (6,000/6,000 + 8,000)/4,000 | 2.14 | |
| $20,000 (8,000/6,000 + 8,000)/5,000 | | 2.29 |
| | | |
| **Computerized Design and Drafting:** | | |
| $30,000 (12/12 + 18)/4,000 | 3.00 | |
| $30,000 (18/12 + 18)/5,000 | | 3.60 |
| | | |
| **A.M.H. Depreciation:** | | |
| ($2,400,000/120)(4,000/4,000 | | |
| + 5,000)/4,000 | 2.22 | |
| ($2,400,000/120)(5,000/4,000 | | |
| + 5,000)/5,000 | | 2.22 |

\*   Differences due to rounding.

labor cost from $2.14 to $3.21 and a decrease in B's labor cost from $2.29 to $1.44.

Cost level two service allocations are indirect costs that must eventually be allocated to products. In this case, however, the cause and effect relationship must acknowledge the inter-relationship between service cost pools as well as service provided to product lines. First, prototypes are dropped as an allocation basis because they ignore the effect of computer time spent on the prototype. This is the main cost driver of the drafting and design cost pool. Therefore, computer hours provided by drafting and design to both products A and B are used in the allocation basis. In addition, because reciprocal services exist between drafting and design, this relationship is first solved to determine the final cost to be allocated to A and B. This results in an increase in product A's drafting and design allocation from $3.00 to $5.43 and a decrease in product B's allocation from $3.60 to $1.65.

## Exhibit 4-5

### NEW COST POOLS AND ALLOCATION BASES

|  |  | Product A | Product B |
|---|---|---|---|
|  |  | (Unit Cost)* | |
| **Level 1: Cell** | | | |
| Direct Labor: | | | |
| Set up | $6,000 x .75/4,000; | 1.13 | .30 |
|  | $6,000 x .25/5,000 | | |
| Mat'l Handl. | $5,000 x .60/4,000; | .75 | .40 |
|  | $5,000 x .40/5,000 | | |
| Maintenance | $4,000 x .70/4,000; | .70 | .24 |
|  | $4,000 x .30/5,000 | | |
|  | | | |
| Indirect Labor: | | | |
| Scheduling | $2,000 x .5/4,000; | .25 | .20 |
|  | $2,000 x .5/5,000 | | |
| Quality Ctrl. | $3,000 x .5/4,000; | .38 | .30 |
|  | $3,000 x .5/5,000 | | |
| Total Labor | | **3.21** | **1.44** |

**Level 2: Service**

Design = $20,000 + 2,000/
   (2,000 + 2,000 + 1,000)  Drafting = $26,087
Drafting = $10,000 + 2,000/
   (2,000 + 6,000 + 2,000)  Design  = $15,217

| | Product A | Product B |
|---|---|---|
| Design = {$26,087 x 6,000/ | | |
| (2,000 + 6,000 + 2,000)}/4,000 | 3.91 | |
| Drafting = {$15,217 x 2,000/ | | |
| (2,000 + 2,000 + 1,000)}/4,000 | 1.52 | |
| Design = {$26,087 x 2,000/ | | |
| (2,000 + 6,000 + 2,000)}/5,000 | | 1.04 |
| Drafting = {$15,217 x 1,000/ | | |
| (2,000 + 2,000 + 1,000)}/5,000 | | .61 |
| Total Design and Drafting | **5.43** | **1.65** |

**Level 3: Plant**
Revised A.M.H. Depreciation:

| | Product A | Product B |
|---|---|---|
| {($3,000,000/96)(5 x 4,000/5 | | |
| x 4,000 + 15 x 5,000)}/4,000 | **1.64** | |
| {($3,000,000/96)(15 x 5,000/5 | | |
| x 4,000 + 15 x 5,000)}/5,000 | | **4.93** |

\*  Differences due to rounding.

Finally, at the plant level, depreciation of automated materials handling equipment must be allocated. Unlike the previous allocation, however, current cost and a revised technical service life are used to more accurately determine product cost. Also, the automated machine time per cell is allocated to each product resulting in a significant difference in cost for product B.

This example illustrates fundamental differences that arise in the definition of cost with new cost drivers in an automated environment. Essentially these new cost drivers dictate new allocation bases. In turn, the cost pool definition must reflect the revised denominator basis of allocation. The broader the allocation basis, the more homogeneous and less diverse is the cost pool. Conversely, the more cost drivers, the more desegregated the cost pools. An optimal tradeoff must be found between possible product cost mis-estimation caused by poorly defined cost pools and excessive computations and record keeping.

## COSTING IN AN FMS ENVIRONMENT

FMS product costing methods vary widely across firms. For instance, cost pools may be very aggregated and periodically recognized, or conversely be very desegregated, traced to individual product and inventoried. An example of the former method includes aggregating direct and indirect cost pools and treating them as a periodic expense on the grounds that tracing them to individual products is (a) too arbitrary (b) too time consuming and (c) too inconsequential. At the other extreme, dozens of cost pools may be compiled at the plant, FMS and individual machine cell level. The plant and FMS pools would reflect all support services required by the parts family being processed. Examples would include DNC programming, engineering, quality control and so on.

Support department costs, once aggregated into appropriate pools, must be allocated to the product. One or more allocation bases should be used for each pool. Utilities might use kilowatt hours, while shipping might allocate costs based upon frequency, size and weight of orders. At the machine level, one obvious candidate for an allocation basis is time. Although many firms continue to use direct labor as an allocation basis, this makes little sense in a highly automated environment. Machine time can be defined as run time. Alternatively, total elapsed time can include material handling, inspection and wait time, in addition to run time. These times can be based upon engineered specifications or actual production times. Bar codes can define the entry and exit intervals from one DNCM to another within the FMS.

If times are similar across products, then a simple average time or units of production may be used as an allocation basis. On the other hand, should any or all of the time components differ significantly between products, then individual time by product should be tracked. The particular time measure chosen, run or elapsed, raises several issues. If run time only is used, then presumably only DNCM will be charged using this basis. This leaves the material handling, robotic and quality control equipment depreciation to be spread evenly over all units. Wait time is not charged, suggesting that no opportunity cost is attached to non value added production cycle time. Should individual products require different amounts of time with respect to material handling, robotic and quality control equipment, then elapsed time by product is a better measure than run time.

Should production time prove not to be a feasible allocation basis for FMS costs, manufacturing operations are another reasonable candidate for allocation. For example, if the automatic insertion of integrated circuits is a cost pool, then the number of inserts per product would be a possible allocation basis. Manufacturing operations can be broken down into various sub-components or pools such as soldering or polishing and the particular manufacturing operation involved can be used to allocate the cost. Alternatively, if similarities exist between different types of operations, a relative complexity factor could be assigned to each operation and overhead allocated on that basis. For example, I.B.M. employs such an allocation procedure, where it determines the complexity based upon engineering studies.

Because such a high proportion of FMS costs are fixed, the

denominator level of activity has an important bearing upon unit depreciation allocations. A predetermined normal capacity level, whether defined as run hours, elapsed time, or estimated operations should be used, allowing for non work days, downtime and non optimal scheduling. This normal capacity should be defined over the feasible number of production shifts. Predetermined normal capacity should be used rather than actual. If actual production is used to allocate depreciation expense and the actual product mix on the shared equipment differs from estimated, then one product will unavoidably incur an unfavorable mix variance solely as a result of the other product's revised production schedule. Furthermore, unfavorable volume variances due to underproduction are not strictly speaking costs of producing the product.

The above concepts will be partly demonstrated in the following example. Exhibit 4-6 includes cost and revenue data for four different products produced on an FMS. Direct labor costs represent work performed for scheduling, loading and unloading and inspection of units. This cost is not readily traceable to particular units. Indirect labor includes computer and engineering support. Unlike direct labor, it is found to vary with the number of operations related to each product. Distribution costs represent shipping and ancillary expenses. Two cost drivers, mileage and weight, explain in approximately equal proportions much of the distribution cost incurred. Depreciation expense is incurred for AMH, individual cell machinery and tools and fixtures.

Traditional cost allocations are found in Exhibit 4-7. Raw material is variable by product. Given that time is not traceable to each product, direct labor is allocated based on the number of units produced. Traditional overhead items include indirect labor and all equipment depreciation and both are allocated based on machine time. Distribution and product development are expenses of the period. It is assumed that all units produced are sold.

A revised allocation scheme, shown in Exhibit 4-8, reveals striking differences in individual product margins. Only raw material remains invariant from the prior allocation scheme. Because distribution costs vary by product line, cost drivers must

## Exhibit 4-6

### FLEXIBLE MANUFACTURING COST DATA

|  | **Products** | | | |
|  | **A** | **B** | **C** | **D** |
| Number of Units | 1,200 | 2,400 | 800 | 1,400 |
| Distribution: Miles | 500 | 1,500 | 200 | 400 |
| ($1,020)    Pounds | 1,500 | 2,000 | 800 | 600 |
| Direct Labor ($6,000) | | | | |
| Raw Material Cost | $1,500 | $4,000 | $900 | $1,800 |
| Product Development ($400) | | | | |
|    Hours Spent | 12 | 4 | 20 | 15 |
| Indirect Labor ($1,200) | | | | |
|    Number of Operations | 5 | 5 | 12 | 12 |
| AMH Depreciation ($800) | | | | |
|    Total Minus | | | | |
|    Estimated Run Time | 25 | 25 | 60 | 60 |
| Cell Machinery Depr. ($1,000) | | | | |
|    Estimated Run Time | 5 | 25 | 15 | 12 |
| Tools and Fixtures ($900) | 5 | 25 | 15 | 12 |
| Sales Price Per Unit | $3 | $4 | $4 | $5 |

be found that affect these costs. Mileage and weight are two equally good explanatory drivers. However, because mileage and weight vary between products, both must be included in the allocation scheme. In this case, multiple cost drivers are significantly more accurate than a single driver. Rather than treating product development as an expense of the period, it can be

Exhibit 4-7

## TRADITIONAL ALLOCATION SCHEME

**Products**

| | A | B | C | D | Total |
|---|---|---|---|---|---|
| Revenues | $3,600 | $9,600 | $3,200 | $7,000 | |
| Less Product Costs: | | | | | |
| Raw Material | $1,500 | $4,000 | $900 | $1,800 | |
| Direct Labor Based | | | | | |
| on Units | $1,242 | $2,484 | $828 | $1,446 | |
| Overhead per Machine | | | | | |
| Hour:* | $ 342 | $1,710 | $1,026 | $ 821 | |
| Gross Margin | $ 516 | $1,406 | $ 446 | $2,933 | $5,301 |
| | | | | | |
| Less Period Costs: | | | | | |
| Distribution | | | | | $1,020 |
| Product Development | | | | | $ 400 |
| Net Margin | | | | | **$3,881** |

* ($1,200 + 800 + 1,000 + 900)/(5 + 25 + 15 + 12) = $68.42 per hour

traced back to product using hours, thus improving profitability analysis by product line. Overhead costs are no longer pooled and allocated using a single denominator level of activity. Instead, two cost pools are formed.

The first pool combines indirect labor and AMH depreciation because the individual product costs of the two pools vary in exactly the same proportion relative to their respective cost drivers. While in reality such perfect covariation is unlikely, this serves to illustrate that quasi-redundant pools should be eliminated so as to lessen computational complexity. AMH depreciation, it should be noted, is based on the difference between total time and run time. This represents maintenance, wait and transportation time that varies between products. Run time would be a poor allocation basis in this case. Because products A and B have similar activity levels, as do products C and D, each pair is considered a product family for allocation purposes.

**Exhibit 4-8**

## REVISED ALLOCATION SCHEME

### Products

| | A | B | C | D | Total |
|---|---|---|---|---|---|
| Revenues | $3,600 | $9,600 | $3,200 | $7,000 | |
| Less Product Costs: | | | | | |
| Raw Material | $1,500 | $4,000 | $900 | $1,800 | |
| Distribution based 50:50 | | | | | |
| on mileage & | 97.92 | 294.27 | 39.27 | 78.54 | |
| on weight | 156.06 | 208.08 | 83.13 | 62.22 | |
| Product Development | | | | | |
| based on hours | 94.00 | 31.20 | 156.80 | 117.60 | |
| Pool 1: Indirect Labor & | | | | | |
| AMH Depreciation* | 294.12 | 294.12 | 705.88 | 705.88 | |
| Pool 2: Cell Depreciation | | | | | |
| and Tooling** | 166.67 | 833.33 | 500.00 | 400.00 | |
| Gross Margin | $1,291.23 | $3,939.00 | $ 814.92 | $3,835.76 | $ 9,881 |
| | | | | | |
| Less Period Costs: | | | | | |
| Direct Labor | | | | | $(6,000) |
| Net Margin | | | | | $ 3,881 |

\*  ($1,200 + $800) * Proportion of number of operations
\*\* ($1,000 + $900) * Proportion of run time

Cell machine depreciation is allocated based on run time individually to each product because bar coding enables tracking machine time in this way. Tools and fixtures are similarly tracked to particular products and therefore pooled with machine depreciation. Contrary to the initial allocation, direct labor is treated as a period expense because it does not have a justifiable cost driver. The revised allocation scheme arguably gives a clearer picture of product profitability because only non-traceable product costs are period expenses. Appropriate cost pools and related cost drivers are also found which more accurately reflect true product cost. The argument that all units produced are sold and that therefore allocations are a non issue because profits are identical under either allocation scheme is unsound. This ignores inaccuracies that result in product line profitability analysis.

## IMPLEMENTATION OF ABC

Many U.S. firms are implementing Activity Based Costing on a trial basis in parts of their operations. There are certain problems in implementing ABC. The first is a problem that arises in any shared overhead allocation scheme with fixed costs. Most overhead activities have fixed as well as variable and semi-variable cost components. It is not obvious what purpose allocations of purely fixed costs serve when they do not vary in the near term with any level of cost driver activity. For example, such items as property taxes, office depreciation, and research and development are basically fixed costs which in the short term do not vary directly with any particular activity drivers. Although activity drivers can be found for most overhead costs, it may not be particularly meaningful to allocate certain cost pools.

Related to this is the problem of fixed cost interdependence between products. With variable overhead, each product line is allocated its fair share of overhead based on activity cost drivers. With fixed overhead allocations, one product's fixed cost allocation can be influenced by a change in the actual level of activity of another product. To avoid this interdependence, predetermined rates and activity levels should be used.

Another problem relates to the feasibility of accurately allocating many cost pools, using a reduced set of cost drivers, to hundreds or possibly thousands of products. Theoretically, each activity should have its own cost driver. Realistically, surrogate drivers should be found to reduce the complexity of such schemes. Doing so however, inevitably results in increased inaccuracies in the allocations, which is what motivated the initial decomposition of the overhead activities. Practically speaking, surrogate drivers can usually be found for aggregated product lines, which will provide a superior allocation scheme than the existing one.

It should be noted that while allocations to product are unitized, semi-variable overhead activity costs only change within a discrete range of activity level, X set ups for an incremental Y units of product for example. Although semi-variable overhead activities are approximated by unitized (X/Y) allocations to product within discrete activity ranges, technically speaking, unit set up costs within a discrete range do not vary. If semi-variable overhead costs are significant, caution should be exercised in interpreting these inflection points.

A final issue is how to integrate the Activity Costing database with the firm's traditional cost pools. The latter are usually defined in terms of external financial reporting. It may be necessary to download certain generic cost pools into a spreadsheet format, for subsequent activity costing purposes. None of the above implementation problems are insurmountable. Simply reallocating costs, however, does not guarantee that the firm is pareto efficient relative to its competitors. The question is, given the limitations of the new system, is the firm comparatively better off with or without it?

The benefits of an effective Activity-based Costing system are several. First and foremost, a complete overhead activity analysis focuses the firm's efforts on non-value added costs and ways to reduce or eliminate them. A focus on overhead activities should lead to reduced transaction complexity, as managers reduce unnecessary overhead. Overhead is no longer treated as an unavoidable or sunk cost, but as avoidable in the long term.

A second benefit is that product costs, even with a limited number of cost drivers applied to aggregate product lines, become more accurate than under previous direct labor or machine hour allocations. Special decision situations, such as make or buy, are more realistically evaluated. More importantly, this improves product line profitability analysis and long term strategic planning. Equally important, new allocation bases can induce appropriate behavioral responses from a control point of view. To the extent that the new activity allocations are regarded as less arbitrary more meaningful by managers, they provide an incentive to both reduce and control costs.

# SUMMARY

This chapter discussed the Activity Accounting model in the context of today's manufacturing environment. Costing issues related to CAD/CAM, Cellular, and FMS manufacturing environments were addressed. Cost allocation in ABC is based on the premise that products consume activities, and the latter drive cost. A cost driver is needed to transfer cost from an activity pool to the product. ABC differs from traditional costing in that:

* All direct and indirect costs are considered as possible candidates for inclusion in product cost.

* Cost centers are determined based on an activity framework, not on physical production flow.

* Cost drivers play a leading role in the allocation process.

The inclusion of all indirect cost in Activity-based Costing results from the fact that a material proportion of cost in today's manufacturing environment may appear fixed, but in reality varies with many different overhead activities related to products. Furthermore, products do not influence indirect costs in as uniform a manner as they did previously. While the result of ABC usage is more accurate product costs, its ultimate significance lies in the fact that a renewed emphasis is placed upon the elimination of non-value added activities.

## REFERENCES

1. R. Cooper and R. Kaplan, "How Cost Accounting Distorts Product Cost." Management Accounting (April 1988): 20-27.

2. J.K. Schubert, "The Pitfalls of Product Costing." Journal of Cost Management (Summer, 1988): 16-26.

3. Ibid.

4. R. Cooper, "The Rise of Activity-Based Costing—Part Three: How Many Cost Drivers Do You Need and How Do You Select Them?" Journal of Cost Management (Winter 1989): 34-45.

# BIBLIOGRAPHY

Bennett, R.E., J.A. Hendricks, D.E. Keys, and E. J. Rudnicki. Cost Accounting For Factory Automation. Montvale, N.J.: National Association of Accountants, 1987.


Berliner, C. and J.A. Brimson. Cost Management For Today's Advanced Manufacturing. Boston, Mass.: Harvard Business School Press, 1988.


Bruns, W.J. and R.S. Kaplan. Accounting and Management Field Study Perspectives. Boston: Harvard Business School Press, 1987.


Cooper, R. "The Rise of Activity-Based Costing—Part Three: How Many Cost Drivers Do You Need and How Do You Select Them?" Journal of Cost Management (Winter 1989): 34-45.

_____ "You Need a New Cost System When..." Harvard Business Review (Jan.-Feb. 1989) : 77-82.

_____ "The Rise of Activity-Based Costing—Part One: What Is an Activity-Based Cost System?" Journal of Cost Management (Summer 1988) : 45-53.

_____ The Ingersoll Milling Machine Company. Case # 9-186-189. Boston, Mass: Harvard Business School Press, 1988.


Foster, G. and C.T. Horngren. "Flexible Manufacturing Systems: Cost Management and Cost Accounting Implications." Journal of Cost Management (Fall, 1988): 16-24.

_____ "Cost Accounting and Cost Management in a JIT Environment." Journal of Cost Management (Winter 1988) : 4-14.


Johnson, H. and D.E. Loewe. "How Weyerhaeuser Manages Corporate Overhead Costs." Management Accounting (August 1987) : 20-26.

Kaplan, R. "The Four Stage Model of Cost Systems Design." Management Accounting (Feb. 1990) : 22-26.

_____ "One Cost System Isn't Enough." Harvard Business Review (Jan.-Feb. 1988) : 61-66.

Miller, J. and T.E. Vollman. "The Hidden Factory." Harvard Business Review (Sept.-Oct. 1985) : 142-150.

O'Guin, M. "Focus the Factory with Activity-Based Costing." Management Accounting (Feb.1990) : 36-41.

Patel, J. "Adapting a Cost Accounting System to Just in Time Manufacturing: The Hewlett-Packard Personal Office Computer Division" in W.J. Bruns and R.S. Kaplan, eds., Accounting and Management Field Study Perspectives. 229-267. Cambridge, Mass.: Harvard Business School Press, 1987.

Shank, J.K. and V. Govindarajan. "The Perils of Cost Allocation Based on Production Volumes." Accounting Horizons (Dec.1988) : 71-79.

Turk, W.T. "Management Accounting Revitalized : The Harley Davidson Experience." Journal of Cost Management (Winter 1990): 28-39.

Turney, P.B. "Using Activity-Based Costing to Achieve Manufacturing Excellence." Journal of Cost Management (Summer 1989) : 23-31.

# Chapter Five

# CONTROLLING COST IN AUTOMATED ENVIRONMENTS

Many manufacturers, in their drive to automate and reduce direct labor, lose sight of the amount of overhead that permeates the automation process. While decreases in direct labor are easily traceable to new production processes, increases in general overhead are much less obvious. The result is that many U.S. manufacturers have seen an escalation of their overhead costs, both historically and relative to foreign competition. It is currently estimated that for a cross-section of U.S. manufacturing, overhead on average accounts for about 35% of product cost. This contrasts with estimates of 25% for Japanese manufacturing, which ironically is automated to an even greater degree.

This chapter discusses the operational control and performance measurement aspects of managing costs in today's high overhead manufacturing environment. The emphasis is on how today's cost systems can provide timely feedback on the **efficiency** and **effectiveness** of the operations being performed by a firm. The chapter begins with an introduction to the concept of manufacturing and non-manufacturing non-value added costs. This is followed by a separate discussion on the Cost of Quality aspects of production.

Budgeting considerations in an automated environment are then presented. This is followed by an analysis of the performance/control measurements that need to accompany the introduction of technology on the shop floor. Non-financial measures are also discussed. Finally, the chapter concludes with a discussion of the issues a firm faces when implementing new performance measurements.

## NON-VALUE ADDED COSTS

Examples of overhead costs that do not directly add value to product, yet are responsible for a significant amount of product cost are shown in Figure 5-1. These non-value added costs include pre- and post-production expenses as well as support services. Accountability is a prerequisite of cost control. If these costs are not tracked to product lines or divisional managers, then little incentive exists for reducing them. Instead, these non-value added costs will simply be viewed as a necessary evil, to be absorbed in some arbitrary fashion by more profitable product lines. Insufficient attention to these costs in newly automated environments seems to have compounded the problem for many firms.

How can these costs be controlled and ultimately reduced or eliminated? The primary method of reducing non-value added production costs is to focus on the transactions behind each cost, i.e. the cost driver. In some cases, the transaction can be eliminated; in others, better controlled. For example, engineering changes can be significantly reduced by building stability into the production process. These changes cause a ripple of new overhead transactions through all facets of production each time they are issued. If engineering changes are reduced, then non-value added activities will decrease proportionately.

Another example involves product design. Economical product design can significantly reduce non-value added as well as value added material and labor by focusing on parts redundancy. As parts reduction is designed into the product, non-value added costs

**Figure 5-1**

## NON-VALUE ADDED COSTS

### Pre-Production Costs

- Redesign
- Prototypes
- Production Planning
- Engineering Changes

### Support Costs

- Systems
- Personnel
- Marketing
- Legal
- Treasury

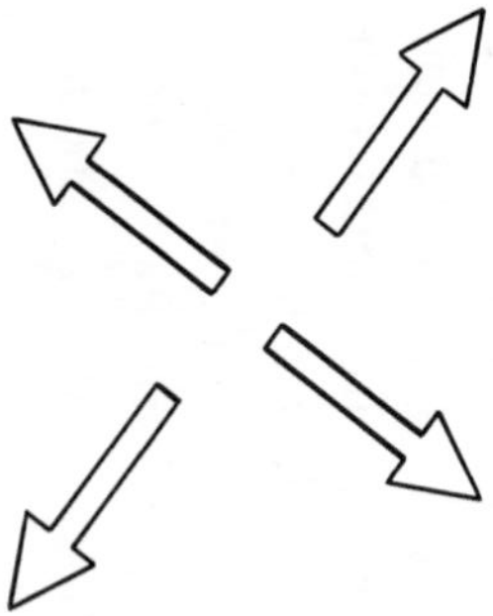

### Production Costs

- Inventory Costs
- Materials Handling
- Maintenance
- Energy
- Purchasing and Receiving
- Space
- Set Ups and Tooling

### Logistic Costs

- Distribution
- Warehousing
- Shipping
- Warranty
- Service

will correspondingly decrease. Inventory costs will decline, quality control will improve, set ups and tooling changes will decrease and logistic costs will be reduced. In similar fashion, each non-value added activity should be analyzed for possible cost reductions.

Another manner in which non-value added production activities can be reduced is by simplifying all production related processes. Just-in-Time is an example of this. The emphasis is on reducing materials handling, decreasing inventory holding costs and freeing up costly space. Eliminating redundant electronic data entry between buyer and supplier, and reducing inspection and quality control costs are also Just-in-Time goals. Non-value added costs can also be reduced by reconfiguring plant layout. Cellular manufacturing and group technology are methods of accomplishing this. Re-designing production layouts can result in tooling changes and set ups being reduced, labor flexibility increasing, and materials handling and downtime decreasing. Similar work simplification can be performed on non-value added support costs and logistics, as well as production processes.

Non-value added costs by expense pool should be tracked back to the driver that affects the cost. If the cost is correctly traced and then allocated to the product or product family causing it, then the first step towards responsibility accounting has been made. Once a manager is held responsible for a cost, and this is built into the performance incentive system, then cost reduction becomes possible. Without adequate responsibility accounting, there is little incentive to reduce mushrooming non-value added costs.

## Support and Logistics Costs

Figure 5-1 also summarizes many non-value added support and logistics costs. These expenses are substantial and traditionally under the control of the supplier, not the user of the service. There is little incentive for the supplier to reduce non-value added cost, unless behaviorally motivated to do so. Support costs are typically taken as a given in the yearly budget projections and then allocated over some common denominator level of volume, such as accounts receivable dollars for collection costs for example, or dollars of sales for interest costs.

An alternative to unquestioned acceptance of service allocations is to obtain market price for the desired service.  This is analogous to negotiating transfer prices for a product within the firm, when market externalities exist.   Just as market price serves as a constraint on internal transfer pricing, so the discipline of the marketplace can control internally sourced services.  For example, in-house legal and recruiting services can just as easily be performed outside the firm.  Increasingly, firms are contracting out services, such as data processing, consulting and distribution in an effort to cut overhead costs.  External contracting provides a control on in-house support services.  Caution must be exercised however in applying these policies.  To the extent that market frictions exist, the market price may reflect predatory pricing and not long term cost.

Another method of reducing non-value added administrative costs is to cost more accurately relative to the users of the services and the overhead activities that the users generate.  This differs from traditional overhead allocations in that the dollars of overhead spent are carefully analyzed relative to the activities generated and the cost drivers employed.  For example, accounts payable might be a function not only of invoices paid, but also the heterogeneity of suppliers, the number of discounts to be taken, and the purchase requisitions to be verified.  Payroll complexity might vary as a function of number of employees, frequency of payments and number of payroll deductions.  The basic premise is that the complexity of the support function should be decomposed by activity; appropriate cost drivers selected; and allocations made on that basis.  This eliminates cross-subsidization that arises when a single volume measure of output is used for the allocation.

As certain support costs do not vary with activities, this leaves unresolved the issue of how to correctly cost fixed non-value added support costs.  For example, the treasurer's salary and automobile depreciation are non-value added fixed costs of the Treasury department that are not related to any particular activity. If some quasi-activity basis is used to allocate these costs, such as dollars of accounts receivable, this implies that total fixed costs vary with the volume of activity chosen, which is not the case. Furthermore, low volume users will have their fixed cost charges subsidized by high volume users. Generally, the majority of support and logistics costs are variable or semi-variable with some basis of activity. Very few support costs are truly fixed.

A final and extremely important consideration in cost driver determination is its effect not only on the accuracy of resultant product costs, but also on human behavior. To the extent that overhead costs are controllable, their allocation can be useful for control purposes and be built into the incentive system. If the number of parts designed into a product for example becomes a surrogate cost driver for many related overhead activities and is controllable in the long term, then engineering design should be measured against this standard. The method of cost allocation chosen serves to elicit the desired behavior. If on the other hand, a cost driver such as machine hours arbitrarily absorbs overhead, there is little control value in using such a method. An excessive number of parts will continue to be designed into the product.

Very conceivably, the most accurate allocation method will not always be the most behaviorally desirable one. If the most appropriate cost drivers are not controllable, then management should reconsider their utilization. Assume for example that certain overhead cost pools, including utilities, supplies, maintenance and machine depreciation were allocated based on production volume. An alternate cost driver might be chosen with the eventual goal of reducing the above non-value added overhead activity. Cycle time might be a preferable basis. This would subsume volume and include time per unit produced. The ultimate control goal in this case would be to decrease cycle time per unit, with a resulting positive effect on non-value added overhead cost reduction. This new allocation basis is more behaviorally congruent with the goals of the firm.

## COST OF QUALITY

Quality undoubtedly ranks with cost as one of the two predominant customer considerations when purchasing a product. Either factor alone is a necessary but insufficient condition for obtaining business. Quality, therefore, deserves particular consideration in terms of its cost impact. Morse et al [1] consider total quality costs, costs that are associated with both preventing quality errors, as well as the cost of incurring defects. The issue at hand is a standard one; in effect, at what point is the incremental benefit of greater quality control outweighed by its marginal cost? Empirical evidence suggests that upwards of 50% of firms do not track quality non-conformance. Furthermore, those that do, do not use the management accounting system.

It is worthwhile examining both the prevention and incurrence categories of quality cost in more detail. Prevention costs vary inversely with failure rates. Such costs include quality engineering and training; preventative maintenance; in-process inspection and supervision; and quality circles and awards. Appraisal costs may be considered to be another aspect of defect prevention. They focus on which products are meeting technical specification. These costs involve all aspects of raw material, work-in-process and finished goods inspection; in process inspection; and production accuracy and field testing. Offsetting preventative measures of quality control is the cost of not catching defective items. These costs may be classified as either internal or external failure costs. Internal failure includes the cost of scrap and rework, lost time, additional inspection and testing of reworked products, disposal costs, and design changes. External failure costs are incurred once defective items leave the plant, and involve such items as production recalls, returns and allowances, warranty work, and most importantly, lost future sales attributable to defective work. Total quality costs are summarized in Exhibit 5-1.

The question arises as to the optimal point at which to minimize total quality costs. While slogans such as "Zero Defects" and "Quality is Job 1" are appealing, such goals are not attainable without significant incurrence of prevention and appraisal costs.

## Exhibit 5-1

### TOTAL COST OF QUALITY

**Prevention**
* Quality Engineering
* Employer Training
* Preventative Maintenance
* Process Inspection
* Supervision
* Quality Circles
* Awards

**Appraisal**
* Raw Material Inspection
* Work-in-Process Inspection
* Finished Goods Inspection
* Product Specification
* Tolerances
* Field Testing

**Internal Failures**
* Scrap
* Rework
* Lost Time
* Additional Inspection
* Disposal Costs
* Design Changes

**External Failures**
* Product Recalls
* Returns
* Allowances
* Warranty Work
* Future Lost Sales

Figure 5-2 depicts the tradeoff between prevention and appraisal costs and overall failure costs. As can be seen, as quality improves, prevention and appraisal costs increase exponentially. The reason for the non-linear increase is that beyond a certain standard of very high quality, the goal of zero defects becomes increasingly costly to attain. Conversely, as quality increases, failure costs also decrease exponentially. Initially, failure costs of significantly poor quality are high, particularly in terms of productivity recalls and lost future sales. However, as quality improves to a high level, incremental internal and external failure costs are lower.

The net result is that an optimal equilibrium point theoretically exists, where total prevention and appraisal costs equal total failure costs, as depicted in Figure 5-2. The problem with implementing such a concept is that explicit internal and external costs of quality are frequently not tracked to particular product lines. This makes the operationalization of this equilibrium cost-benefit analysis more of a subjective than objective judgment.

101

**Figure 5-2**

# COST OF QUALITY

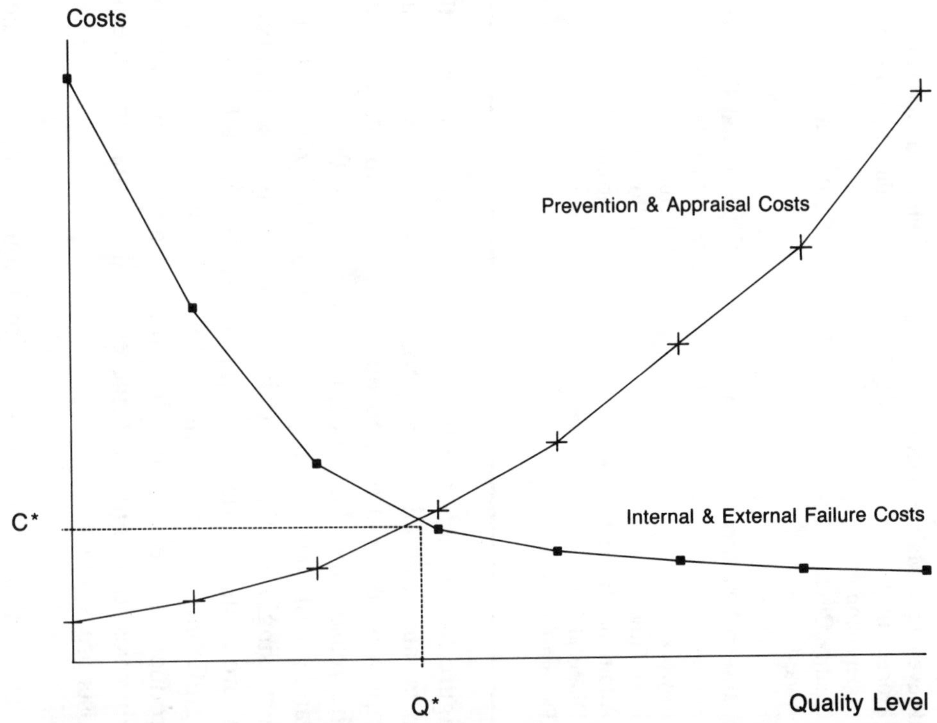

While complete cost information with respect to categories of prevention and appraisal cost of quality may not be available, alternate measures exist which do permit the firm to indirectly approximate an optimal cost-benefit quality tradeoff. One approach is to trade off the relationship between prevention and appraisal costs, as shown in Figure 5-3. As prevention costs increase, appraisal costs decrease. If the firm can approximate how a $1000 decrease in prevention costs translates into related appraisal costs, then the firm can assess a Pareto efficient mix of prevention and appraisal for a desired quality level.

Pareto inefficient mixes involve a disproportionate amount of prevention costs that are not offset by a corresponding decrease in appraisal costs or vice versa. This is reflected by all points that lie off the Pareto optimal curve. A firm can assess its prevention and appraisal effectively by compiling periodic costs for these categories and plotting them against physical measures of quality. In this way, the relative efficiency of the cost inputs can be compared in terms of desired quality levels.

Another worthwhile approach is to use divisional ratio analysis to track total quality costs to total manufacturing costs, or total quality costs to total divisional assets for example. Divisional responsibility can also be tracked through budgetary goals over time. Quality attainment is not a short term objective. The trend in the above ratios should be scrutinized.

The total cost of non-conformance can be broken down into its constituent parts and tracked through time. This is demonstrated in Figure 5-4, which shows the trend in prevention and appraisal costs, and how this impacts internal and external failure costs. These trends can be reported on a quarterly basis, using an annual cumulative carry forward. In this way, actual quality costs by cost category can be compared to budgeted amounts. Long term trends can be assessed relative to long term quality goals. Over time, investment in prevention and appraisal costs must be more than offset with reductions in internal and external failure costs. The net result should be a downward trend in total quality costs.

**Figure 5-3**

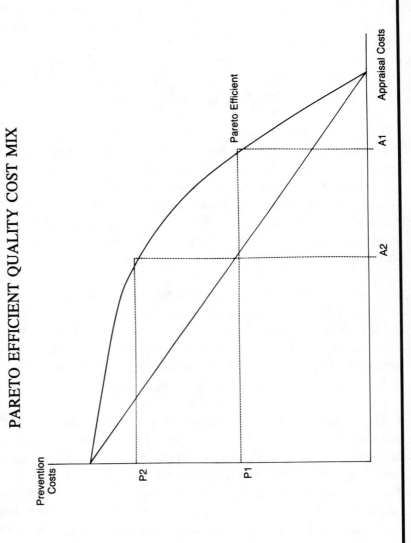

PARETO EFFICIENT QUALITY COST MIX

**Figure 5-4**

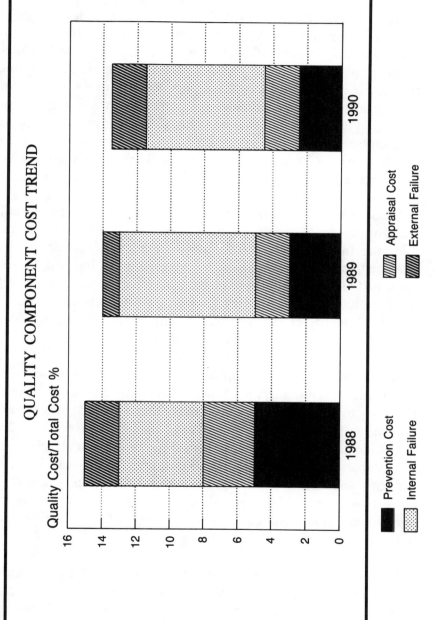

QUALITY COMPONENT COST TREND

## Japanese Practices

Japanese firms are particularly adept at controlling quality. The results of numerous field studies of Japanese industries reveal several interesting findings. First of all, contrary to U.S. firms, organizational responsibility for quality tends to be pushed down to the lowest level. Quality standards are not immutable. Rather, they are constantly revised. This philosophy implies that the total quality cost of nonconformance overlooks one important cost, that of lost <u>additional</u> business based solely on superior quality in the marketplace. If quality is viewed as an important marketing tool that can increase revenues, this may well supercede quality cost expenditure considerations.

In Japanese firms, process control is heavily stressed by Quality Control personnel during production on the shop floor rather than after the fact. Exacting machine maintenance, spotlessly clean plants and severe calibration standards exemplify Japanese process control. Quality monitors are prominently displayed throughout the plant. These include display boards, awards, quality trends and statistical quality control charts. Roving quality inspectors assign demerits for below standard quality output.

Above all, quality is emphasized over output volume. This means that when defects are found, immediate corrective action is taken. In the extreme, this may mean halting production, preventing defective parts from being made for inventory. Two characteristics of Japanese manufacturing highlight this preoccupation with quality above volume. The first is below capacity scheduling, this allows buffer time in production for corrective action. The second is small lot sizes, which permit corrective action to be taken before a large lot of defective items is produced.

Incoming raw materials are presumed to meet company standards, and contrary to U.S. policies, are usually not inspected. Suppliers work hand in hand with manufacturers to ensure that exacting raw material standards are met. Raw material handling is also emphasized. Studies report that Japanese workers are more careful in their handling of incoming parts, work-in-process and finished goods than their U.S. couterparts. Careful attention is also paid to the details of packaging to minimize damage.

The same care given to products is also given to worker training. New workers are assigned to experienced teams. Worker flexibility and cross training is also given to minimize downtime, boredom and to foster a team approach. Quality Control Circles are worker teams designed to generate suggestions for improvement in defect reduction, as workers are most aware of process problems. Quality is not viewed as a white collar top down responsibility but as a bottom up approach.

Industrial departments in Japan are responsible for tabulating internal and external causes of quality failure and tracking trends through time. A quality control department keeps track of quality and coordination, and quality training and awareness throughout the plant. While random sampling is often the basis for quality control in Western plants, the Japanese have not adapted this approach. First, an acceptable level of defective items for a given sample size is not taken for granted. Often, all items are inspected rather than randomly sampled, as zero defects are the goal. Second, the first and last items of a production run may be sampled in order to see if tolerances are significantly different at the beginning versus the end of the run.

A similar lack of concern for traditional standards is evidenced in over-engineering many production standards. For example, if a product was designed to last five years, then the materials would be constructed to last ten. Tolerances designed to operate within a predetermined range are extended beyond the required tolerance range and so on. This seeming disregard for traditional sampling and tolerances suggests that cost-benefit considerations are not a paramount concern to Japanese firms. Instead, customer goodwill engendered by such practices is implicitly presumed to be a significant intangible benefit that will more than offset the incremental cost.

Recent takeovers of U.S. plants by Japanese manufacturers provide a controlled experiment in the effects of differential American and Japanese management practices. Significant productivity improvements have been registered by such firms as Sanyo and Motorola once under Japanese management. Yet the economic conditions facing the plants have remained the same, only management practices have differed.

## BUDGETING

Operating budgets should reflect the changing definition of cost in highly automated production systems. New productivity measures should also be defined. Traditional budgeting typically compares operating budgets at standard cost against actual operating performance, in contribution margin format. That is, variable production costs are segregated from fixed costs to enable flexible budgeting analysis of profit at different levels of production activity. As a firm changes technologically, fewer costs are truly variable; overhead cost pools and related drivers become more significant; and not all costs are easily traced to individual products. This suggests that the firm must do an in-depth analysis of product cost behavior, allocation processes and level of cost accumulation prior to budget implementation.

Because increasingly production costs have the characteristics of fixed and semi-fixed behavior, a variant of full cost reporting may be used rather than contribution reporting. Under traditional budget reporting, activity variances are distinguished from production price and quantity efficiency variances. Master budget comparisons are made against standard operating budgets to determine activity variances, while standard budgets are compared to actual production results to measure production efficiencies.

Because so few costs vary directly with production volume, activity variances within certain production ranges now have less meaning. A preferable and more accurate budgeting alternative is for the firm to derive flexible budgets only for discrete break points of activity, where semi-fixed costs are expected to change. With the exception of raw material which remains directly variable, the budget now assumes significance only for different ranges of activity rather than all levels of activity.

In a highly automated environment, another budgetary consideration that arises is that appropriate cost drivers for each overhead item should now be used to project costs. This differs from traditional budgeting, in which only one driver or allocation basis is used to allocate overhead. Variable overhead in this case is presumed to change directly with the allocation basis. Fixed overhead is typically viewed primarily as a sunk cost to be absorbed. In the new manufacturing environment, individual cost pools should be budgeted using the appropriate cost driver. A common denominator such as direct labor or machine hours should not be used, as these are poor explanators of individual pools of overhead cost behavior.

A final budgetary consideration should be at what level to consolidate the information. Ordinarily, production budgets are summarized at the departmental level for costing and control purposes. Given that the traditional definition of a work-in-process department no longer exists in a highly automated environment, the appropriate level of budgetary control must be reassessed. One possibility is that indirect costs not directly traceable to individual products, such as automated materials handling equipment, might be budgeted to sub-assemblies or families of relatively homogeneous products. Then, within each product family, costs that are sufficiently material and are directly traceable to individual products can be budgeted.

In summary, the changing nature of fixed and variable costs, overhead pools and related cost drivers, and product family definition all fundamentally alter traditional budgeting techniques. Several of these new budgetary aspects are illustrated in Exhibits 5-2 and 5-3. Under traditional budgeting, raw material, direct labor and variable overhead all vary linearly with the projected budgetary activity. Within each activity level, these costs also vary by product, reflecting the particular raw material, labor and overhead usage and price mix of product. A common denominator, in this

**Exhibit 5-2**

## TRADITIONAL FLEXIBLE BUDGET

| | 10,000 units | | | | 20,000 units | | | |
|---|---|---|---|---|---|---|---|---|
| | A | B | C | TOTAL | A | B | C | TOTAL |
| Raw Material | $20,000 | $10,000 | $15,000 | $45,000 | $40,000 | $20,000 | $30,000 | $90,000 |
| Direct Labor* | 12,000 | 15,000 | 3,000 | 30,000 | 24,000 | 30,000 | 6,000 | 60,000 |
| Variable Overhead:** | | | | | | | | |
| Material Handling | 6,000 | 7,500 | 1,500 | 15,000 | 12,000 | 15,000 | 3,000 | 30,000 |
| Indirect Labor | 18,000 | 22,500 | 4,500 | 45,000 | 36,000 | 45,000 | 9,000 | 90,000 |
| Fixed Overhead: | | | | | | | | |
| Depreciation | | | | 120,000 | | | | 120,000 |
| Maintenance | | | | 20,000 | | | | 20,000 |

\* Direct Labor varies by product and is presumed to be linear with units produced.

\*\* Variable Overhead is allocated based on a percentage of direct labor dollars.

110

# Exhibit 5-3

## ACTIVITY-BASED FLEXIBLE BUDGET

| | 10,000 units | | | | | 20,000 units | | | | |
|---|---|---|---|---|---|---|---|---|---|---|
| | | A | B | C | TOTAL | | A | B | C | TOTAL |
| Raw Material | --- | $20,000 | $10,000 | $15,000 | $45,000 | --- | $40,000 | $20,000 | $30,000 | $90,000 |
| Direct Labor (Unload at $8 each) | $30,000 (fixed) | 2,000 (250) | 600 (75) | 1,000 (125) | 33,600 | $40,000 (fixed) | 4,000 (500) | 1,200 (150) | 2,000 (250) | 47,200 |
| Variable Overhead: | | | | | | | | | | |
| Material Handling (orders at $12 each) | 6,000 (fixed) | 1,800 (150) | 3,600 (300) | 2,400 (200) | 13,800 | 6,000 (fixed) | 3,600 (300) | 7,200 (600) | 4,800 (400) | 21,600 |
| Indirect Labor (inspections at $45 each) | 22,000 (fixed) | 9,000 (200) | 5,625 (125) | 6,750 (150) | 43,375 | 22,000 (fixed) | 18,000 (400) | 11,250 (250) | 13,500 (300) | 64,750 |
| Fixed Overhead: | | | | | | | | | | |
| Depreciation | 120,000 | | | | 120,000 | 120,000 | | | | |
| Maintenance (machine hours at $6/hour) | --- | 7,200 (1,200) | 3,000 (500) | 12,000 (2,000) | 22,200 | --- | 14,400 (2,400) | 600 (1,000) | 24,000 (4,000) | 39,000 |

Numbers in parentheses are activity cost drivers.

case direct labor dollars, is used to allocate all variable overhead items. In other words, these items are presumed to vary directly with direct labor dollars. Only maintenance and depreciation are considered purely fixed.

A revised budget analyzes cost behavior more precisely, that is whether fixed, variable or semi-variable cost behavior exists. It also examines drivers by cost pool. Only raw material remains unchanged. Direct labor is analyzed and found to be semi-variable. A fixed component of $30,000 exists at 10,000 units, which increases to $40,000 at 20,000 units. Remaining direct labor costs are linearly variable with loading and unloading activity. This activity varies significantly by product line.

Raw material handling is found to have a fixed cost component of $6,000 and a variable portion that changes with the number of orders processed. Handling cost is not proportional with raw material value or number of units by product line, so individual product analysis is necessary. Indirect labor also is a mixed cost, with $22,000 fixed and the remainder variable with inspection activity. Because automated materials handling depreciation is a sunk cost not directly traceable to any product line, it is segregated from the product line budgets. Finally, maintenance which was previously considered to be purely a fixed cost is now found to be solely variable with machine hours and allocated accordingly to each product.

## CONTROL MEASURES

Not only does the nature of the budget change in an automated environment, but so understandably do the related control measures. Traditionally, production accounting reports emphasize price and quantity variances, and to a lesser extent mix and yield variances, associated with raw material, direct labor and variable overhead. Fixed overhead price and volume variances are also usually reported. These variances are no longer very significant in a high tech production environment.

To begin with, an excessive focus on raw material price variances may lead to greater inventory because of increased purchasing caused by volume discounts. Secondly, direct labor is now a very small part of overall product cost. Furthermore, many of the different variable overhead cost pools are not individually related to a common denominator. Variable overhead variances cease to be very meaningful unless closely and causally linked to the particular allocation basis. Finally, excessive focus on volume variances leads to possible inventory build-ups, because fixed overhead is buried in inventory as a product cost rather than recognized as a period expense. Not only are traditional reported variances suspect, but their timing is obsolete. Typical monthly accounting reports do not allow prompt corrective action at the production level when the variance actually occurs.

New operational controls are proposed in Figure 5-5. These control measures are radically different from previous raw material, labor and overhead variances. The primary difference is that the focus is now on production efficiency rather than accounting overhead measurements. As production time subsumes many facets of efficiency, various measures are proposed. These include machine time switchover from one product to another, as lengthy set ups are now eliminated. Throughput or cycle time measures the total production time inclusive of run, transportation and wait time. Downtime indicates the extent to which the machines are operational, while machine utilization rates and scheduling are other time measures of production efficiency.

An example of operational time variances is included in Exhibit 5-4. The opportunity cost of under-utilized equipment is decomposed into a cell utilization variance and a cycle variance. Unfavorable utilization reflects the extent to which production was below normal capacity, the volume upon which overhead costs should be based. Utilization rates can no longer be improved simply by stepping up production for inventory, as inventory turns also are measured. Unfavorable cycle time is an indication of the degree to which actual production per hour was below estimated engineered cycle time. Similar variances can be constructed for other measures of production.

113

**Figure 5-5**

## PERFORMANCE MEASUREMENTS

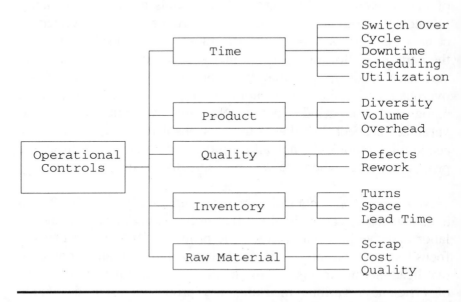

Because new production systems are designed for heterogeneous manufacturing, the diversity and volume of products per dollar of overhead is another measure related to performance attributes. Product diversity should be high relative to volume of output. Quantity and cost variances can be calculated for different products. Defects and rework are indications of quality, while inventory management is best measured by reduced space requirements and increased inventory turns per sales dollar. Trends can be calculated for these figures. Finally, raw material, scrap, quality and inventory levels are broader measures of performance than price variances which overlook inventory levels, or usage variances which ignore supplier quality.

In the absence of buffer stocks, performance between production cells is interdependent. This means that control measures must emphasize total plant performance, not just cell efficiency. Motorola for example has eliminated all labor and overhead

**Exhibit 5-4**

---

## OPERATIONAL VARIANCES

| | |
|---|---|
| Standard Cycle Time | 18 units per hour |
| Actual Cycle Time | 15 units per hour |
| Normal Capacity | 12,000 hours |
| Actual Utilization | 9,000 hours |

| Actual Cycle | Standard Cycle | Standard Cycle |
|---|---|---|
| Actual Utilization | Actual Utilization | Normal Capacity |
| 15 * 9,000 | 18 * 9,000 | 18 * 12,000 |

| 27,000 unfav. | 54,000 unfav. |
|---|---|
| Cycle Variance | Utilization variance |

---

variances at one of its plants to decrease the sub-optimal effect of focusing on cell rather than plantwide efficiency related to these costs.

Both financial and non financial performance indicators of efficiency should be tracked. A hierarchical measurement system, as shown in Figure 5-6, should include the business, plant and shop floor objectives. At the highest level, the business should focus on such financial and non financial measures as earnings per share growth, market share and new product development. These measures encourage product innovation, market leadership and investment in leading edge technology. At the plant level, financial performance should include target cost objectives as well as overall inter-plant efficiency measures. At the lowest level, the shop floor, cost accounting and productivity measurement assume a crucial role. Traditional financial measures of performance should be expanded to include non financial measures. These new micro level measures are the focus of the alternative control systems under discussion.

**Figure 5-6**

## PERFORMANCE OBJECTIVES

Earnings per Share Growth

Relative Performance
Target Costs

Value Added
Non-Value Added

Overall Productivity

New Products
Market Share

☐ Shop Measures    ◼ Firm Goals

☐ Plant Objectives

Shop floor control measures can be broken down into value and non-value added activities. This distinction is worthwhile because it forces the firm to focus on activities that do not add value to the product. By emphasizing non-value added activities, the control system can signal how to reduce or eliminate these costs. Value is added to the product only when it is being processed, representing between 10% to 50% of total product cost. The largest non-value added waste activities include product travel time between work stations, wait time, the number of parts per product, and storage space requirements. Many indirect costs correlate highly with the amount of time a product spends in the plant. Supplier lead times are crucial to minimizing investment in production, as is time spent in actual production. Rapid tooling changes and plant layout improvements minimize wait time in production. Lengthy leadtimes are an indication of production inefficiency that increase

**Exhibit 5-5**

---

## NEW SHOP CONTROL MEASURES

Value Added:

| **Raw Material** | **Worker Flexibility** | **Equipment Productivity** |
|---|---|---|
| %age of Total Cost | Tasks Performed | Schedule Attainment |
| Scrap | Direct Labor Productivity | Throughput Time |
| Defects | Indirect Labor Productivity | Maintenance |
| Rework | | Downtime |
| | | Set ups |

Non-value Added:

| **Waste** | **Inventory** | **Lead Time** | **Customer** |
|---|---|---|---|
| Space | Turnover by Type | Design | Warranty Claims |
| Wait Time | Turnover by Product | Tooling | Order Time |
| Travel Time | Obsolescence | Layout Changes | Backlog |
| Parts per Product | Space | Equipment Repair | Stockouts |

---

indirect labor and work-in-process inventory. Similarly, increasing the number of parts tends to drive up all indirect costs proportionately (Exhibit 5-5).

The full cost of inventory is only beginning to be appreciated. In addition to traditional holding and financing costs, product obsolescence is an important consideration. Control systems must recognize the non-value added cost of holding inventory by measuring the number of inventory units by product line; the turnover ratios for raw material, work-in-process and finished goods; and product obsolescence costs. Another non-value added cost that is seldom measured is lead time for product introduction. U.S. lead times for product development are much longer than Japanese lead times. Quick market response time is even more important as product life cycles continue to decrease. The cost of unfinished orders, the time it takes to complete an order, backlogged orders and warranty claims are all indications of production inefficiency.

Value added conversion costs directly related to production include control measures for raw material, worker flexibility and equipment productivity. The measures proposed are much more in tune with present day production realities than traditional price and volume variances. For example, manufacturing firms have decreased the number of their suppliers and increased the longevity of their relationships. Raw material price variances become irrelevant with long term relationships built around a few suppliers. Instead, because defective raw material is very costly in terms of subsequent production inspection and rework, the new focus is on incoming raw material quality, rework and measures of scrap.

The value of raw material as a percentage of total cost is important in attaining total cost objectives. Ways of minimizing materials handling is also important. Many of these measures subsume traditional raw material usage variances and instead concentrate on more important factors such as total product cost, quality and reliability of suppliers. Narrowly defined measures of direct labor rate and quantity variances should be expanded to include labor productivity measures, worker flexibility, minimization of downtime and indirect labor efficiency. Direct labor flexibility can be measured by focusing on idle time and number of products worked upon. Indirect labor is also a significant part of product cost. Efforts should be made to increase efficient utilization of programmers, engineers and support staff.

Finally, equipment productivity is not presently captured by overhead price, efficiency and volume variances. These variances focus on small components of overhead cost, use inappropriate bases of allocation, and reinforce overhead absorption by increasing production and inventory levels. Capital production efficiency can best be measured by cycle time. Amount of time required for set-ups and tooling changes are further measures of production efficiency. Machine downtime and preventative maintenance indicate how well the machines are being serviced. These production measures of efficiency are much more meaningful an indication of capital productivity than spending and volume overhead variances.

A recent empirical study examined how certain measures of shop floor productivity correlated with total firm productivity, both through time and across plants.[2] Productivity was defined as total output relative to inflation adjusted labor, material and capital investment. New capital investment and equipment productivity improvements, once adjusted for learning effects, accounted for some 50% of total factory productivity. Good inventory management also correlated strongly with overall productivity. Decreasing work-in-process by 10% produced a 9% increase in total factory productivity. In addition, every 1% reduction in waste led to a 3% improvement in productivity. Finally, when engineering change orders tripled, total factory productivity decreases of between 3% to 16% were recorded. This study suggests that several of the value and non-value added control measures previously discussed bear a direct relationship with total factory productivity. Reporting erroneous measures will discourage improvements in factory productivity.

## IMPLEMENTATION ISSUES

Performance measures must be consistent with economically sound productivity goals. The purpose of the measures should be to induce desired behavioral changes. When implementing performance measures, the lowest level of responsibility should be identified. Controllability must be within the purview of the department or departments being measured. To the extent that responsibility for a measure lies across departments, this should be the appropriate unit of performance measurement. Budgets should be set by first analyzing the activities of the unit. Present activities should be compared to alternate methods of reducing costs. Support departments should constantly be making efforts to streamline their activities, and justify the cost of their services rather than building costly overhead empires.

The question remains of how best to measure the proposed value and non-value added productivity measures. The simplest and most useful measures are found directly on the shop floor. One method is to track performance trends graphically through time, for example defects per 1000 units or number of reworked pieces. These performance trends can be used as motivational devices for the group or department responsible. Another method is to track time of production using computerized cards or bar codes, which indicate when products and processes are started and completed. Employee time by labor grade can also be tracked to products by computerized cards. These "real" time measures are a simple and inexpensive record keeping device that improve both costing and control.

Statistical process control is another control measure that is useful for determining when a realized observation exceeds the bounds of statistical expectations. Traditional standard engineered costs should allow some variation above and below standard. This applies equally to non monetary measures of performance. Establishing confidence intervals around a mean expectation allows a decision rule for investigation to be used, as shown in Figure 5-7. Only observations that are significantly different from the mean at 95% probability, or two standard deviations, are investigated. Once the observed process falls within the statistical parameters and is relatively stable, then additional efficiency improvements can be sought. Statistical process control should of course be measured in "real" time for immediate corrective action. Historical reports are of little utility. "Six sigma" charts cover the walls at Motorola, recent winner of the coveted Malcolm Baldridge Award. Such charts cover all productivity aspects, inclusive of white collar productivity.

As dozens of measures have been proposed to replace traditional material, labor and overhead variances, the question arises as to possible redundancy in the metrics. Several possibilities suggest themselves. One is to focus on a few key metrics that correlate well with others. Cycle time is such a metric. As cycle time decreases, many productivity measures improve. Possible improvements include less handling time and rework, fewer engineering change orders, less inventory and downtime etc. It is highly likely that reducing cycle time will improve many other control metrics. This is therefore a good barometer of productivity. Cycle time however will not account for all the variance

**Figure 5-7**

## STATISTICAL PROCESS CONTROL

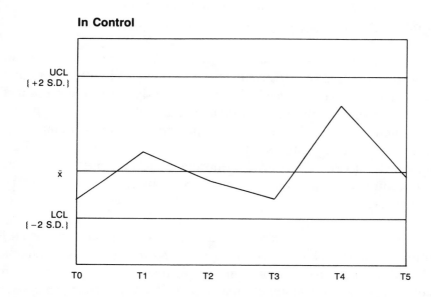

**In Control**

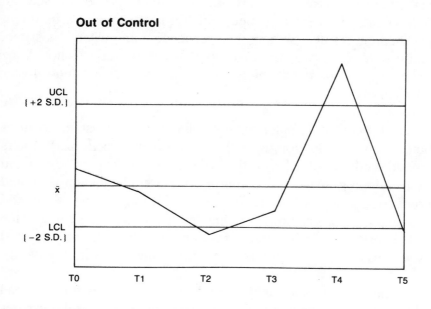

**Out of Control**

121

in productivity. It is necessary to track which factors are and are not responsible for improvements in cycle time. Is it due to less rework or is it attributable to better scheduling? Having many control measures enables a better understanding of overall productivity.

Another approach is that adopted by Northern Telecom. First, control measures of performance are designated by managers and performance goals are set. Weights are assigned to the measures based on their relative importance, such that the sum of the weighted measures is 100. Actual performance is then compared to the theoretical limit, as a measure of overall productivity. This approach effectively rewards improvement in control measures differentially, based upon relative contribution to total factory productivity.

What organizational changes are needed to assure successful implementation of new control systems? First, incentive systems should be designed to measure performance through time and across interdependent functional units. Overall performance sub-optimization occurs when short term results are emphasized and performance measurement is too narrowly focused. Second, burgeoning middle management which is not accountable for direct production results should be reduced, and where possible, eliminated. Disproportionate staff to line ratios should be redressed. Too many chiefs and too few indians don't foster productivity.

Third, successful implementation of new control systems requires bottom up participation, as well as top down direction. Workers most directly involved with the production process are best suited to developing reasonable control measures. Not only should production workers become involved with the process, so should pre- and post-production participants. This so because non-value added costs are also incurred prior to production (e.g., prototyping) as well as after production (e.g., warehousing and warranty work).

A final consideration is that suitable activity bases for overhead allocation should be adopted, consistent with the control measures required. For example, if cycle time is a good surrogate for many overhead cost drivers, then allocations based on cycle time will reinforce performance results designed to decrease time. Alternatively, if material burdening is used as an allocation method, then presumably controlling overhead burden rates will reduce overhead costs related to materials. Using an arbitrary allocation basis will not only misreport product cost, it will also have little control validity.

## SUMMARY

The non-value added concept greatly reinforces the process of controlling and reducing cost. Manufacturers can now work towards eliminating pre- and post-production non-value added costs as well as the actual production conversion cost. Non-financial measures should play a significant role in the control function. Timeliness characterizes operational control in today's factories, a trend that is facilitated by information technology. The emphasis today is on real-time information and continuous improvement, not obsolete and overly aggregated control reports. Finally, total cost of quality must be considered. A myopic view ignores all the internal and external failure costs associated with substandard quality. A comprehensive control system is designed to provide immediate feedback on all of the above parameters.

## REFERENCES

1. W.H. Morse, H. Roth and K. Poston, <u>Measuring, Planning and Controlling Quality Costs</u>. Montvale, N.J.: National Association of Accountants, 1986, 19.

2. R.H. Hayes and K.B. Clark. "Why Some Factories Are More Productive Than Others." <u>Harvard Business Review</u> (Sept.-Oct. 1986): 66-73.

# BIBLIOGRAPHY

Berliner, C. and J.A. Brimson. Cost Management For Today's Advanced Manufacturing. Boston: Harvard Business School Press, 1988.

Chow, W.B. "No-Nonsense Guide to Measuring Productivity." Harvard Business Review (Jan.-Feb. 1988): 110-118.

Clark, J. "Costing for Quality at Celanese." Management Accounting (Nov. 1989): 25-30.

Dixon, J.R., A.J. Nanni and T.E. Vollman. The New Performance Challenge: Measuring Operations For World Class Competition. Homewood, IL: Dow Jones-Irwin, 1990.

Edmonds, T.P., B. Tsay and W. Lin "Analyzing Quality Costs." Management Accounting (Nov.1989): 25-30.

Garvin, D.A. "Japanese Quality Management." Columbia Journal of World Business (Fall 1984): 3-12.

Hayes, R.H. and K.B. Clark. "Why Some Factories Are More Productive Than Others." Harvard Business Review (Sept.- Oct. 1986): 66-73.

Howell, R. "World Class Manufacturing Controls: Management Accounting For The Factory Of The Future". In R. Capettini and D.K. Clancy, eds., Cost Accounting, Robotics and The New Manufacturing Environment: 2.1-2.22. Sarasota, Fl.: American Accounting Association, 1987.

Howell, R.A. and S.R. Soucy. "Operating Controls in the New Manufacturing Environment." Management Accounting (Oct. 1987): 25-32.

Howell, R.A., J.D. Brown, S.R. Soucy and A.H. Seed. Management Accounting In The New Manufacturing Environment. Montvale, N.J.: National Association of Accountants, 1987.

Johnson, H. and D.E. Loewe. "How Weyerhaeuser Manages Corporate Overhead Costs." Management Accounting (August 1987): 20-26.


Kim, I. "A Microeconomic Approach to Quality Cost Control." Journal of Cost Management (Fall 1989): 11-17.


Morse, W., H. Roth and K. Poston. Measuring, Planning And Controlling Quality Costs. Montvale, N.J.: National Association of Accountants, 1986.


O'Brien, T.M. "Measurements in the New Era of Manufacturing." In A.M. King and N.E. Hadad, eds., Cost Accounting For The '90's: Responding To Technological Change: 63-83. Montvale, N.J.: National Association of Accountants, 1988.


Reeve, J.M. "The Impact of Variation on Operating System Performance." In P.B. Turney, eds., Performance Excellence In Manufacturing And Service Organizations: 75-91. Sarasota, Fl.: American Accounting Association, 1990.


Schonberger, R.J. Japanese Manufacturing Techniques. New York: Free Press, 1982.

# Chapter Six

# INVENTORY MANAGEMENT: THE JIT SYSTEM

This chapter will present the impact of a JIT system on inventories in a production environment. The essence of JIT manufacturing is to simplify all activities of the business. Thus, support activities such as set ups, quality control, and material management are all simplified if not entirely eliminated in a JIT environment. Many indirect activities of traditional plants are then performed by designated direct labor personnel. For example, tooling changeovers are increasingly performed by production workers on line rather than by support personnel. Line workers also perform machinery maintenance and set ups. Material handling pools may disappear or be reduced when suppliers deliver directly to manufacturers. Finally, raw material warehousing costs are eliminated and work-in-process storage is greatly reduced.

In addition to reduced inventory carrying cost, space requirements also decrease, materials handling is minimized, quality improves and cycle time decreases. Generally speaking, many overhead items that do not directly add value to the product are reduced or eliminated. An example of such cost reductions is shown in Exhibit 6-1. Although based on a sample of only 5 firms,[1] the results show distinct reductions in manufacturing lead time and all components of inventory. Set up times, space, cost of raw material and quality also improve significantly. Similar improvements are documented in other studies.[2]

Anecdotal evidence of JIT improvements has been documented at several large Japanese and U.S. firms. Toyota, for example is reported to have reduced space, time and inventory from a factor of 15 days to 1 day. Stanadyne Corporation decreased lead times from 8 weeks to 2 weeks. Brunswick Marine, a boat manufacturer, has cut floor space in half and increased inventory turns threefold. Harley-Davidson, the U.S. motorcycle manufacturer, at one time on the brink of bankruptcy, decreased inventories by 50% and set ups by 75%.

While such JIT improvements are commendable, their implementation is not as widespread as it may appear. An extensive survey of over 1000 firms reported balanced production flows and frequent supplier deliveries, traits characteristic of JIT environments, to be

**Exhibit 6-1**

---

COST REDUCTIONS IN JIT

| | Range of Improvement (%) |
|---|---|
| Manuafcturing Lead Time | 83 - 92 |
| Inventory: Raw Material | 35 - 73 |
| Work-in-Process | 70 - 89 |
| Finished Goods | 0 - 100 |
| Changeover Time | 75 - 94 |
| Labor: Direct | 0 - 50 |
| Indirect | 21 - 60 |
| Space | 39 - 80 |
| Cost of Quality | 26 - 63 |
| Purchased Material | 6 - 11 |

---

Source: H. Johansson, "The Effect of Zero Inventories on Cost" in Cost Accounting for the 90's: The Challenge of Technological Change. Montvale, N.J.: National Association of Accountants, 1986, p. 145.

in the range of 40-50% of total respondents, while purely pull production remained an elusive target for the majority (87%) of firms.[3] These field results quite convincingly demonstrate the existence of JIT advantages. However, either because of environmental constraints or inappropriate management practices, these benefits remain unrealized for many firms.


## INVENTORY VALUATION

In JIT environments, balanced work flows strive to eliminate work-in-process between work stations that are not self-contained. This increased production flexibility improves work scheduling and significantly decreases work-in-process inventory buildup. All of these production characteristics reduce customer lead time, in turn decreasing the need for buffer stocks of finished goods.

Purchasing is also significantly affected as firms strive to improve supplier quality and decrease raw material inventory holding costs. Long term contracts with fewer nearby suppliers are encouraged. High quality raw material is expected of suppliers and inspection is increasingly their responsibility. Deliveries are frequent and in small lot sizes, decreasing inventory holding costs. As vendors become computer networked with raw material buyers, paperwork is eliminated. Where feasible, goods are delivered directly to the production floor, as required by the producer, eliminating storage, handling, and holding costs.

Figure 6-1 reflects the impact of JIT production policies on raw material, work-in-process and finished goods inventory held by a firm. Purchasing and raw material inventory are drastically affected by new buyer-supplier relationships. Work-in-process is reduced because of new production technologies and processes, and finished goods is decreased because of the characteristics of demand pull production. It should be noted that zero inventory components are a theoretical goal, unlikely to be attained in reality. Further, successful JIT implementation is highly dependent upon individual peculiarities facing the firm, such as a highly flexible

**Figure 6-1**

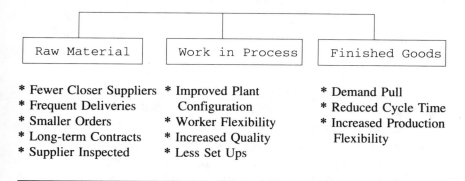

INVENTORY REDUCTION METHODS

| Raw Material | Work in Process | Finished Goods |
|---|---|---|
| * Fewer Closer Suppliers | * Improved Plant | * Demand Pull |
| * Frequent Deliveries | Configuration | * Reduced Cycle Time |
| * Smaller Orders | * Worker Flexibility | * Increased Production |
| * Long-term Contracts | * Increased Quality | Flexibility |
| * Supplier Inspected | * Less Set Ups | |

pull system, a reconfigured plant layout, short production cycle time, and close long term vendor relationships.

## Raw Material

The changing firm relationship with suppliers has already been described. Several key aspects of this new relationship affect the valuation of raw material inventory. As the number of suppliers is greatly reduced, the long term contractual commitments of the firm to its suppliers increases. Suppliers in turn assume greater responsibility for quality, inspection and JIT deliveries. Having fewer regular suppliers but more frequent deliveries can result in more paperwork per supplier, that is, the number of invoices increases. To eliminate the necessity of repetitive data entry for both supplier and buyer, many firms are turning towards electronic data interchange and batching of invoices. This involves the electronic exchange of transactions between buyer and seller.

Several firms have instituted Electronic Data Interchange (EDI).[4] Where inter-firm computer systems are incompatible, a third party network may alleviate the incompatibility. Navistar has materials delivered only hours before they are required for production. The firm is electronically linked to its suppliers. General Motors has several plants which have EDI. All invoices are paid electronically through automated funds transfer with the firm's banks. This requires a three way electronic link between vendor, buyer and banker. Ford has a similar set up that involves an electronic exchange of invoices for production, purchase orders, requests for quotes and electronic funds transfer.

Likewise, Chrysler can notify its suppliers electronically of parts requirements and make adjustments to material requirements schedules as required. These electronic systems not only reduce human error as data entry is lessened, but decrease cost and speed up operations as well. Although paperless transactions are not a requirement of JIT, the characteristics of JIT production encourage the adoption of EDI.

Theoretically, if raw material is delivered just prior to production, there is no need for a raw material inventory account. The firm may simply debit the transaction directly to Material-in-Process and debit or credit a variance account for any deviation from standard cost.

| | | |
|---|---|---|
| Material in Process | xxx | |
| Price variance | xxx | |
| Accounts Payable | | xxx |

In reality, a small stock of several days' production may be held to buffer production scheduling as required. These goods may require an inventory account in which production requisitions are recorded via either a raw material kanban or a bar code that electronically checks out the part and quantity.

**Work-in-Process**

Work-in-process inventory has undergone several valuation changes as a result of JIT. Traditional work-in-process valuation involves raw material, direct labor and overhead product costs.

Under process costing for homogeneous units, beginning and ending inventory often have different degrees of completion for each product cost, requiring the calculation of equivalent units of production for correct work-in-process and finished goods valuation. Under job costing for heterogeneous units, individual raw material, labor and overhead product costs are tracked to each unit of product, rather than averaged as in process costing.

In a JIT environment, work-in-process inventory valuation is generally simplified. First, production configuration is now designed for homogeneous production cells of similar products. Different work-in-process stations are greatly reduced. In many cases, this decreases the heterogeneity of product flow between work stations, enabling greater utilization of process rather than job costing. The product or product families by cell are relatively homogeneous and costs may be averaged over these identical or similar units.

Second, because cycle times are reduced, machine flexibility is increased and production is pulled through the system, contingent upon demand. This improved response time allows the firm to respond to more erratic demand patterns. There is generally much less unfinished beginning and ending work-in-process. Without differing degrees of completion of beginning and ending inventory, the calculation of equivalent units is reduced to an average cost per unit, greatly simplifying costing calculations. Third, the cost pools themselves are redefined. Direct labor, where insignificant in terms of total product cost, is now collapsed into overhead. This reduces costs into two pools, raw material and conversion costs, rather than the traditional pools, which include direct labor. If the firm wishes to continue tracking labor rate and efficiency variances however, it must maintain actual labor charges for comparison against standard inventory labor debits.

At month end, physical inventory count is greatly simplified by the use of standardized kanban and regular cycle counting. At the extreme, physical counts may not even be required if the degree of work-in-process is sufficiently low. If this were the case, raw materials and conversion costs could theoretically be charged

131

directly to finished goods. Then at the end of the period, a physical count of work-in-process inventory would be done and an adjusting entry could be made between finished goods and work-in-process for this amount. This method is described below under normal "backflushing" techniques of valuation for finished goods inventory. Assuming however the more common case where some work-in-process inventory valuation is involved, then an adaptation of traditional process costing is useful.

Assume the firm manufactures two components, X and Y, for final assembly. Its product costs include direct labor, raw material and overhead. A work-in-process department exists for each component. Two service departments, Maintenance and Materials Handling are allocated in a reciprocal fashion to each work-in-process department, depending upon utilization. Subsequent to JIT implementation, the two departments are consolidated into one manufacturing cell and the support department costs are allocated directly to the cell. Materials handling is allocated based on 20% of raw material charges. Maintenance is allocated proportionately with machine hours at a rate of $25 per hour. Direct labor is no longer broken out, but included as a conversion cost. There are 50 units in beginning inventory, and 75 units in ending inventory that are 50% complete. 550 units are completed during the period. The firm uses weighted average costing. Ancillary data is included in Exhibit 6-2.

Exhibit 6-2 reveals two new cost pools, one for raw material and one for conversion costs. Because weighted average is used, beginning inventory and period raw material costs are combined. In addition, overhead related to raw materials handling is included in the pool, because these costs are directly traceable to the product. Conversion costs include the departmental depreciation for machinery as well as electricity. In addition, as direct labor is not very material, it is pooled with conversion costs. Finally, maintenance is no longer treated as a general overhead allocation, but is included in conversion costs, based upon machine hours. Standard equivalent unit calculations and allocations to finished goods and ending work-in-process are shown in Exhibit 6-3, based upon these new cost pools.

**Exhibit 6-2**

## JIT PROCESS COSTING DATA

| | |
|---|---:|
| Beginning Inventory Costs: | |
| Raw Material X | $10,000 |
| Raw Material Y | $5,000 |
| Conversion Costs | $500 |
| | |
| Period Costs and Hours: | |
| Raw Material X | $80,000 |
| Raw Material Y | $40,000 |
| Direct Labor | 60 hours @ $12 |
| Machine Hours A | 50 |
| Machine Hours B | 30 |
| Machine Depreciation | $24,000 |
| Electricity | $1,250 |

### JIT WORK-IN-PROCESS COST POOLS

| | |
|---|---:|
| Raw Material Cost Pool: | |
| Beginning Inventory | $15,000 |
| This Period | $120,000 |
| | |
| Raw Material Handling: | $24,000 |
| 0.2 X 120,000 | |
| Total | **$159,000** |

| | |
|---|---:|
| Conversion Cost: | |
| Beginning Inventory | $500 |
| This Period - Direct Labor  (60 X 12) | $720 |
| Maintenance  (80 X 25) | $2,000 |
| Depreciation | $24,000 |
| Electricity | $1,250 |
| Total | **$28,470** |

The primary difference between traditional and JIT process costing is the cell basis of allocation and the formation of new cost pools for subsequent product allocation. A cell now replaces several work-in-process departments. Pools are formed that best reflect the product's cost. Direct traceability of overhead is encouraged and direct labor is no longer treated as a separate cost

**Exhibit 6-3**

## JIT INVENTORY VALUATION

| | Beginning | Started & Completed | Ending |
|---|---|---|---|
| Raw Material Equivalent Units | 50 | 500 | 75 |
| Conversion Cost Equivalent Units | 50 | 500 | 37.5 |

| Equivalent Unit Cost: | | |
|---|---|---|
| Raw Material | $159,000/625 | $254.40 |
| Conversion Costs | $ 28,470/587.50 | $ 48.46 |
| Total | | $302.86 |

| Valuation: | | | |
|---|---|---|---|
| Finished Goods | 550 | X  $302.86 | $166,573.00 |
| Ending Inventory: | | | |
| Raw Material | 75 | X  $254.40 | $ 19,080.00 |
| Conversion Costs | 37.5 | X  $  48.46 | $   1,817.25 |

pool. To the extent that cost pools do not accurately reflect the equivalent units to which they are allocated, inventory will be mis-estimated. It should be noted that if beginning or ending work-in-process is insignificant, then the equivalent unit allocation becomes a non-issue. An average product cost across pools can simply be assigned to the number of units produced.

## Finished Goods

Finished goods can be treated in different ways under JIT. As explained, if the firm has a significant amount of beginning and ending work-in-process inventory, then tracking costs is worthwhile. Costs must be assigned not only to the units transferred out but also to those remaining in work-in-process. To do otherwise would misstate both the work-in-process and the finished goods inventory. Another advantage of tracking work-in-process costs is for control. If costs are not tracked during production, then cost feedback occurs after the fact, which may be too late for corrective purposes. Costs only become known once the goods are transferred out to finished goods.

If production is fairly stable, it may be assumed that on average raw material and conversion costs are one half complete with respect to ending inventory work-in-process across different production cells. This assumption simplifies the equivalent unit valuation. Assuming the firm uses standard costs, then the journal entries would be very similar to traditional entries. If raw material were delivered directly to the production area, then the following entries would be made:

| | | |
|---|---|---|
| Work-in-Process (Standard) | xxx | |
| Accounts Payable | | xxx |
| Raw Material Variances | | xxx |

| | | |
|---|---|---|
| Work-in-Process (Standard) | xxx | |
| Conversion Costs | | xxx |
| Conversion Cost Variances | | xxx |

| | | |
|---|---|---|
| Finished Goods | xxx | |
| Work-in-Process | | xxx |

| | | |
|---|---|---|
| Cost of Goods Sold | xxx | |
| Finished Goods | | xxx |

The only noticeable difference from traditional entries is the absence of a raw material inventory account and altered cost pools. Should ending work-in-process be insignificant, posing no inventory valuation and control problems, then work-in-process may simply be bypassed via the following entry.

| | | |
|---|---|---|
| Finished Goods | xxx | |
| Accounts Payable | | xxx |

| | | |
|---|---|---|
| Conversion Cost Variances | xxx | |
| Raw Material Variances | | xxx |

| | | |
|---|---|---|
| Cost of Goods Sold | xxx | |
| Finished Goods | | xxx |

Again, this assumes that raw material is put into production as delivered. This pull or "backflush" system of journal entries records transactions only at termination of the production and sales cycle, eliminating detailed costing during the process. It effectively focuses only on outputs. Again, it should be stressed that such an approach is justifiable only if ending work-in-process is insignificant, resulting in no material misstatement of inventory values. Also, adequate production controls must exist so that cost control during the production process is not sacrificed.

## JIT and EOQ

JIT, due to its profound effect on inventories, redefines the traditional EOQ model used in inventory policies. Two cost pools are traditionally associated with optimal inventory policies. Raw material inventory policy is determined by minimizing the total of ordering and carrying costs, while optimal work-in-process inventory is based upon minimizing set up and carrying costs. Because demand uncertainty usually exists, finished goods inventory policy should include the possibility of stockout costs. Minimizing carrying cost suggests small lot production. However, this increases the frequency and therefore the cost of orders. Likewise, reducing set up costs requires longer production runs which increases the amount of inventory carried.

Optimal inventory is traditionally determined in the following manner. Total ordering, or alternatively set up, and carrying cost can be defined as:

$$TC = PD/Q + CQ/2 \qquad (1)$$

where    TC = total order or set up cost and carrying cost
          P = the cost of an order or the cost of a set up
          Q = the number of units ordered or production lot size
          D = annual demand
          C = carrying cost of one unit per year

To minimize the total cost requires setting the equation equal to zero and taking the derivative of total cost relative to quantity. This is the Economic Order Quantity (EOQ) where the change of total cost relative to quantity is at a minimum.

$$EOQ = [2DP/C]^{1/2} \tag{2}$$

Substituting the above parameters into equation (2) yields the optimal inventory quantity. The point at which to reorder is simply a function of usage and lead time. If safety stock is needed to cope with uncertain demand then this can be included as well.

$$R = U * L + SS \tag{3}$$

where $\quad$ U = daily usage
$\quad\quad\quad$ L = number of days of lead time
$\quad\quad$ SS = safety stock

The most subjective components of equation (1) are P, the order or set up cost and C, the carrying cost. Evidence exists suggesting that firms do not fully incorporate all cost components into EOQ analysis. Order costs are not simply delivery charges and transaction costs of paperwork. They also include raw material handling costs which are significant, as well as scheduling and purchasing activities.

Set up costs typically ignore quality and rework costs, product diversity, routing and idle time and scheduling changes. Further, to assess the true cost of decreased set ups, it is necessary to know the opportunity cost of extra capacity. This cost is usually not provided by the accounting system. Finally, warehousing and financing inventory carrying costs overlook product obsolescence and significant material handling cost. The latter are estimated to be in the order of 10-20% of product cost. JIT helps focus on reducing this cost. Another problem that arises with EOQ implementation is the level at which to optimize inventory. If the production capacities of different assembly lines are not integrated in the analysis, then optimization at one department is thwarted by potential production bottlenecks at other departments.

The above suggests that the firm should correctly cost all ordering, set up and carrying costs of inventory. Once this cost analysis is performed, true inventory costs emerge. Rather than attempt to minimize a possibly inaccurate cost, it makes more economic sense to try and simply reduce the inventory itself to a minimum and eliminate certain costs. The most logical candidates for cost reduction in JIT are order and set up costs.

Order costs are reduced by entering into long term supplier agreements. Supplier proximity is a key consideration. Long term commitments improve raw material quality and permit optimal pricing by reducing uncertainty. Suppliers deliver only what is needed when raw material is put into production. Electronic data links exist between buyer and supplier and deliveries are often specified at point of production. This eliminates much transportation, storage, handling, paperwork, inspection and volume purchases due to discounts. Effectively, all order cost components are significantly reduced or eliminated.

Set up costs can be eliminated with quick changeovers due to production innovations. Reconfigured plant layouts reduce cycle time and handling costs. Smaller batches lead to increased focus on quality, as defective items cannot be hidden in inventory. Once order and set up costs are reduced, only carrying costs remain. With supplier cooperation and flexible manufacturing machinery, raw material and work-in-process inventories can be reduced to minimal levels.

Finished goods inventory is a function of the uncertainty inherent in product demand. With improved cycle time however, the need for buffer inventories of finished goods decreases. Producing to demand becomes more feasible. These changes are described in Figure 6-2. Initial EOQ, or Q, shifts significantly to the left to Q*, that is decreases, as order and set up costs are reduced and total carrying costs decrease. Theoretically, Q* tends to 1 as costs are minimized. Conversely, should order and set up costs not decrease

**Figure 6-2**

---

## REDUCED INVENTORY COSTS

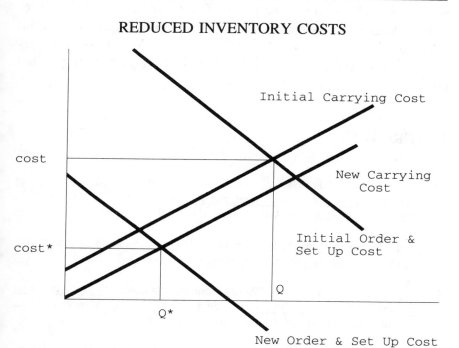

in proportion to reduced carrying costs, quantity could actually increase. This highlights the importance of reducing order and set up costs for JIT management.

## SUMMARY

JIT is a philosophy with an emphasis upon small batch size and waste reduction. When combined with cellular manufacturing, it leads to radical changes in the method of inventory valuation as well as control measures on the shop floor. Both raw material and work-in-process inventories are greatly reduced as supplier relationships change and production layouts are transformed. Inventory valuation is significantly simplified as cost pools are reduced and unfinished units eliminated. At the same time, responsibility accounting increases within production cells. This leads to a renewed emphasis on quality.

The benefits of JIT are more than just reduction in inventory. Among other benefits is the complete re-evaluation of value and non-value added costs on the factory floor. Reduction of such non-value added items as space, rework, wait time and set ups are all changes that accompany a JIT system. When successfully implemented, JIT can also have a significant impact upon product costing.

## REFERENCES

1.  R.A. Howell, J.D. Brown, S.R. Soucy and A.H. Seed, Management Accounting in the New Manufacturing Environment. Montvale, N.J.: National Association of Accountants, 1987, p.9.

2.  A.T. Sadhwani and M.H. Sarhan, "Electronic Systems Enhance JIT Operations." Management Accounting (Dec. 1987) : 25-30.

3.  H. Johansson, "The Effect of Zero Inventories on Cost" in Cost Accounting for the 90's : The Challenge of Technological Change. Montvale, N.J.: National Association of Accountants, 1986, p. 145.

4.  M.F. Barton, S.P. Agrawal and L.M. Rockwell, "Meeting the Challenges of Japanese Management Concepts." Management Accounting (Sept. 1988): 49-53.

## BIBLIOGRAPHY

Barton, M.F., S.P. Agrawal and L.M. Rockwell. "Meeting the Challenge of Japanese Management Concepts." Management Accounting (Sept. 1988): 49-53.

Calvasina, R.V., E.J. Calvasina and G.E. Calvasina. "Beware the New Accounting Myths." Management Accounting (Dec. 1989) : 41-45.

Cappettini, R. and D.K. Clancy. Cost Accounting, Robotics and the New Manufacturing Environment. Sarasota, Fl : American Accounting Association, 1987.

Foster, G. and C.T. Horngren. "Cost Accounting and Cost Management in a JIT Environment." Journal of Cost Management (Winter 1988): 4-14.

Karmarkar, U. "Getting Control of Just in Time." Harvard Business Review (Sept.-Oct. 1989) : 122-131.

Patell, J. "Adapting a Cost Accounting System to Just in Time Manufacturing: The Hewlett-Packard Personal Office Computer Division." In W.J. Bruns and R.S. Kaplan, eds. Accounting and Management Field Study Perspectives: 229-267. Cambridge, Mass.: Harvard Business School Press, 1987.

Robinson, M.A. and J.E. Timmerman. "Vendor Analysis Supports JIT Manufacturing." Management Accounting (Dec.1987) : 20-24.

Sadhwani, A.T. and M.H. Sarhan. "Elecronic Systems Enhance JIT Operations." Management Accounting (Dec.1987) : 25-30.

_____, M.H. Sarhan and D. Kiringoda. "Just-in-Time: An Inventory System Whose Time Has Come." Management Accounting (Dec.1985): 36-44.

Schonberger,R.J. Japanese Manufacturing Techniques. New York: Free Press, 1982.

Turk, W.T. "Management Accounting Revitalized: The Harley Davidson Experience." Journal of Cost Management (Winter 1990): 28-39.

# Chapter Seven

# JUSTIFYING CAPITAL INVESTMENT

This chapter is dedicated to the complex task of justifying investments in advanced manufacturing technologies such as Numerically Controlled machines, CAD/CAM, FMS, and CIM. As previously discussed, extant cost systems provide insufficient relevant information to properly evaluate benefits that can ensue as a result of automation on the factory floor. This chapter reviews the utility of the discounted cash flow model traditionally used in capital budgeting. Other evaluation techniques are also discussed, as is the post-audit evaluation process. Finally, the performance of recent high-tech capital investments by various firms is presented.

## STRATEGIC CONSIDERATIONS

Investing in advanced technology such as RE, FMS or CIM requires strategic decision making. Many of the long term ramifications of these decisions in a technologically competitive and changing production environment however are simply not known. As such, strategic considerations do not readily lend themselves to customary capital budgeting analysis. While elaborate statistical methods exist for combining joint distributions of independent events, the problem is more acute than simply incorporating uncertainty into a discounted cash flow analysis.

142

When distributional assumptions about environmental uncertainty do not exist, these methodologies are of little use.

In such situations, strategic positioning becomes an overriding consideration. For example, should a competitor adopt an FMS that enables it to offer greater product heterogeneity, more customized service, greater product reliability, and shorter lead time, there is little doubt that a firm's own discounted cash flow assumptions regarding such an investment will be of limited value. If it does not adopt the technology, it will cease to be a player in the marketplace.

Strategic decisions involve overall corporate goals such as market share, product reliability, customer satisfaction and improved production performance. Each of these goals in turn may be broken down into sub-goals. Manufacturing performance may focus on reducing materials handling, decreasing set ups and improving real time variance reports. None of these production benefits may be readily quantifiable, or if so, the numbers may be highly suspect. Yet these are some of the strategic production advantages of investing in the new production technology.

Investing in Computer Aided Design (CAD) leads to some obvious costs and benefits in terms of manual labor savings, and yet the overriding consideration may be strategic. If interactive design enables greater design creativity and ultimately fewer parts to be incorporated into the product, then the attendant benefits reach into virtually all areas of production cost, inventory management, and product reliability. These strategic considerations far outweigh more immediate cost-benefit considerations, but are virtually impossible to incorporate into a traditional discounted cash flow analysis.

Simmonds Precision Products is a case in point. When electing a CAD/CAM system, it chose the system purely for strategic reasons.[1] They included (1) strengthening the organization's visibility in the marketplace; (2) enabling production of high quality low cost production with fewer errors; (3) faster customer turnaround; (4) and more integration of manufacturing and

143

engineering. Interestingly, Simmonds did not attempt to quantify any of these strategic advantages in its capital budgeting decision.


## INVESTMENT SCOPE

Figure 7-1 depicts the estimated expenditures for automated equipment among a representative cross-sample of respondents between 1985-1990. Almost one half of the respondents indicated expenditures to be in the $1 to $10 million category, a fairly small level of investment relative to the size of the surveyed firms for a 5 year period. Over half of the surveyed firms had annual revenues in excess of $50 million. The majority of firms (80%) intended to limit their capital expenditures to under $50 million. The relatively small size of these investments suggests that many firms are not prepared to invest the sums necessary to make wholesale changes in their production technology. Rather, the scope of the outlays indicates a piecemeal approach to investment.

Several reasons for this approach may exist. The first is that extremely large factories are very difficult to manage and can lead to diseconomies of scale beyond an optimal production point. Many firms consider larger factories to be unfocused and more susceptible to excess capacity problems in the event of economic downturn. Rather than investing large amounts in technology, less drastic cellular changes in production layout and processes are being undertaken.

Incremental rather than wholesale changes in machinery are being made, with an emphasis on plant and machinery flexibility. In other words, emphasis is on the ability to convert an existing machine into an alternate form for different production needs. This is important as product life cycles shorten. Possibly, firms are waiting to assess the results of their previous technological investments. While this cautious wait and see attitude may appear reasonable, it may simply be a reflection of the quicker payback typical of smaller investments. An inverse relationship appears to exist between scope of investment and payback period.

**Figure 7-1**

ADVANCED TECHNOLOGICAL EXPENDITURES: 1986–1990

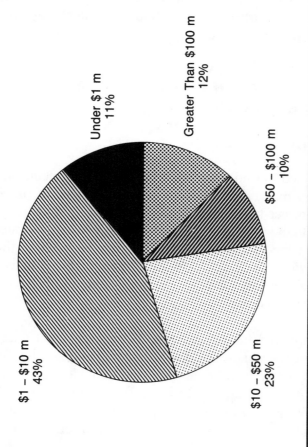

Under $1 m
11%

Greater Than $100 m
12%

$1 – $10 m
43%

$50 – $100 m
10%

$10 – $50 m
23%

Source: R.A. Howell, J.D. Brown, S.R. Soucy, and A.H. Seed, Management Accounting in the New Manufacturing Environment. Montvale, NJ: Nat'l. Assoc. of Accountants, 1987, p. 16.

An incremental approach to investment should consider a portfolio of projects with a strategic focus. New manufacturing investments should be integrated so as to reap the benefits of synergistic effects between design, engineering and production. As discussed earlier, the whole is frequently greater than the sum of the parts. This portfolio approach to investment may offset the risk identified with individual projects.

## DISCOUNTED CASH FLOW ANALYSIS OF ADVANCED TECHNOLOGY

### Quantitative Factors

Several costs and benefits related to investments in advanced technology may be estimated with a fair degree of precision. For instance, direct labor savings may be quantified, as may increases in indirect labor caused by industrial engineering, maintenance and computer support staff. An estimate may be made of the step-like cost behavior of indirect labor at different levels of activity. These semi-variable costs can then be projected for different levels of estimated production activity.

The improved throughput time often associated with advanced technologies has several quantifiable results. The first is that increased demand may be realized per dollar of incremental investment. This obviously impacts revenue projections for the investment. Furthermore, when process time is the cost driver, less cycle time per unit means that units of product will have less indirect costs attached to them.

Closely related to throughput time is inventory level. As cycle time decreases, response time to customer demand is much faster, implying that large buffer stocks of work-in-process and finished goods are no longer necessary. Decreased inventory levels result in several quantifiable cost savings. The first is the decreased financing costs resulting from lower inventory levels, as well as the one time liquidation value of the investment itself. The second is the opportunity cost of reducing floor space which can be put to

146

alternate use. These savings are a significant part of the analysis.

As machine changes are programmable, set up times decrease or disappear with many new production technologies. Improved machinery tolerances and product inspection scanners eliminate human quality control errors. Scrap and rework costs decrease. Spoilage will be reduced and post sale customer warranty work will decline. It should be mentioned that many of the above cost savings will not be found in the cost reporting systems of the firm. Rather, they will have to be estimated on a project by project basis.

## Qualitative Factors

Strategic considerations were previously mentioned as corporate goals that override immediate quantifiable capital budgeting considerations. Market share, a commitment to product innovation and reliability, and industry leadership are all considerations that may or may not be supported by capital expenditure analysis. Because of rapid technological change, useful economic life and equipment residual values are often difficult to predict. Future operating costs, particularly in the face of technological learning and change may also be difficult to quantify.The learning experience of advanced technology in itself may be worth the investment. Without it the firm may find itself lagging further behind in the marketplace in terms of product and production innovation in subsequent technological advances.

The majority of firms place more emphasis on qualitative factors in advanced technology investment decisions than they do on quantitative factors. These intangibles are numerous. Beyond its quantifiable labor savings, CAD for example may lead to improved design and less product parts. The former would impact revenues and the latter production costs and product reliability. While these numbers are very difficult to quantify, they are probably more material than the actual labor cost savings.

An FMS is another example. These systems permit heterogeneous and customized production runs, theoretically at the limit, in lot sizes of one. The impact on future revenue streams is very difficult to assess. Clearly, being able to respond immediately to shifts in customer demand with more flexible machinery will allow the firm to capture some previously foregone opportunities. These additional revenue opportunities may significantly outweigh more quantifiable cost considerations.

Real time performance feedback rather than periodic accounting variance reports is another intangible benefit of newly automated systems. Instantaneous feedback permits immediate identification of problem production areas, allowing corresponding action before entire defective batches of material are produced and cost overruns are incurred. Improved delivery, product reliability and service are additional qualitative benefits.

**Figure 7-2**

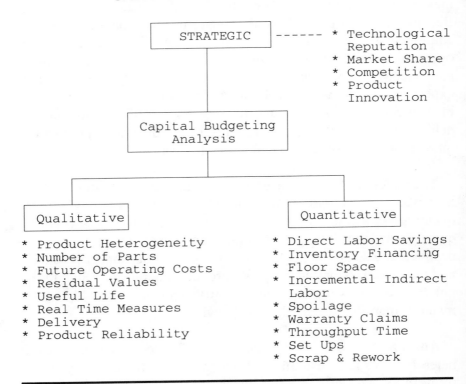

CAPITAL BUDGETING CRITERIA

STRATEGIC ------ * Technological Reputation
* Market Share
* Competition
* Product Innovation

Capital Budgeting Analysis

Qualitative

* Product Heterogeneity
* Number of Parts
* Future Operating Costs
* Residual Values
* Useful Life
* Real Time Measures
* Delivery
* Product Reliability

Quantitative

* Direct Labor Savings
* Inventory Financing
* Floor Space
* Incremental Indirect Labor
* Spoilage
* Warranty Claims
* Throughput Time
* Set Ups
* Scrap & Rework

Quantitative and qualitative capital budgeting considerations in advanced technology environments are summarized in Figure 7-2. As can be seen, quantitative factors include many cost reduction and revenue enhancement opportunities uncharacteristic of traditional manufacturing environments. Development of realistic quantitative estimates requires close cooperation between marketing, corporate planning and manufacturing. These estimates may then be used to perform traditional discounted cash flow analyses as well as payback calculations . Once the numbers indicate whether or not the investment is worthwhile, qualitative factors should be addressed, in conjunction with the strategic implications for the firm.

## A CASE EXAMPLE

ABC produces machine tools. It is considering replacing its boring and drilling equipment, which is near the end of its physical life and has no residual value. The firm is facing two options. The first involves an incremental approach which consists of replacing existing components of the machining system with similar technology with a 10 year life, at a cost of $2.5 million. For expository simplicity, depreciation is assumed to be straight line with no residual value for tax purposes. All other fixed costs are cash expenses. This system has the following annual cost and revenue projections:

| | |
|---|---|
| Production and Sales: | 50,000 |
| Price per Unit: | $35 |
| Cost per Unit of | |
| Raw Material: | $4 |
| Direct Labor: | $5 |
| Var. Overhead: | $3 |
| Fixed Overhead: | $4 |

The second option, an FMS also with a 10 year life, no residual values and straight line write off, is significantly more expensive, $6 million in cost. In addition, installation costs of $600,000 are required. Training and start up costs are estimated at $700,00 and engineering support is projected at $800,000. Compared to the replacement option, the FMS will improve quality and rework, resulting in an estimated 25% reduction in raw material costs. Direct labor will decrease 35% as certain tasks are automated and throughput time will decrease by 20%, resulting in a corresponding increase in realized sales over the replacement option.

Reduced materials handling and cell maintenance of machinery will decrease variable overhead by 15% yearly, but this will be offset by annual increased fixed engineering costs of $30,000. Fixed electrical costs will also increase by $20,000 a year. Inventories however will be reduced by $300,000. This will lead to less financing charges and the space will be put to alternate use, resulting in annual fixed cost savings of $75,000. The discount rate for projects of this sort is 16% and the marginal tax rate is 34%.

Replacing the machinery involves discounting the after tax net inflows over the life of the project, adjusted for depreciation tax effects. In this case, as seen in Exhibit 7-1, the present value of the net inflows exceeds the firm's investment. The payback period of 3.5 years is also relatively short. In contrast, the FMS must capitalize all start up costs, yielding a total investment of $8 million. Once all differential cash flows are accounted for, the net annual after tax cash flows are $1,197,420, which, when present valued over the life of the project do not meet the total original investment. Furthermore, the payback period is approximately 7 years.

Closer inspection however indicates that some of the non-quantitative data are extremely important. Various strategic and qualitative factors have not been included in the analysis. For instance, it is anticipated that although the firm may not invest in this technology, some of its competitors probably will. Also, the FMS will allow much greater product heterogeneity and product reliability. Improved cycle throughput time will also diminish customer response time. While these benefits were considered too

# Exhibit 7-1

## CAPITAL BUDGETING ANALYSIS

| Machinery Replacement | | Flexible Manufacturing System | | |
|---|---|---|---|---|
| Investment | $2,500,000 | Cost | $6,000,000 | |
| | | Installation | 600,000 | |
| | | Start-up | 700,000 | |
| | | Engineering | 800,000 | |
| | | TOTAL | | $8,100,000 |
| | | | | |
| Revenues | | Revenues | | |
| (50,000 x $35) | $1,750,000 | (60,000 x $35) | | $2,100,000 |
| | | | | |
| Expenses | | Expenses | | |
| Full Cash Cost | | Raw Materials | | |
| (50,000 x $16) | 800,000 | (.75 x 4 x 60,000) | 180,000 | |
| Annual Depreciation | 250,000 | Direct Labor | | |
| | | (.65 x 5 x 60,000) | 195,000 | |
| | | Variable Overhead | | |
| | | (.85 x 3 x 60,000) | 153,000 | |
| | | Fixed Overhead | | |
| | | (4 x 50,000) | 200,000 | |
| | | Incr. Fixed Overhead | 50,000 | |
| | | Fixed Overhead Saved | (75,000) | |
| | | Annual Depreciation | 810,000 | |
| Total Expenses | $1,050,000 | Total Expenses | | $1,513,000 |
| | | | | |
| N.I.B.T | 700,000 | | | 587,000 |
| N.I.A.T (@.34) | 462,000 | | | 387,420 |
| Depreciation Addback | 250,000 | | | 810,000 |
| A.T Cash Flow | $712,000 | | | $1,197,420 |
| Total Present Value | **$3,441,096** | | | $5,787,130 |
| (@ 4.8333) | | | | |
| Initial Inventory Liquidation | | | | 300,000 |
| | | | | |
| Total Return | | | | **$6,087,130** |
| | | | | |
| Payback | **3.5 years** | Payback | | **6.8 years** |
| ($2,500,000/712,000) | | ($8,100,000/1,197,420) | | |

**Exhibit 7-2**

## REVISED CAPITAL BUDGETING ANALYSIS

| Machinery Replacement | | Flexible Manufacturing System | |
|---|---|---|---|
| Investment | $2,500,000 | Investment | $8,100,000 |
| Revenues (50,000 x $35 x.75) | $1,312,500 | Revenues (60,000 x $35) | $2,100,000 |
| Total Expenses* $1,513,000 | $1,050,000 | Total Expenses* | |
| Less: Depreciation Adjustment | | | (140,000) |
| N.I.B.T | 262,500 | | 727,000 |
| N.I.A.T (@.34) | 173,250 | | 479,820 |
| Depreciation Addback | 250,000 | | 670,000 |
| A.T Cash Flow | $423,250 | | $1,149,820 |
| Total Present Value (@ 5.650) | **$2,391,363** | | $6,496,483 |
| Initial Inventory Liquidation | | | 300,000 |
| Residual Value (@.386 x $1,400,000) | | | 540,000 |
| Total Return | | | **$7,336,883** |
| Payback ($2,500,000/423,250) | **5.9 years** | Payback ($8,100,000/1,149,820) | **7.0 years** |

* See Exhibit 7-1 for Total Expenses Number.

intangible to quantify, the firm's customers will undoubtedly consider these aspects when weighing competitive bids. The firm projects that over the lifespan of the project, it might lose on average 25% of its customers as a result of not adopting competitive technology. In addition, the assumption of no residual value because of the difficulty of estimation is probably extreme. Additional analysis indicates a probable recovery of $1,400,000 at termination of the project. Finally, the treasurer finds that since future inflows and outflows were not inflation adjusted, a 16% cost of capital is excessive. The real cost of capital for the firm is closer to 12%.

Exhibit 7-2 indicates the revised figures. Once machine replacement revenues are adjusted and net inflows are discounted at the new cost of capital, the total present value no longer exceeds the cost of the investment. The payback period increases from 3.5 to 5.9 years. The FMS analysis indicates significant differences once residual values, depreciation expense and cost of capital adjustments are made. Total returns are increased from $6.1 to $7.3 million, which however is still below the total cost of the investment. The firm must therefore decide whether additional strategic and qualitative considerations warrant the investment, or whether it should pursue alternate investment opportunities.

## ALTERNATIVE EVALUATION METHODS

As has been demonstrated, not all economic and quantitative data may be incorporated in a discounted cash flow analysis when evaluating advanced technologies. In such cases, alternate evaluation techniques exist which may supplement or incorporate existing present value analyses. These methods rest on ordinal ranking of quantitative and qualitative investment criteria. Ordinal rather than interval scaling is used because interval or ratio data that measure different attributes, such as cost savings versus lead time reduction, is impossible to combine mathematically.

A simple example of this approach is the "Q Sort" method. In this case, projects are evaluated on the basis of a set of quantitative and qualitative factors. A binary split of the projects into more and less desirable categories is made. Each category is then successively split into further more and less desirable categories. This proceeds until all projects have been sorted, at which point the implicit ranking of all projects is made, based on all previous binary classifications.

The "Q Sort" method is useful when many investment

alternatives are under consideration. It leaves unresolved however, the judgmental issue of how to incorporate all factors when performing the binary classifications. Scoring or Multi Attribute Decision Models (MADM) are frequently used methods of combining mathematically non-comparable qualitative and quantitative data. They assume more precision than simple cost sort techniques in addressing the relative weighing of all decision attributes. A set of strategic, qualitative and quantitative attributes necessary for investment justification purposes is first outlined. These attributes must then be qualitatively valued, for example on a 5 point scale. Total scores can then be compared to other projects. When all attributes are equally valued, then the factors are unweighted. More realistically, when investment attributes differ in importance, then differential weights should be assigned to each attribute.

An example of strategic, quantitative and qualitative attributes for an FMS investment are shown in Exhibit 7-3. The first column indicates the relative weighing of each attribute under consideration. These weights are tremendously important. They indicate the relative importance of all the quantifiable and non-quantifiable measures that constitute the firm's success in the marketplace. These weights should be derived from a consensus of managerial opinion: technical; financial; marketing and administrative. Once estimated, the weights assigned to the selected attributes become the basis for evaluating all investment proposals.

The value column in Exhibit 7-3 represents the value assigned to the project attributes on a predetermined scale, in this case 0-5. For example, maintaining market share might be assigned the mid point of the range. Similarly, if the project's net present value is positive, it will be assigned a high value and so on. Finally, the confidence column of Exhibit 7-3 represents the probability of attaining the project's stated goal for that particular attribute. These probabilities can be either subjectively input or statistically determined. The lower the confidence level, the lower the probability weight assigned.

**Exhibit 7-3**

## SCORING MODEL FOR A
## FLEXIBLE MANUFACTURING SYSTEM

| Attributes | Weights | Values | Confidence | Product |
|---|---|---|---|---|
| 1. Strategic | | | | |
|   a. Technological | | | | |
|     Reputation | 12 | 4 | 1.0 | 48 |
|   b. Market Share | 10 | 2 | 0.8 | 16 |
|   c. Competitive | | | | |
|     Position | 14 | 3 | 0.7 | 29 |
|   d. Product | | | | |
|     Innovation | 8 | 4 | 1.0 | 32 |
| 2. Quantitative | | | | |
|   a. NPV | 30 | 4 | 0.9 | 108 |
|   b. Payback | 10 | 2 | 0.8 | 16 |
| 3. Qualitative | | | | |
|   a. Product | | | | |
|     Heterogeneity | 4 | 4 | 1.0 | 4 |
|   b. Product | | | | |
|     Reliability | 3 | 2 | 0.6 | 4 |
|   c. Response Time | 3 | 1 | 1.0 | 3 |
|   d. Number of Parts | 4 | 0 | 0.8 | 0 |
|   e. Real Time | | | | |
|     Measures | 2 | 5 | 0.9 | 1 |
|     TOTAL (rounded) | 100 | | | 273 |

The product column (weight x value x confidence) represents the probabilistic weighted average value score for the project. Alternative valuation models incorporating subjective weights and risk measures are feasible. The MADM is however one of the more prevalent valuation models. It is particularly appropriate for advanced technological investment, given the significant qualitative and strategic factors not captured in traditional discounted cash flow techniques.

# POST-AUDIT EVALUATION

The problems that plague capital budgeting in advanced technological environments naturally carry through the post-audit evaluation. Empirical evidence suggests that the majority of firms either do no post-audits of capital investments in high technology environments or else perform sporadic evaluations. The reasons for such casual monitoring appear to be related to difficulties in quantitatively evaluating many of the strategic and qualitative benefits realized by the technology. Just as pre-investment benefits are difficult to project, so post-investment returns are also difficult to measure. Items such as quality, response time, technological reputation and product innovation are not usually captured by the performance measurement system.

A comprehensive post-audit would use multiple performance criteria such as the scoring model discussed earlier, in order to assess the success of a project. Economic returns should be compared to net present value and payback projections. Productivity measures should be determined in the pre-investment analysis for qualitative and strategic criteria. Product reliability, for example, could be determined via survey calls; real time measures by physical shop floor performance measures; and response time by days of lead time required between order and delivery. Actual performance can then be compared to projections for all investment attributes. This data should be subject to audit. Managerial needs should be distinguished from financial reporting requirements throughout the analysis.

More efficient post-audit procedures would have favorable ramifications for subsequent investment decisions. Both the criteria under consideration and the accuracy of the projections would be improved. As most cost accounting systems are not designed to dovetail with capital investment reporting, modifications to the existing cost system might have to be carried out. Input from engineering, marketing and financial planning is crucial in performing these design changes. Because the technology is new, several unanticipated outcomes will undoubtedly be realized. Some will be unexpected benefits, others costs.

# PERFORMANCE RECORD

It is instructive to examine a recent compilation of the record of successes and failures in new advanced technologies, particularly in light of the uncertainty surrounding their adoption. Ettlie recently summarized performance of several advanced technology categories.[2] These included (1) Computer Automated Design and Manufacturing (CAD/CAM); (2) Group Technology (GT) and Cellular Manufacturing (CM); (3) Robotic Equipment (RE); (4) Flexible Manufacturing Systems (FMS); (5) Automated Assembly (AA) and (6) Computer Integrated Manufacturing (CIM). The performance record of each of these technologies will be briefly examined.

Some ambiguity exists in the CAD/CAM designation, alternately referring to drafting systems, engineering design, or integrated design and computerized machine preparation. If one adopts a comprehensive definition of CAD/CAM, there appears to be very strong consensus on productivity gains. These range from 3:1 to 30:1, a rather striking range. When CAD is integrated with manufacturing, returns are higher. Downtime appears to average 30%. In addition to significant labor savings, lead times decrease and output increases significantly. While internal rates of return are not reported, fairly short payback periods of 1-3 years are generally recognized, suggesting that adoption of this technology has been a success.

Group Technology processes parts by families of similar products. Production operations on these families of products are often grouped by manufacturing cell within the plant. GT and CM have been unconditionally successful, as the number of parts decreases; materials handling is reduced; set ups decrease; cycle time improves; and buffer inventories of various parts are eliminated. Exhibit 7-4 summarizes firm reports of GT and CM improvements. Almost without exception, implementation has been successful and payback relatively short.

Of course, the lower the firm's initial productivity, the higher the relative productivity improvements. Generally, system implemen-

157

# Exhibit 7-4

## GROUP TECHNOLOGY and CELLULAR MANUFACTURING

| Application | Payback |
|---|---|
| Various (overview) | Otis Engineering: eighteen months to install, nine months to recapture cost: 2.25 years payback. |
| | Assuming 2,000 new parts a year and 10% existing parts substituted, annual savings of $260,000 to $2.4 million. |
| Manufacturing shop (case study) | GT may lead to less productive system due to loss of flexibility from dedication of equipment in manufacturing cells. |
| GT and cellular manufacturing (overview) | If number of new parts exceeds 10,000 per year, computerized GT is needed. If number of new parts is fewer than 10,000 per year and especially if fewer than 5,000 per year, computerized GT is needed. |
| John Deere GT | GT system stores information on 400,000 parts and system saved firm $6 million in eighteen months. |
| | John Deere manufacturing cells: 70% reduction in the number of departments responsible for manufacturing parts; 25% reduction in the number of machines required; 56% reduction in number of job changes and materials. |
| GT survey | Manufacturing lead time reduction, 55%; set up time reduction, 17%; average batch travel distance reduction, 79%, on-time deliveries increase, 61%; average WIP reduction, 43%. |
| Various GT | GT can save up to 80% of new parts design requirements. |
| | For a company that releases 3,000 new parts a year, a 5% reduction in new designs would save $200,000, assuming every release cost $1,300. |
| | There are several examples of GT paying for itself within 18 months. |

Source: J.E. Ettlie, <u>Taking Charge of Manufacturing</u>. San Francisco: Jossey-Bass, 1988, p. 26.

tation is successful when the number of parts is so high as to warrant GT, in the order of 10,000 parts plus. Average payback is reported to be 2.25 years, with annual savings ranging from $260,000 to $2.4 million. Work-in-process often decreases by half. Also, because of machine interdependence within the cell, downtime generally decreases.

Robotic applications also report quick payback, in the order of 1.5 years, generally as projected in the capital budgeting analysis. Applications range from welding to materials handling and die casting. In this area, users are generally very satisfied with performance relative to expectations. FMS on the other hand are not as clear cut. Performance seems to vary relative to expectations. Survey results are summarized in Exhibit 7-5. Several of the studies report physical but not financial indicators of success. Physical indicators include downtime measures, scrap and lead time reductions. They do not report a more significant indicator, the number of different products produced, a key measure of machine flexibility.

A comprehensive survey of over 400 FMS in Europe and North America report profitability increases ranging from 100% to 300%. Per se however, these numbers are not illustrative of investment success. Without the distribution of these profits relative to the magnitude of the initial investment, which is substantial, there is little room to gauge the internal rate of return of the projects. Productivity improvements are not always as anticipated. Flexibility of the machinery is not being realized, which could affect long term returns and justification for the investment.[3] Anecdotal evidence suggests that a significant portion of firm returns are realized through plant reconfiguration in anticipation of system installation.

Automated assembly is an extension of robotic installation to the entire assembly line. Ettlie reports on several firms' experience with automated assembly. These include General Electric's Louisville dishwasher plant; numerous Chrysler Corporation projects; Buick City; and Black and Decker's robotic gear box

# Exhibit 7-5

## FLEXIBLE MANUFACTURING SYSTEMS

| Application | Payback |
| --- | --- |
| Various (overview and survey) | Two to three-year payback period; 50% reduction in lead time; scrap level down from 25% to 5%; machine tool utilization up 20%. |
| Hitachi Seiki: three FMSs | Productivity (two shift hours of operation utilization): after 15 months of operation, FMS 112 and 113 productivity was approximately 90%; downtime averaged about 5%. For FMS 114, productivity was about 60%, downtime about 10%. FMSs can introduce two new component designs within two days. Break-even point for the new component is between two and seven pieces compared to a general purpose machine. |
| MBB FMS in Augsburg, West Germany | Lead time on a Tornado is eighteen months versus thirty months for planes on conventional machines. Reduced standalone NC and personnel by 44%; reduced required floor space by 30%; capital investment costs down 9%. Annual total costs down 24%; floor space reduced by 39%; achieved 50% higher flexibility. |
| Survey of 400 FMS installations in average Europe & North America | 30% savings in labor costs; 13 to 15% savings in 50% or material costs; more savings on both inventory and work in progress; average of 40% reduction in lead times; average of 30% increase in machine utilization; more than 50% reduction in floor space; 14 to 27% reduction in total production costs; increase of 112 to 310% in operating profits. |
| Various flexible system applications | Predicted average payback is three years. Actual paybacks in systems average 2.7 years (N = 5, 1985) and 2.1 years (N=9, 1986). Achieved cycle time: 98% (N=11, 1985); 94% (N=17, 1986). Uptime: 87% (N=12, 1985); 95% (N=23, 1986). Utilization (two shifts): 70% (N=11, 1985); 62% (N=21, 1986), versus approximately 10% higher average utilization than standalone NC. |

Source: J.E. Ettlie, Taking Charge of Manufacturing. San Francisco: Jossey-Bass, 1988, p. 32.

## Exhibit 7-6

## COMPUTER-INTEGRATED MANUFACTURING

| Application | Payback |
|---|---|
| GE Steam Turbine Division, Schenectady, New York: CIM, cellular manufacturing concept | 35 to 40% increase in throughput, "80% out of the tape business." |
| Rolls-Royce: CAD/ (DNC) introduced throughout operations (for example, wheel disc line; blade cell first) | One-year payback (equivalent to $5.6 million); lead CAM times on wheels and discs reduced from twenty-six to six weeks, number of operations reduced from twenty-one to five; 2 million British Pounds blade line: 90% reduction in lead time to four weeks, uptime is 72% (82% targeted by end of 1986); requires two operators (cell first) versus traditional line of twenty-one to twenty-five operators. |
| GE Bromont (Quebec); CIM plant for compressor airfoils; five-year automation plan 20% complete | After six months, 520 worker hours to produce airfoil set versus 540 at Ruthland plant (target is 420 hours); fifteen of 500,000 parts returned to Evandale assembly plant (0.003%); 1.8% absenteeism rate; 10% of each worker's time is spent in training. |
| Ingersoll Milling Machine Company: CIM Program | Since 1970s, "spent more than $100 million" to modernize shops and offices; "In 1980 and 1981, he {Gaylord} spent more than $1 million to link Ingersoll's three U.S. divisions to a common computer database."<br><br>Over five years, savings of $1 million per year. |
| Various CAD/ CAM: five case studies and review (data mostly on MRP systems) | Average inventory reduction of 35% (N=3); average WIP reduction of 28% (N=2); inventory accuracy increased an average 49% (N=4) to an average level of 96%. |

Continued on Next Page

161

**Exhibit 7-6 continued**

## COMPUTER-INTEGRATED MANUFACTURING

| Application | Payback |
|---|---|
| U.S. pump mfg. modernization & "streamlining manufacturing operations," using robots & JIT or CIM | Invested $9 million; got back $10 million in annual savings; eliminated $11 million from inventory, and returned a net of $2 million to balance sheet. "Reduced throughput from 25 to 2 days; eliminated 19 of 24 forklift trucks. Increased inventory turns from 5 to 30. Reduced deployed deliveries from 40% to 2%; reduced workforce from 6% to 1%. |
| Auto Parts Supplier: JIT and cellular manufacturing program (technology secondary) | Invested $4.5 million; inventory was reduced from $3.5 million to $1 million, with an additional savings of $560,000 in annual carrying costs; throughput was cut from three weeks to four hours, and inventory turns increased from five to fifteen; staff was reduced from 239 to 200; subcontracted work decreased from 5% to none. |
| Johnson Wax: five year automation plan, two years completed | Savings of $3.5 million annually; inventory accuracy 99.8%; goal is savings of $6 million annually. |
| Yamazaki Minokamo plant (at heart of plant): full scale operation began May 20, 1983 | Initial capital investment of $65 million; 85% utilization within one year of operation; WIP of twenty-eight days; 100% deliveries by due date; rework volume 1.1%, in first two years, saved $3.9 million in inventory costs and $3 million in inventory costs and $3 million in labor costs for a total of $6.9 million. |
| DEC plant, Enfield Connecticut (after 1 year of operation) | Plant start-up on schedule, fifteen inventory turns, 3% scrap, 40% reduction in overhead; break-even point at 60% of capacity. |
| Computer printer manufacturer | Inventory turns went from three to twenty-four; scrap and rework reduced by 30%; reduced floor space by 70%, throughput times by 50%; payback in less than 1.9 years. |

Source: J.E. Ettlie, <u>Taking Charge of Manufacturing</u>. San Francisco: Jossey-Bass, 1988, p. 40-41.

assembly plant in Great Britain. The projects include robotic equipment, scanners and automated manufacturing equipment. Again, reported paybacks are short, under 4 years, and quality improvements are notable.

CIM is the final area surveyed. This encompasses a fully integrated data system; inter-locked design and manufacturing; and supplier as well as customer integration. For most firms, this is a theoretical ideal. Most of these very costly projects are presently in the process of being implemented and the success of their eventual outcome is unknown. CIM projects are summarized in Exhibit 7-6. Most of the released data reflect improvements in qualitative performance criteria. Very little hard data has been released with respect to the financial returns of these investments.

Several possible explanations exist for the paucity of economic data. One is that positive returns on such large scale projects are realizable only in the long term, over a 5 to 10 year period, and firms are therefore reluctant to release preliminary data. Another is that given competition in the marketplace, the proprietary nature of the data is essential. A third less sanguine speculation is that actual returns are below forecast.

Summarizing, the financial and strategic performance of these various advanced technology investments has been mixed. Generally, the smaller investments, such as CAD/CAM, GT and Robotics, have performed well in terms of financial payback. There is always a possibility that a response or self-selection bias may exist in the reported studies. Namely, there is less incentive to report unfavorable rather than favorable investments, or to report only dramatic improvements, where the base case was initially very low. Even allowing for this reporting bias however, overall evidence seems fairly positive.

In the case of FMS and CIM, there is a paucity of information concerning financial returns. Negative anecdotal evidence, such as General Motors' Saturn plant or John Deere's FMS experience, suggests that at least in some cases, investment returns have not been as anticipated.

# SUMMARY

New quantitative dimensions for measuring advanced technology investment results were discussed. These measures were included in an example when comparing a replacement decision with traditional machinery as opposed to advanced manufacturing equipment. Incorporation of the cash flow consequences of these new measures is imperative for correct analysis of advanced technology investments. Even more important than quantitative measures however are qualitative and strategic factors related to high technology investments. Because different strategies and qualitative measures are not directly comparable, a scoring model for advanced high technology projects was proposed. This allows the decision maker to include all factors into the analysis and weight them by appropriate confidence levels. To the extent that complete quantitative and qualitative criteria are not included in the analysis, successful post audit of the project is unlikely. Evidence indicates that few firms perform routine investment post audits.

Documented capital expenditure data suggests that neither individual project scope nor total magnitude of corporate expenditures are adequate. Consistent with these observations is the fact that accounting measurements continue to favor quick payback projects. Historical cost ROI measures do not induce a manager to invest in long term more strategically important investments.

Traditional capital budgeting techniques in advanced technology environments have definite shortcomings and limitations. Primary among these is the underestimation of strategic planning. The strategic importance of larger scale longer term investment projects was emphasized. Quick payback piecemeal investments are not a solution to long term multinational competitiveness. Documented evidence of success remains sketchy for these high technology investments. It is in this arena that the future viability of U.S. competitiveness undoubtedly lies.

# REFERENCES

1. R.C. Van Nostrand, "Justifying CAD Learning Systems : A Case Study." Journal of Cost Management (Spring 1988): 9-17.

2. J.E. Ettlie, Taking Charge of Manufacturing. San Francisco: Jossey-Bass, 1988, 19-48.

3. J. Ramchandran, "Postindustrial Manufacturing." Harvard Business Review (Nov.-Dec. 1986) : 69-76.

# BIBLIOGRAPHY

Bennett, R.E. and J.A. Hendricks. "Justifying the Acquisition of Automated Equipment." Management Accounting (July 1987): 39-46.

Berliner, C. and J.A. Brimson. Cost Management For Today's Advanced Manufacturing. Boston: Harvard Business School Press, 1988.

Brimson, J.A. "Technology Accounting." Journal of Cost Management (Winter 1989): 17-27.

Ettlie, J.E. Taking Charge of Manufacturing. San Francisco: Jossey-Bass, 1988.

Hayes, R.H., S.C. Wheelwright and K.B. Clark. Dynamic Manufacturing. New York: Free Press, 1988.

Howell, R.A., J.D. Brown, S.R. Soucy and A.H. Seed. Management Accounting in the New Manufacturing Environment. Montvale, N.J. : National Association of Accountants, 1987.

Kaplan, R.S. "Must CIM be Justified by Faith Alone?" Harvard Business Review (March-April 1986): 87-95.

Meredith, J. "New Justification Approaches for CIM." Journal of Cost Management (Winter 1988): 15-20.


Noble, J.L. "A New Approach for Justifying Computer-Integrated Manufacturing." Journal of Cost Management (Winter 1990): 14-19.


Schonberger, R.J. "Frugal Manufacturing." Harvard Business Review (Sept.- Oct. 1987): 95-100.


Seed, A.H. and R.G. Wagner."Investment Justification for Factory Automation." In Cost Accounting for the '90s : The Challenge of Technological Change: 83-106. Montvale, N.J. : National Association of Accountants, 1986.


Van Nostrand, R.C. "Justifying CAD/CAM Systems : A Case Study." Journal of Cost Management (Spring 1988): 9-17.

# Chapter Eight

# STRATEGIC COST MANAGEMENT

While product costing and control are usually considered to involve short term measurement issues, their long term implications are equally significant. Managerial focus on accurate cost allocations, performance measurement and cost reduction are commendable but longer term competitive considerations must not be ignored. The economic success of Japanese industries attests to the importance of strategic positioning and the role of cost in attaining that position. Once adequate short term costing and control practices are in place, the firm must be prepared to implement further improvements in long term strategic costing.

Three characteristics distinguish strategic costing from everyday product costing and control. The first is a clearly defined long-term costing horizon, in the order of three to five years. Managerial accounting must be prepared to consider cost outflows over the entire, albeit shorter, product life cycle. Uniform cost outflows over the product life cycle are increasingly the exception rather than the rule.

A second characteristic that distinguishes strategic costing from routine costing is the definition of the responsible organizational unit. Generally, the longer the strategic time horizon, the broader the span of control of the unit being measured. In other words, strategic costing does not lend itself to narrow definitions of performance measurement. The locus of organizational control becomes much broader and more diffuse. A final but very important strategic cost difference is that the focus of cost analysis becomes significantly more external to the firm. That is, competitor and industry analysis become increasingly important as the firm tries to assess its relative advantage.

Four emerging paradigms seem worthy of consideration when evaluating strategic costing. Rather than viewing each as distinct, it is worthwhile appreciating their complementarities. Although product life cycles have long been recognized in marketing, **Life Cycle Costing** is a very recent phenomenon. Two significant changes are occurring that obviate the traditional conception of what constitutes cost life cycle: one is rapidly changing environmental technology and hence shorter product life cycles; the other is a significant shift towards disproportionate cost outflows during the early stages of the product life cycle.

A second evolving paradigm is **Target Costing** to market competition, as recently implemented by several large Japanese multinationals. This is clearly an alternative to standard cost plus mark-up pricing as traditionally practiced. Closely related to target costing is the notion of **Value Chain Analysis**. Here, the entire value chain of pre-production, production and post-production is decoupled and analyzed where possible relative to external sources for the intermediate product. A final strategic costing technique available to the firm is **Competitive Cost Analysis**. In this case, a thorough analysis of product cost structure and differentiation is performed relative to the firm's competitors.

Together, these emerging paradigms of strategic cost management are useful techniques for analyzing the firm's ability to compete both domestically and internationally. Strong interrelationships, it should be noted, exist between each approach. Accurate competitor cost analysis is impossible without a thorough understanding of the value chain. Similarly, target costing to market and competitive cost analysis complement each other. Furthermore, target costing is more meaningful when life cycle costs of the product are well understood. This chapter is designed to provide an overview of emerging strategic costing paradigms and to show their significance in ensuring the long term cost competitiveness of the firm.

## LIFE CYCLE COSTING

Reduced product life cycles have made accurate allocation of full cost to product essential. Many products now have estimated life cycles of 3 years or less. At the same time, greater initial outlays of cost are occurring. These joint factors make accurate matching of costs to revenues increasingly important. A primary objective of life cycle costing is to improve this matching and the strategic costing of the firm.

The relative mix of pre and post-production costs under traditional and new production environments is shown in Figure 8-1. As indicated, the proportion of initial engineering and design outlays to total cost is increasing in new production environments. One reason for this phenomenon is that product design determines the bulk of subsequent production costs, and to a lesser extent, post-production logistical costs. For instance, fewer parts can be designed into the product or the design can take account of existing product part families.

As indicated in Figure 8-1, production and logistics costs decline as a proportion of total cost in new production environments. Lower costs are designed into the product. In addition, reconfigured plant layouts, newly automated equipment and Just in Time inventory practices improve costing efficiency relative to traditional costing. The net result is that total cost tends to be more skewed towards the initial phase of product development relative to latter phases in new versus traditional production environments. Logistics costs can be reduced during the start up phase by designing component assembly as late as possible into the production process. This reduces separate product line inventory requirements and related costs up to the point of differential component assembly, and allows more rapid and economical

**Figure 8-1**

TRADITIONAL AND NEW PRODUCTION COSTS

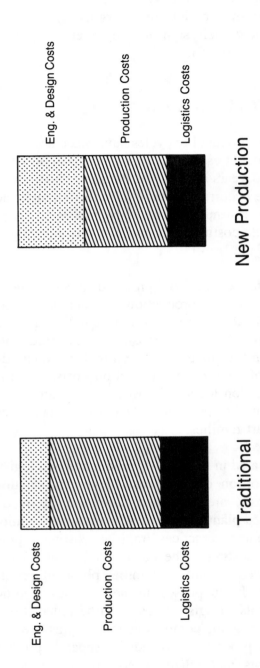

customer response. Improved design can also reduce both the subsequent frequency and amount of warranty work. The frequency of warranty work is affected by the reliability of products. The complexity of actual warranty work will be affected by the initial product design. Heightened awareness of the importance of early engineering and design upon subsequent production and post-production costs has led to increased life cycle costs in the initial development stages of the product.

Coupled with this shift in cost distribution over time is the decreasing life cycle of the product itself. As summarized in Figure 8-2, much shorter product life cycles make it crucial to carefully allocate and match more pre and post-production costs to products. Should a firm attempt to recover periodic expenses, it would effectively be skewing its revenues to match its cash outlays. This could be very sub-optimal from a long term profit perspective. For example, if a high price for the product was initially charged, this might maximize short term profits. On the other hand, several negative consequences might result. One is that high margins attract competition. Another is that depending on demand elasticity for the product, a high price might prevent the firm from capturing a larger market share. In addition, production economies of scale will not be realized at lower levels of volume.

Two important implications can be drawn. The first is that the firm should make every effort to reduce burgeoning developmental costs. While justifiable, given the goals of reducing subsequent production and logistics cost, caution must be exercised in not spending more on initial design then justified by subsequent production and post-production cost savings. The second implication is that product mis-costing must be avoided. Typically, development costs are treated as period costs and therefore not capitalized or matched to subsequent product specific revenues. Managers should strive to accurately track all developmental costs to product lines and write them off over the product life cycle.

**Costs Tables** are one method of improving control during the life cycle.[1] Cost tables are computerized cost relational databases that function as decision support systems. They are particularly

171

**Figure 8-2**

# LIFE CYCLE COSTS AND REVENUES

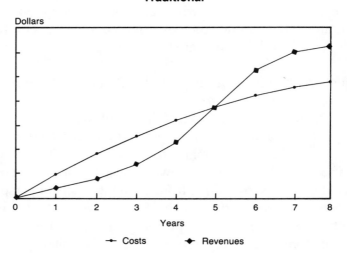

**Traditional**

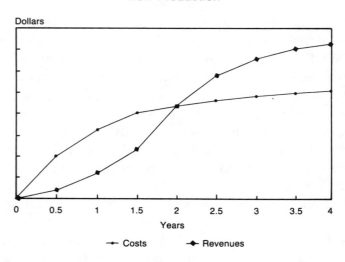

**New Production**

useful for pre-production cost estimation. Japanese firms use cost tables to both estimate the cost of new products, as well as control and reduce costs of existing products. As in value decomposition analysis, production subsets of activity such as drilling or assembly are broken down. A cost table then provides alternative unit costs by activity for different levels of activity intensity, such as depth of drilling or number of parts assembled. Cost tables essentially determine engineering specifications by production activity and by degree of performance intensity of the activity.

Indirect as well as direct cost tables may exist. In this way, alternative product designs that demand different degrees of direct and indirect cost activity can be accurately estimated. As anywhere form 50% to 80% of total life cycle cost may be committed before production ever takes place, cost tables are invaluable for life cycle costing. Accurate cost estimates may be made before production takes place and ways found to reduce total cost by activity. Cost reduction during the life cycle is also encouraged, as new cost combinations are sought and existing technological costs of certain activities are replaced with lower cost substitutes.

## TARGET COSTING

Japanese cost management is frequently governed by principles of target costing. Market price is first examined for a product under consideration. The unit cost necessary to be competitive in the marketplace is then determined for a pre-determined level of production. Target cost becomes a tool for decreasing the cost of a product, not only at inception, but throughout the product life cycle. The focus is on ex ante cost planning for design and production rather than ex post cost control. Target costs are determined at the outset prior to production. Subsequently, continual efforts are made to reduce standard costs rather than treating them as immutable.

Target costing is widely practiced in Japan in various industrial sectors. These include machining, automobiles and electronic products. It is particularly appropriate in environments where product life cycles are short, product heterogeneity exists and production involves a great deal of assembly work. It is less readily implemented in mature process manufacturing sectors, because less room exists for productivity improvements.

Precisely how is target costing implemented? The usual procedure is to examine a potentially lucrative product market. The sales price in the market is a starting point from which a desired profit, or return on sales, is calculated. This target profit defines "allowable" cost, which is the maximum cost allowed for the product, if required return on sales is to be realized. The latter is defined by firm and trade information available to the public. In essence, the procedure is market rather than cost driven. Based on current data, the firm's "drifting" or current standard cost is determined. This requires exact full costing of all expenses directly related to the product line under investigation. The eventual goal is to reduce the current drifting standard cost to the ultimate allowable standard cost in order to meet the target profit. The difference between drifting and allowable cost is target cost, as depicted in Figure 8-3.

Illustrating the above with a numerical example, assume the market price for the product under consideration is $120, with an estimated market volume of 1,000 units. If the required profit margin is 25%, as shown in Figure 8-3, then total allowable cost is $120 * 1,000 - 0.25 ($120 * 1,000) = $90,000, or $90 per unit. It becomes the responsibility of engineering and cost accounting to attain this cost. Investigation reveals that current standard or drifting cost is $120 a unit. Hence the target cost reduction is $30 a unit.

How is target cost reduction attained? The method most frequently employed is value engineering. In Japan, value engineering includes cost reduction of all types of pre-production, production and post-production activities. Based on a limited survey of only 25 firms, the most frequent types of costs considered were found to be conversion costs of production, research and development, and distribution costs. These cost categories accounted for some 85% of cost containment effort.[2] In

**Figure 8-3**

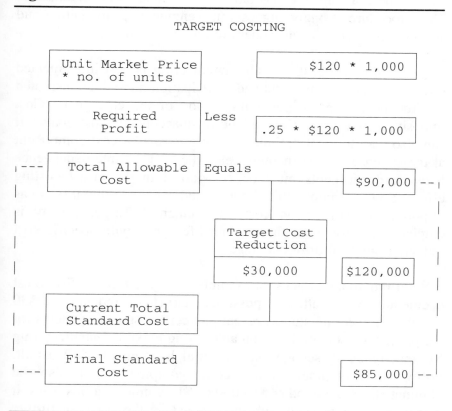

TARGET COSTING

| | |
|---|---|
| Unit Market Price * no. of units | $120 * 1,000 |
| Required Profit | Less .25 * $120 * 1,000 |
| Total Allowable Cost | Equals $90,000 |
| Target Cost Reduction | $30,000 / $120,000 |
| Current Total Standard Cost | |
| Final Standard Cost | $85,000 |

addition, in highly automated environments, computer software is a major cost component that seems like a promising area for target costing. Value engineering can be used in conjunction with other methods of reducing non-value added costs, such as Just-in-Time and Group Technology manufacturing.

It is interesting to note that the trend towards cost reduction is leading to a de-emphasis on standard costing and traditional cost control of production variances. As production processes continually evolve during life cycle costing, standard costs take on less significance. In addition, shortened product life cycles may not warrant the time consuming process of determining standard costs for each product. In fact, certain Japanese firms, such as the Japanese Conveyor Corporation, use target costs to set standard costs. The challenge then becomes the attainment of standard cost. This procedure strongly suggests that engineering, marketing and accounting must work in tandem in cost reduction efforts.

To attain target costing, value engineering is best implemented through worker involvement and participation rather than instituted by "top down" management imposition of the cost goal. Cost imposition may lead to unrealistic or unacceptable cost goals. It can also lead to local optimization of a particular cost component at the expense of cost increases elsewhere. Cost interdependence between departments must be recognized in the target costing effort. So for example, initial design and eventual reliability are as important as conversion cost containment. Target costing is emphasized throughout the product life cycle, with specific cost reduction goals at different stages.

Returning to the target cost example of Figure 8-3, the firm must decide how best to attain, if possible, a target cost reduction of $30 a unit. Engineering studies reveal that certain sub-components for the product can be produced on an existing Flexible Manufacturing System, reducing set ups and material handling by $12 a unit. Software development for robotic equipment will also be eliminated, saving another $15,000 or $15 a unit. On this basis, it was decided to proceed with the product, in the hopes of further cost reduction once production was implemented.

Over the course of the product's life cycle, worker involvement and suggestions led to a reduction in estimated defective units, with resultant savings of $8,000 or $8 a unit, for a total target cost reduction of $35 a unit. In this way, the final standard cost was actually below allowable cost, permitting the firm to realize its required profit goal.

Target costing is a strategic philosophy that encourages firms to be competitive in areas essential to their future growth. It is an alternative to traditional capital budgeting approaches which require that certain hurdle rates be met. Target costing essentially turns the traditional investment question on its head. Rather than asking should we invest, given cost and revenue projections, target costing asks how do we attain target cost, given the investment that must be made in order to remain strategically competitive?

## VALUE CHAIN ANALYSIS

The underlying economic structure of the firm is dictated by its production technology. This includes several factors. The first is realizable economies of scale under optimal production capacity. Whether or not these economies are being realized is of paramount concern to the firm. Second is the degree of vertical integration. To what extent is the firm a fully integrated producer? Is the resulting decrease in manufacturing flexibility caused by extensive integration offset by increase in production economies at each stage of the production value chain? Finally is the firm's production technology state-of-the-art and cost competitive relative to other producers? Value chain analysis is a potentially worthwhile tool for answering these questions.

For vertically integrated firms, value chain analysis is an important strategic costing tool. It is designed to identify sources of cost competitive advantage or disadvantage for the firm. A value chain is a sequential set of activities that extends beyond traditionally defined boundaries of production (Porter, 1985). The value chain can be considered to range from initial raw material sourcing to end user delivery of finished product. A value chain analysis consists of breaking down composite costs into a strategic sequence of activities in order to better understand cost behavior at each stage of the process.

Value chain analysis differs in several respects from more traditional analyses. First, the entire value chain is considered, not just a subset of production activity. Second, market prices of intermediate products are considered at each stage of the analysis. By performing such a study, the firm is better able to plot its strategic alternatives for products at all stages of the value added process.

In delineating the value chain, attention must be paid to costs that are external as well as internal to the firm. These costs are often significant and may exceed total internal costs. Raw material supplier costs for example may account for as much as 50% of manufacturing cost. At the other end, customer post-production costs, while not as material, are also significant. To sustain a competitive advantage, the firm must monitor the entire value chain, not just its own production processes.

An example of exploiting supplier links would be working with the supplier in determining optimal packing, inspection and delivery systems. Proximity of suppliers and frequency of deliveries may alter raw material costs. In similar fashion, customer links may be formed to reduce non-value added post production costs. Warranty work may be reduced by utilizing customer information input. Distribution channels may be consolidated or altered, and advertising campaigns jointly shared. In short, creative cost reduction efforts aimed at significantly decreasing supplier and customer non-value added costs can be as significant as decreasing internal non-value added expenses for the firm.

Once the value chain is defined, the second major step is to determine profitability at each step of the value chain. To do so requires an external market price for the intermediate product under production. Calculating profit at each step in the value chain ensures greater controllability than simple cost accounting allocations between successive production operations. This is essentially no different than using external market prices as a control in measuring the validity of successive external cost transfers across cost centers of the vertical production chain.

As production is sequentially completed at each successive point in the value chain, wherever possible external market prices should be used, with cumulative cost, to determine incremental product profitability. In this manner, true value or non-value added profitability emerges, suggesting sub-contracting alternatives.

Value chain analysis is summarized in Figure 8-4. Including external pre- and post-production costs suggests where non-value

**Figure 8-4**

## VALUE CHAIN ANALYSIS

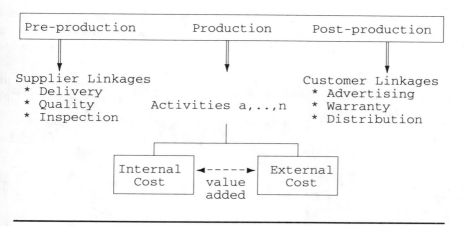

added restrictions might exist outside the firm. Internal non-value added savings are indicated by production activity decomposition, cost aggregation by activity, and external pricing comparisons.

Depending on the bottom line provided by this analysis for the value chain components, the firm has several options: it can source externally; integrate forwards or backwards; or, based on cost driver analysis, try to reconfigure or reduce activity costs. Market growth, production capacity and investment base are all important considerations in determining which strategies to follow for a particular value chain component.

## COMPETITIVE COST ANALYSIS

A final area of strategic cost analysis that complements and to a degree overlaps with life cycle costing, target costing and value chain analysis is competitive cost analysis. Firms must continually reassess the cost competitive position of their products. A clear understanding of competitor cost, as well as internal firm costs, enables these comparisons to be made.

**Table 8-1**

## COMPETITOR COST ANALYSIS

| | SEC, 10K, 8Q | Fin'l Analysis | Industry Reports | Predicast by SIC code | Dun & Bradst. | Gov't Sources |
|---|---|---|---|---|---|---|
| Sales | ■ | ■ | | ■ | | |
| Cost of Goods | ■ | | | | ■ | |
| Trade Volume | | ■ | ■ | ■ | | ■ |
| Assets | ■ | ■ | | | ■ | |
| Labor | ■ | | | | ■ | |
| Overhead | ■ | | | | ■ | |
| Quality | | | ■ | | | |
| Raw Materials | ■ | | | | ■ | |
| Research | | ■ | ■ | | | |

To successfully perform such an analysis requires three components: an understanding of what information to analyze; obtaining the information; and using correct methods of analysis. Table 8-1 summarizes many useful sources by type of information. The matrix is by no means comprehensive. Other sources and types of information may be obtained. Also, the particular information extracted from a source may not correspond with that depicted in Table 8-1. What clearly should emerge however, is an appreciation of the many databases that do exist and their utility in competitive cost analysis.

S.E.C. data often is useful for obtaining product line information related to sales and component parts of costs of goods sold. Industry data and financial analysts' reports are also very worthwhile sources of information for obtaining price changes, growth projections, and expenditure analysis. Brokerage firms and credit rating agencies are worthwhile sources. Trade and governmental associations and independent data gathering agencies are also invaluable data sources.

Types of analyses include fundamental information related to competitors' sales price and mix, real market growth, gross margins and return on assets deployed. If firm margins are above or below competitor's, the analysis should attempt to determine why this is so. Is it due to less productive deployment of fixed assets, higher labor utilization or uncompetitive raw material prices? Asset investment figures will indicate which competitors are obtaining a higher or lower return on assets. Research and Development expenses will be a gauge of future dominant players in the market.

Once the current information is gathered, the most challenging part of the exercise remains, namely how to derive reliable cost competitive figures. Several methodological approaches may be used. One involves traditional ratio analysis. By decomposing parts of the Balance Sheet and Income Statement, comparative ratio analysis may reveal where the firm is at a cost advantage or disadvantage.

Another approach is to use statistical methods such as cross-sectional regression or time series analysis based on historical records. For example, by examining competitive product cost mix over time, a statistical relationship may be determined. Isolating price changes within the particular product sector allows real growth and number of units sold to be determined.

Cost of Goods Sold interrelationships between raw material, direct labor and overhead may be decomposed by looking at accumulated depreciation changes, number of units produced, existing labor rates and raw material supplier prices. Likewise total competitor revenue may be decomposed into price, mix and activity variances. All the information necessary to perform such an analysis is publically available. Price, market volume, and changes in relative market share is all useful information that may help to explain why certain product lines are growing or shrinking.

The problem of obtaining reliable competitive cost information however should not be minimized. Several of the following problems may arise:

* Competitive cost structure may differ.
* Lines of business may not be directly comparable.
* Transnational differences may exist in production and currency translation.
* Difficulties may arise in obtaining labor rates or material prices.

The above suggests that successful competitor cost analysis depends upon the type of business, production characteristics and product line reporting requirements. In certain cases, reliable information may simply be impossible to obtain.


## SUMMARY

It is imperative that costing strategies be continually reassessed. To do so requires the firm to adopt a long term planning perspective across inter-divisional units, and to externally redirect its focus. Several strategies have been proposed. These include life cycle costing, target costing, value chain analysis and competitive cost analysis. Each of these paradigms includes the afore-mentioned characteristics. Namely, a long term focus is adopted; a wider span of performance measurement is defined; and market price and competitor costs are continuously monitored.

Another common characteristic of these strategies is that complete cost decomposition across the value chain takes place. Every effort is made to convert periodic expenses into product costs. Market prices are closely monitored not only for the final product, but also for the intermediate stages of production. This permits comparative assessments of competitor costs at all points in the value chain. External sourcing is always a consideration.

Continual monitoring of competitor costs and prices prevents the firm from involuntarily subsidizing long term "losers" and improves the firm's ability to spot long term "winners." A strategic approach also prevents the firm from maximizing short term contribution margin at the expense of long term profitability. The benefit to be realized form strategic costing suggests that it should become an integral part of the firm's long term planning.

## REFERENCES

1. T. Yoshikawa, J. Innes, and F. Mitchell, "Cost Tables: A Foundation of Japanese Cost Management." Journal of Cost Management (Fall 1990): 30-37.

2. M. Sakurai, "Target Costing and How To Use It." Journal of Cost Management (Summer 1989): 39-50.

## BIBLIOGRAPHY

Berliner, C. and J.A. Brimson. Cost Management for Today's Advanced Manufacturing. Boston: Harvard Business School Press, 1988.

Jones, L. "Competitor Cost Analysis at Caterpillar." Management Accounting (Oct. 1988): 32-40.

Kaplan, R. (ed.). Measures For Manufacturing Excellence. Boston: Harvard Business School Press, 1990.

Kelder, R. "Era of Cost Accounting Changes." In R. Capettini and D.K. Clancy, eds., Cost Accounting, Robotics and the New Manufacturing Environment: 3.1 - 3.29. Sarasota, Fl: American Accounting Association, 1987.

Peavey, D.E. "Battle at the GAAP? It's Time for a Change." Management Accounting (Feb. 1990): 31-36.

Porter, M.E. Competitive Advantage. Glenwood, IL: Free Press, 1985.


Sakurai, M. "Target Costing and How To Use It." Journal of Cost Management (Summer 1989): 39-50.


Shank, J.K. and V. Govindarajan. Strategic Cost Analysis. Homewood, IL: Irwin, 1989.


Shank, J.K. "Strategic Cost Management: New Wine or Just New Bottles?" Journal of Management Accounting Research (Fall 1989): 47-65


Susman, G.I. "Product life Cycle Management." Journal of Cost Management (Summer 1989): 8-22.

# Part Three

# CORPORATE IMPLEMENTATION OF NEW COST SYSTEMS

# Chapter Nine

# JUST-IN-TIME AT TELLABS

**Duane "Duke" Dahmen**
**Project Manager, JIT Programs**

Since Tellabs was founded in 1975, its revenues have grown steadily, doubling in the last five years (see Exhibit 9-1). Tellabs' early success came from selling voice-frequency signaling and transmission units as well as other subsystems to telephone companies.

Today, both local and long-distance telephone companies continue to represent the majority of Tellabs' customers. The product line, however, has expanded beyond special services. Tellabs manufactures and markets digital cross-connect systems, high-speed digital networking systems, network management systems, statistical multiplexers, switching multiplexers, echo cancelers, distributive data bridges and teleconferencing systems, as well as special services products. Products are used in private and public voice, digital and data networks, as well as hybrid networks.

## MOTIVATION FOR CHANGE

Despite dramatic growth at Tellabs, the company recognized there was room for improvement both in terms of production

187

productivity and product quality. Inadequacies that were barely noticeable in some areas, were evident in others. Production, for example, was housed in two separate facilities. As described by Jim Slanina, process engineering manager at Tellabs:

> "We used to build modules in one building, put them on a truck, run the truck across the street, unload the truck, and put the modules into systems. We then put the finished systems back on the truck, brought them back to the first building and shipped them out. We actually bought a truck to go back and forth across the street."

Also, shop order quantities were inordinately high, and set up time was lengthy. This led to large batch production runs which

## Exhibit 9-1

### FINANCIAL STATEMENTS
(In thousands of dollars, except per share data)

SELECTED FINANCIAL DATA

|  | 1989 | 1988 | 1987 | 1986 | 1985 |
|---|---|---|---|---|---|
| Net Sales | $181,280 | $155,430 | $136,098 | $115,811 | $99,980 |
| Gross profit | $ 80,183 | $ 66,454 | $ 56,749 | $ 46,096 | $35,807 |
| Net earnings | $ 7,052 | $ 13,459 | $ 10,725 | $ 8,410 | $ 6,963 |
| Average number of shares outstanding | 12,609 | 12,948 | 13,076 | 13,120 | 13,327 |
| Earnings per common share | $0.56 | $1.04 | $0.82 | $0.64 | $0.52 |
| Total assets | $157,839 | $140,639 | $131,065 | $116,432 | $105,878 |
| Long-term debt | $ 4,361 | $ 4,407 | $ 4,917 | $ 5,441 | $ 5,954 |

caused fatigue-induced high defects near the end of a run, along with excessive inventories. Throughput times were high due to a non-optimal plant layout. Furthermore, customers complained about unacceptable high defect rates that led to expensive rework.

In conjunction with Bill Sandras, a JIT expert at Hewlett-Packard at the time, Tellabs decided to fundamentally change its production processes:

> "The underlying principle of Just-in-Time is to continually improve the company's ability to respond to change with a minimum of waste. Waste is defined as any non-value added activity above the theoretical minimum required to provide customers with the company's product." [Bill Sandras]

## IMPLEMENTING JIT

Tellabs' manufacturing process consists primarily of printed circuit board and systems assembly. The process is typical of manufacturing methods commonly used in traditional electronics. Production is characterized as low volume/high mix. Prior to JIT implementation, lead time for a standard product was from 8 to 12 weeks. Typically, the first two weeks involved requisitioning parts from raw material inventory and then completing the automatic insertion of resistors and chips into the boards by machine. A week was then required for parts prepping and the completion of any hand insertions. The fourth week entailed components wave soldering and final assembly. The final two weeks were devoted to testing, inspection and movement to finished goods.

The actual JIT pilot included a subset of production, accounting for some 10 percent of total output. The pilot program was initiated on the third shift with a pilot team of committed change agents. Four months of preparation and training were necessary before actual implementation occurred. During preparation for JIT implemen-tation, many traditional mind-sets had to be overcome. The following "traditions" were particularly problematic:

## Tradition One

Raw material was issued to the factory floor with shop "picks." While as many as 50 jobs could be in process, not all were ready for the parts to be inserted. This resulted in a sizeable amount of raw material taking up space on the factory floor.

Over time, each production process had been established as a functional work area with a supervisor and an assigned crew. The job of the work area was to perform that function only by completing the assigned "job" and sending it to the next process. It was common for the supervisor of one of these work areas to maintain at least one week's worth of inventory in his or her area. If the supervisor had been "burned" a couple of times by running out of work, then his/her tendency would be to hold even more than a week's worth of material for "just in case" emergencies. This fact, in conjunction with normal sizes of from 100 to 1,000 pieces, accounted for ever increasing inventories of work-in-process.

## JIT Change One

Upon implementation of JIT, shop "picks" from the stock room were discontinued. The process was changed from a "push to a pull" system. All previously defined functional work areas were set up as U-shaped work cells, 10 in all. Rather than operating job batches independently between work-in-process departments, production was completed within a cell in much smaller lot sizes. This new production flow is detailed in Exhibit 9-2.

For example, previously the Automatic Insertion production department would receive parts in anticipation of running a job. The problem of not having complete jobs to run caused lost setup time and excessive stock piling of in-process inventory. Under the new work cell configuration, printed circuit boards, integrated circuits and reeled parts, such as resistors and capacitators, were moved into the Automatic Insertion department.

This reduced the previous requirements for space in the stock

**Exhibit 9-2**

## CELLULAR PRODUCTION FLOW

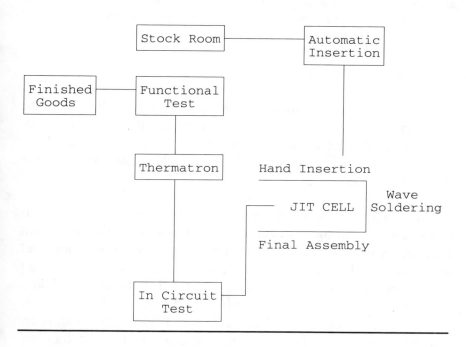

room. It also eliminated the need to order parts when a new job order came in. Instead, the parts were pulled without having to order from the stock room and the job run only when all the parts were available.

The functional personnel were divided into teams to meet the new requirements. Initially, after the cells were set up, they were overmanned. This "extra" staffing assisted in manning the cells when personnel were being pulled out for training in new job responsibilities. The 52 job grades within the manufacturing area were eventually reduced to two, electronic associate and technician. This helped to abate the "not my job" syndrome that had been evident prior to implementation of the cells, thus encouraging worker task flexibility.

**Tradition Two**

When the work-in-process inventory shrank to very low levels, supervisors were finding that employees were stretching out the work. Many employees considered it preferable to slow down the work pace rather than be moved somewhere else.

**JIT Change Two**

Knowing what to build and when was the challenge. The decision was made to implement a Kanban system in conjunction with Materials Requirement Planning II. Production scheduling, bill of materials and inventory records were used to generate material requirements.

Maximum limits of quantity were then established for all processes by cell, the Kanban level. No more than the maximum Kanban quantity was allowed in each cell. Once the Kanban level was reached, the feeder cells shut down until the receiving cell worked out the backlog. For example, the Test Repair cell had a maximum Kanban of 10 assemblies. Upon reaching 10, the preceding feeder cell, Hand Insertion, would be shut down until the test cell could determine what was the cause of the test failures. Once the problem was identified, this information would be relayed to the Hand Insertion cell and the problem would be corrected.

**Tradition Three**

A common phenomenon was to assess blame towards the preceding work area when errors occurred. Rather than focusing on the actual cause of the defect and then eliminating it, more time was devoted to searching for the department responsible for the defect.

**JIT Change Three**

Each of the cells was made responsible for building assemblies from start to finish. This provided a greater sense of ownership and pride in cell activities. Time spent searching for someone to blame was now focused on process improvements to eliminate the cause of defect.

## Tradition Four

Throughout the process came quality inspection. Inspectors existed at various points in every functional department. The most stringent quality check was the one that occurred just prior to moving the product to the finished goods warehouse.

## JIT Change Four

The inspection function was absorbed into the cell process, with instructions that identified checks to be performed on the previous station's work. The new rule: Never pass along a known defect! The focus moved from end-of-line inspection to roving process inspections, and finally to defect collection at the cell level. This defect information was reviewed by team members at weekly meetings.

The process data was broken down by team members into a Problem "story board." A story board was a problem resolution tool taught to every Tellabs employee during a company-wide program called Total Quality Commitment or TQC. JIT would identify the problems, while TQC techniques provided methods and tools to eliminate them. The story board tool walked the users through a step-by-step method of problem analysis and resolution.

Critical in the quality improvement process was allowing time for team members to solve issues within each respective work area. It was also extremely important to provide tools to help team resolve the many problems uncovered by JIT.

## Tradition Five

High inventory levels of finished goods were necessary to meet expected customer demand. The amount of material in finished goods was generally determined by the marketing group to assure availability when a customer called. Damages caused from excessive handling were common and often blamed on vendors.

## JIT Change Five

As product cycle time decreased from 10 weeks to two days, the need to keep large amounts of finished goods was also reduced. The product once kept in finished goods was now kept in the systems assembly area where the finished assemblies were configured into systems, or sent out as line items per customer request. The factory pull system by this time was originating in the systems area when material was pulled for a customer order. When a pre-identified quantity was taken, a signal was sent to the cell to initiate a replenishment order.

For example, if the Kanban was 50 pieces, five tickets of 10 pieces each would be attached to an assembly every 10 assemblies apart. As the systems cell pulled the card and arrived at a ticket, it would be delivered to the adjacent board cell, which would begin the 10-piece replenishment cycle.

## Tradition Six

Once the printed circuit boards were completed, they were moved to the finished goods area until the time to be pulled for a customer order. Because of the high level of finished goods, the product could sit on the shelf for an extended period of time. However, if an engineering change was issued while the product was in finished goods, it would have to be reworked to meet current standards. As a result, the rework department was as large as many of the functional work areas. Another danger was that if a mistake had been made in the first four weeks of the process, but was only detected in terminal testing, the one to four weeks of material in process was also in need of rework.

## JIT Change Six

Because the product was built only when customer orders depleted the Kanban, the total amount of finished goods was drastically cut. This provided a number of advantages:

* Less material in finished goods meant less rework exposure;
* Eliminating the move to finished goods cut material handling;
* Less paperwork was needed for product transfers; and
* Less handling decreased product damage.

## Tradition Seven

Materials handling was a continual problem that arose primarily for two reasons. The first was due to the plant layout and the excessive amount of inventory on the factory floor. At any given time, 30-40 percent of new jobs on the floor were waiting for back ordered parts. As a result, parts were often "borrowed" from one job to complete another. Distances between processes also resulted in excess handling. As the product criss-crossed the plant, an assembly was estimated to move about 12 football fields in length from start to finish.

A second problem arose because a static bag was used to envelop the assemblies in order to prevent electrostatic damage during handling. During the old process, one assembly was calculated to be removed from the bag over a dozen times.

## JIT Change Seven

The new JIT role was "no job starts until it has all its parts." This allowed the factory to keep excess inventory off the floor and minimized materials handling. Once the cells were configured, this also reduced time and material handling, and all but eliminated the need to put assemblies into static bags.

## SUMMARY AND RESULTS

The above traditions and JIT changes are summarized in Exhibit 9-3. Positive productivity results are also included. When these results were quantitatively assessed at year end, the numbers were impressive:

* Work-in-process decreased by some 90 percent;
* Lot sizes shrank five-fold;
* Throughput time decreased from 6 weeks to 2 days;
* Floor space went down 50 percent;
* The labor time was reduced some 45 percent; and
* Defective boards dropped by half.

JIT focuses on the elimination of waste. In his book <u>Just-In-Time: Making It Happen</u>, Bill Sandras emphasized always doing "one less at a time." A large amount of inventory hides problems.

**Exhibit 9-3**

---

### JIT SUMMARY

| **Tradition** | **Change** | **Result** |
|---|---|---|
| "Push" raw material release | Pull system | Decrease in work-in-process |
| Large batch processing | Production cells | Shorter cycle times; Less space and set ups |
| Uneven work scheduling | Work-in-process Kanban | Improved quality |
| End-of-line inspection | Cell responsibility | Less rework |
| High levels of finished goods | Finished goods Kanban | Less finished goods |
| Significant materials handling | Plant reconfiguration | Less materials handling and damage |

---

JIT and TQC methods use a step at-a-time approach to expose system constraints. When the constraints are eliminated, the process of one less at a time continues until the next constraint is identified. The process must be one of continuous evaluation and improvement. Reviewing processes for non-value-added activities provides insight into simplification and waste reduction.

The continuous improvement cycle remains active at Tellabs in a growing number of departments throughout the company. Although Tellabs has developed a strong JIT manufacturing operation, it is still developing the JIT pull system with its vendors. The process is one of continuing education and partnering. To survive in today's marketplace, old beliefs must be dispelled:

* More inventory does not automatically lead to better customer service;
* Large lots do not guarantee better efficiency;
* Long lead times do not imply on-time delivery;
* Specialized staffing does not assure quality; and
* Large functional departments are not mandatory for serving customers well.

During implementation, the project leader often commented "We don't have many million dollar problems but we probably do have a million five-dollar problems." JIT is the foundation that allowed Tellabs to improve quality and increase competitiveness. The educational value of implementing JIT and TQC processes has provided Tellabs with more than just the benefits of reduced inventory, space, lead times and cost. It has provided a means to compete and survive.

# Chapter Ten

# CAPITAL INVESTMENT AT CATERPILLAR

**Chris Schena**
**Manager, Corporate Accounting**

In recent years accounting investment techniques have been criticized as inappropriate for evaluating new technology because they focus primarily on direct labor reduction. Benefits generated by modern machinery and equipment however are mainly in indirect "hidden cost" areas.

Complex manufacturing processes and diversified product lines have made investment decisions a challenge for accountants. For that reason, Caterpillar has always required its cost accountants to become intimately familiar with products and manufacturing processes. Active interaction with functional groups such as design engineers, manufacturing processors, and purchasing personnel is encouraged.

The Caterpillar Accounting Training Program is designed to provide accountants with the necessary skills and understanding of all facets of the business. This program requires accountants to hold job positions for several months in various departments with an emphasis on engineering and manufacturing. To further emphasize the committment to relevant investment decisions at Caterpillar, an Investment Analysis function involving senior

198

company cost accountants was created in the 1960s. The responsibility of the Investment Analysis function is to provide both quantitative and non-quantitative criteria for individual investment proposals which can be reliably used by management to determine whether a proposed investment will support the company's long term financial objectives.

## HISTORICAL PERSPECTIVE

Caterpillar Inc., a multinational company headquartered in Peoria, Illinois designs, manufactures and markets earth-moving, construction and material handling equipment/engines. Caterpillar has been in business since the merger of the Holt and Best companies in 1925. The company grew significantly after World War II, expanding its manufacturing facilities and distribution network overseas. In the decade between 1970 and 1980, sales grew rapidly from $2.1 billion to $9.2 billion. Employment grew from 66,000 to 84,000 and annual capital expenditures increased from $113 million to $836 million.

In the early 1980s, Caterpillar was affected by severe worldwide reduction in demand for earth-moving equipment and engines. This was precipitated by financial crises in lesser developed nations, as well as new aggressive competition emerging with new management techniques and business philosophies. Over-capacity in the industry resulted in intense price competition and declining margins. Cost reduction became a matter of survival throughout the industry.

During these difficult years, Caterpillar reduced costs through traditional means such as employment attrition, automation, material sourcing changes and so on. Caterpillar also reduced its world-wide floor space by about 30 percent and capital expenditures from an all time high of $836 million in 1981 to $229 million by 1985. Following three successive years of losses totalling almost $1 billion, Caterpillar recognized that in order to remain financially viable, some fundamental changes in design, procurement, manufacturing, and distribution had to take place.

In the middle 1980s, Caterpillar embarked on an ambitious two billion dollar capital investment plan. The nature of the changes generated by the plan were far reaching. Caterpillar recognized it would be difficult to properly assess the merits of such a major investment using traditional evaluation approaches. Instead, a more creative and comprehensive evaluation methodology was needed that would take into account reductions generated by quality improvements, production flexibility, improved throughput, and system integration.

A three phase approach was used for financial evaluation of the proposed investments (Exhibit 10-1):

1. financial evaluation of the macro vision
2. division of the macro vision into bundles, and their economic analysis
3. bundle monitoring

The Discounted Cash Flow Model continued to be used at Caterpillar as the most appropriate investment analysis methodology. Caterpillar's particular application of this method however, is what has differentiated it from other manufacturers.

## MACRO PLAN

In late 1984, a multi-discipline team sponsored by the Vice-President of Manufacturing, Pierre Guerindon, was formed. Its charter was to develop a strategy which would position Caterpillar in a cost and quality leadership position into the next century. The proposal addressed Caterpillar's entire manufacturing strategy and its use of technology. A document entitled "Plant with a Future" (PWAF) was published, which provided the strategy, tactics and milestones necessary for Caterpillar to remain the industry leader. This vision was shared with the worldwide organization and each facility had the opportunity to provide its input into the strategy.

The PWAF would be achieved through Flexible Manufacturing Systems, Automated Material Handling Systems, Computer Integrated Manufacturing Systems, and Cellular Rearrangement

**Exhibit 10-1**

# INVESTMENT PLAN FOR MODERNIZATION

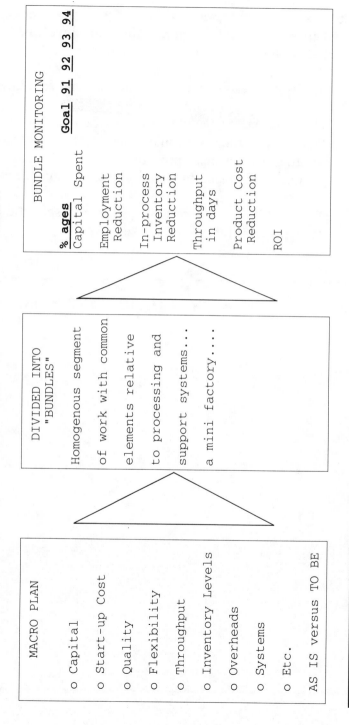

MACRO PLAN

o Capital

o Start-up Cost

o Quality

o Flexibility

o Throughput

o Inventory Levels

o Overheads

o Systems

o Etc.

AS IS versus TO BE

DIVIDED INTO
"BUNDLES"

Homogenous segment

of work with common

elements relative

to processing and

support systems.....

a mini factory.....

BUNDLE MONITORING

| % ages | Goal | 91 | 92 | 93 | 94 |
|--------|------|----|----|----|----|
| Capital Spent | | | | | |
| Employment Reduction | | | | | |
| In-process Inventory Reduction | | | | | |
| Throughput in days | | | | | |
| Product Cost Reduction | | | | | |
| ROI | | | | | |

with Just-in-Time Material Flow. The changes envisioned were broad in scope, would require substantial investment and would affect all Caterpillar plants worldwide.

The PWAF strategy was structured around four key principles:

* CONSOLIDATE manufacturing space world-wide
* SIMPLIFY product design, manufacturing processes, and operating and business procedures
* AUTOMATE machining quality control and materials handling processes
* INTEGRATE engineering, logistics and shop floor functions into one single information system.

**Exhibit 10-2**

---

### PWAF STRATEGIC PRINCIPLES

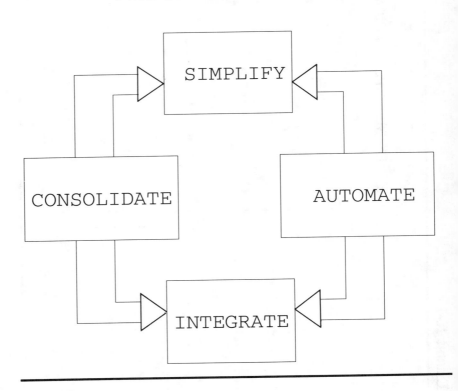

The PWAF was more than just a manufacturing plan. Its scope affected all areas of the business, including engineering, finance, employee and labor relations, purchasing, materials and manufacturing. Not only would overall operating expenses be reduced, but product quality would be improved and customer response time and manufacturing would hasten introduction of new products for competitive advantage.

By mid-1985, most manufacturing facilities had provided their input and submitted a first estimate of the investment and resources necessary to implement the strategy. Certain issues soon became obvious:

* Total investment would surpass any previous expenditures.
* The investment strategy had to be viewed as a synergistic combination of technologies, development of new logistic structures and deployment of new computer systems to support the new environment.

Caterpillar executives called upon management accountants for their participation in the modernization investment evaluation. The idea of a massive investment in all plants posed a revolutionary problem. Was this massive investment the right strategy for the company? What if some strategic portions were approved and others were not? Would the total plan succeed? What kind of cost reductions were quantifiable?

To address the above questions, the first step required addressing the viability of the <u>total</u> strategy, that is investments, logistics and systems at the corporate level. In the feasibility study, this assessment was achieved by comparing two scenarios. The cost and benefit of producing future product lines and volumes within existing manufacturing and organizational environments was labelled the "AS IS" condition. The cost and benefit projections of producing the same future product lines and volumes with the proposed investment in new technologies was labelled the "TO BE" condition.

The most critical financial step of the MACRO PWAF VISION

was the Operating Plan definition. Each manufacturing plant worldwide was required to develop an Operating Plan for both the AS IS and TO BE environments, including such components as plant layout, material flow, employment levels, indirect material, assets, inventory turnover, etc. The Operating Plan had to provide enough concise detail to accurately describe AS IS and TO BE plant operation scenarios. The operating plant characteristics were used to identify cost drivers for each scenario. The TO BE operating plan was designed around the four PWAF principles of consolidate, simplify, automate and integrate.

A consolidated Financial Model was the vehicle used to assess the economic viability of the overall strategy. It translated the Operating Plan into dollars, and isolated such things as total costs and expenses, investment and product cost (Exhibit 10-3). A ten year pro forma comparison of operating expenses and resources was prepared. The internal rates of return and net present values of each scenario were calculated using a traditional Discounted Cash Flow methodology. A summary showing total investment requirement, start-up costs, inventory reduction, cost reduction, IRR and NPV, as well as other relevant non-financial factors was presented to the Executive Office for approval of the overall modernization concept.

Since the macro plans were at a feasibility stage, the Executive Office required more detailed review of each specific plan. Based on the figures, the green light was given to pursue a more detailed analysis, to ensure that each portion of the plan was justified on its own economics. As a result, each plant was required to break its total plan into manageable projects. Each project was then to be presented to the Board of Directors as an individual business proposal.

## ECONOMIC ANALYSIS OF BUNDLES

Traditionally Caterpillar had justified most machinery and equipment acquisitions on a one-for-one basis, whether simple replacement of the asset or a new investment in modernization. Because of the synergistic nature and scope of the new proposal,

**Exhibit 10-3**

## PWAF COST/BENEFIT ANALYSIS

| OPERATING PLAN |
| --- |
| - Plant Layout<br>- Organization<br>- Employment by Function<br>- Indirect Material Expenditures<br>- Assets<br>- Inventory Turnover |

| OPERATING ANALYSIS |
| --- |
| - Improved Quality<br>- Improved Availability<br>- Lower Non-quality Cost<br>- More Flexibility<br>- Effective Communication<br>- Increased Teamwork |

| FINANCIAL MODEL |
| --- |
| - Cost and Expenses<br>  • by account/type<br>  • organizational unit<br><br>- Cost and Expenses<br>  • buildings<br>  • machines<br>  • inventory<br><br>- Product Costs |

| FINANCIAL ANALYSIS |
| --- |
| - Reduced Operating Costs<br><br>- Competitive Costs<br><br>- Return on Investment<br><br>- Reduced Product Costs |

traditional approaches to investment evaluation were not applicable. As manufacturing and accounting personnel modelled the modernization of their facilities, they encountered difficulties in capturing the complete financial impact of the changes. The model needed to include direct labor savings, as well as economies generated by quality improvement and flexibility of operations. Just-in-Time practices, related inventory reductions, improved manufacturing flows, and system integration changes also needed to be assessed. In other words, all costs, direct as well as "hidden," and benefits had to be accounted for.

To deal with this complex situation, the MACRO PWAF PLAN was divided in to 77 distinct projects called **bundles**. Individual bundles were defined as "homogenous segments of work or product that had common elements relative to processing and support systems." Each bundle had three operating characteristics:

* The functions/processes it comprised, had to be synergistically related to each other through sharing of common manufacturing processes, material handling systems, sequencers, tool management and computer systems. All of these systems were necessary to make the complete manufacturing plan work.
* A bundle represented a GATE-to-GATE process, from receiving of the various parts or components through delivery of a finished and assembled product to the next bundle or assembly line.
* It defined an area or mini-factory that could be independently managed.

The bundles were the vehicles used for the investment evaluation and capital expenditure approval. The following were the major elements in the bundle analysis.

## 1. Introduction

The introduction included a problematic statement that defined the plant's current business situation with regard to cost of products manufactured and their relative competitiveness. Product quality and delivery concerns as well as levels of inventory and other problems were also included. The specific bundle was positioned relative to the entire plant's plan, to ensure that it fit within the total strategy. Finally, the introduction provided a list of the AS IS versus the visionary TO BE business characteristics on manufacturing process (age, capability etc.), product cost, quality, delivery and inventory. Some of the key elements included in this list were management system changes, adoption of a pull manufacturing concept as opposed to the current push practice, improved material flow and handling, increased inventory turns and the integration of operations.

## 2. Plan Base

This was a very crucial step in the evaluation process. Before manufacturing plans and processes were designed and investments contemplated, one had to decide which products and components the facility would make versus purchasing from outside sources.

This was done by taking the following factors into consideration:

* components which were proprietary
* components which were crucial to the quality/performance of the final product
* components for which the plant was cost competitive
* parts that could be easily purchased from outside, with industry or world economies of scale, and which offered no differentiation advantages
* parts or components which negatively affected the plant manufacturing flow

## 3. Plan Concept

This section provided all the technical information necessary to understand the proposal. It included a description of all recommended machinery and equipment, as well as material flow diagrams and explanations on how key operating principles interrelated. Other descriptions included work flow in the various cells or flexible manufacturing systems, gate-to-gate processes, process control, and how the material was being procured. Just-in-Time process flow, control of direct and indirect costs, and information flow was also considered. The operating characteristics of the AS IS and TO BE environments were also described in this section (Exhibit 10-4).

## 4. Resource Plan/Data

The resources required included capital expenditures of machinery and equipment, in addition to expenses such as tooling and systems. Every time new technologies were adopted, the company incurred significant start-up costs for items such as rearrangement of existing machine tools, installation of new equipment, disruption to the production flow, and training and systems implementation. Also included in this section was the identification of personal skills required, training, organizational structure, people involvement, and labor relations.

## 5. Identify Alternatives

Another critical step in the process was to identify all relevant alternatives. As a general rule, Caterpillar's methodology recom-

**Exhibit 10-4**

## "AS IS" vs "TO BE" CHARACTERISTICS

| AS IS | TO BE |
|-------|-------|
| 1. Manual Scheduling From Forecast | Order Driven Mechanical Scheduling |
| 2. Long Lead Times - monthly buckets (EOQ/ELM) | Lead Time Reduced to Hours (Day of Need Environment JIT) |
| 3. Large Inventory (PF in-process rough, finished product) | 1/2 Month of Inventory |
| 4. Manual Handling | (Automated) Mechanical Material Handling |
| 5. Material Flows Between Buildings and Machine Lines | Material Flows Within Building and Cells |
| 6. Receiving - Central | Point of Use |
| 7. Manual Design Detailing Checking | CAE/CAM |
| 8. Standalone Testing Function | Integrated with Fabrication and Assembly |
| 9. Lengthy Set up Standalone Machines | Reduced or Eliminated Set up Flexible Random Processing |
| 10. Inspection - after the fact | Closed Loop Automatic Feedback |
| 11. Manual Tool Management | Adaptive Control: Auto Tool Management |
| 12. Separate Design & Processing | CAE/CAM and Manufacturability Functions Integrated |
| 13. Supplier Communications Clerical/Manual Interfaces | On-line Communication with Supplier |
| 14. Etc...... | Etc...... |

mended considering at least the three following alternatives:

* Continue AS IS i.e. the present manufacturing processes were updated for potential obsolescence.
* Invest in the TO BE manufacturing processes. Several sub-alternatives were sometimes considered to allow for various automation levels.
* Purchase the finished product from a supplier.

The rationale of each alternative was provided, together with an analysis of strengths and weaknesses.

## 6. Integration/Systems/Simplification
Each bundle had to specify its systems needs and rationalize its position within the total plant system plan. Integration was a major focus, including day-of-need planning, design/processing integration and factory floor integration.

## 7. Financial Model
A detailed Financial Model had to be developed based on the above operating principles and alternatives. The accountant was held responsible for fully understanding the product, processes and organizational structure in order to challenge the Operational Model for reasonableness. After the reasonableness of the AS IS and TO BE plans were assessed, the Financial Model had to meet some basic objectives:

* Provide a reasonably consistent and comprehensive means of displaying the accounting of the cost and benefits of the two operational plans.
* Determine the best and most economic criteria for the financial evaluation of the differences between the two plans. The plan had to yield costs equal to or better than competitive costs and provide an acceptable return on the investment. The key to assuring credible results was that all alternatives had to be designed around producing the same product mix at the same volume.

A five step process was followed to complete the investment analysis evaluation:

* Identify Alternatives
* Evaluate Benefits
* Budget Cash Flows
* Discount Cash Flows
* Evaluate Results

As mentioned earlier, a minimum of three alternatives were considered in each modernization study. The same alternatives, if feasible, were retained for the investment analysis.

Benefits were then determined for the overall change in operating conditions from AS IS versus TO BE. An **Operating Plan Checklist** developed by management accountants was used to bridge the language of manufacturing and accounting. This Operating Plan Checklist translated process characteristics into specific general ledger accounts. The checklist was also used as a tool in presenting Operating and Financial Plans to upper management. The Operating Plan Checklist shown in Exhibit 10-5 identified the benefits generated from modernization improvement from increased productivity, manufacturability, production flow, improved quality, increased flexibility, throughput and system integration, along with benefit category impacted.

The third step was to budget a 10 year cash flow statement for each alternative using the relevant operating plans. Operating Plans inherently had a set of assumptions for each alternative that could be translated into cash flow, for instance, number of employees by class in each department; estimated annual tooling expenses; percentage of scrap, inventory in number of days, investment, support costs. These cash flows analyzed the ongoing operational costs for each alternative. Included in these budgeted ongoing costs were wages and fringes for all employees. Indirect materials and expenses included things like tools, supplies, automotive materials and real estate taxes.

In addition, there were certain up front costs. In the continue

210

**Exhibit 10-5A**

## MODERNIZATION PROJECTS – OPERATING PLAN CHECKLIST

| CATEGORY | INCREASED PRODUCTIVITY | MFG' ABILITY | IMPROVED FLOW | IMPROVED QUALITY | IMPROVED FLEXIBILITY | INCREASED THROUGHPUT | SYSTEM INTEGRATION |
|---|---|---|---|---|---|---|---|
| **MATERIAL** | | | | | | | |
| • Fewer Steel Codes | | x | | | | | x |
| • Improved Steel Utilization | x | x | | | x | | x |
| • Use of Mill Edge (Untrimmed steel) | | x | | | | | |
| **DIRECT LABOR** | | | | | | | |
| • Hourly Reduction | x | | | | | | |
| • Higher Classification Impact | x | | | | | | |
| **INDIRECT LABOR** | | | | | | | |
| • Scrap, RSSM | | | | x | | x | |
| • Rework | | | | x | | x | |
| • Inspection | | | | x | | x | |
| • Material Distribution | | | x | x | | x | |
| • Clerical/Stock Follow-Up | | | x | | | x | |
| • Machine Repair | x | | | | x | | x |
| • Equipment Repair | x | | | | x | | x |
| • Automotive Repair | | | x | | | | |
| • Tool Room | | x | | | x | | |
| • Tools Disbursement | | x | | | x | | |
| • Tool Grinding | | x | | | | | |
| • Prototype Test | | | | | x | | |
| • Rearrangement | | | | | x | | |
| **MANAGEMENT/WEEKLY** | | | | | | | |
| • Foreman Reduction | x | | x | x | x | | |
| • Manufacturing/Engineering | | x | | | | | |
| • Office Automation | x | | | | | | x |

Exhibit 10-5B

## MODERNIZATION PROJECTS – OPERATING PLAN CHECKLIST

| CATEGORY | INCREASED PRODUCTIVITY | MFG' ABILITY | IMPROVED FLOW | IMPROVED QUALITY | IMPROVED FLEXIBILITY | INCREASED THROUGHPUT | SYSTEM INTEGRATION |
|---|---|---|---|---|---|---|---|
| **INDIRECT MATL & EXPENSE** | | | | | | | |
| • Scrap | | | | x | | x | x |
| • Scrap Recoveries | | x | | x | | | x |
| • Material Cleaning | | | x | | | x | |
| • Paint/Rust Proofing | x | x | x | x | x | x | |
| • Rental Software | | | | | | | x |
| • Lease DP Hardware | | | | | | | x |
| • Perishable Tools | | x | | | | | x |
| • Machine Repair | x | | | | x | | x |
| • Durable Tool Repair | x | | | | x | | x |
| • Automotive Repair | | | x | | x | | x |
| • Misc. Supplies | x | | x | x | | | x |
| • Gas & Oil | x | | | | | | |
| • Weldrod | x | x | x | x | x | | |
| • Subcontracted Services | x | | x | | | | |
| • Engrg. Changes & Prototypes | | | | | x | | |
| **OTHERS** | | | | | | | |
| • Power & Gas | x | | | | | | x |
| • Freight | | | x | | x | x | |
| • Warranty Expense | | x | | x | | | |
| **INVENTORY** | | | | | | | |
| • Rough | | | | | | x | |
| • In Process | | | x | | | x | |
| • Finished | | | | | | x | |
| • Prime Product | | | | | | x | |
| • Indirect | x | | | | x | x | |
| • Replacement Parts | | | | | x | x | x |

AS IS alternative, these up front costs included replacement of equipment to continue manufacturing. In the TO BE alternative, the up front costs included the machinery, equipment, tooling, and systems in addition to start-up costs such as rearrangement of floor space, training and learning curves. The levels of raw material, work-in-progress and finished inventories in the two alternatives was another important consideration. These inventories were valued and considered an up front investment in all alternatives.

The fourth step was to discount the cash flows using the company's cost of capital. Of the three common methods of investment analysis, the Payback Method is a simple but conceptually deficient technique. It simply determines how many years it takes to recover the investment. The return **of** the investment is emphasized instead of the return **on** the investment. If the payback period is more than some maximum acceptable level, the proposal is rejected. The major shortcoming of the payback technique is that it ignores the time value of money, and fails to consider savings after the payback period, thus leading to a deceptive measure of profitability.

The Return on Assets Method is based on accounting income calculations following GAAP, rather than upon cash flows. The timings of the cash flows are ignored.

Caterpillar used the Discounted Cash Flow Method as the most realistic basis for evaluating investment projects. Simply because operating environments are becoming more sophisticated, it was felt, that was not a reason that the method should be abandoned. The quality and relevance of an investment analysis resides in the quality of the alternative and Operating Plan identified. Only thorough initial work can help identify all the "hidden costs" associated with the factory of the future, including automation, systems, and flexibility with JIT.

The final step was to evaluate the results. The entire plant management group was responsible for approving the plant's Operational Model and Financial Model. A very important element was the analysis of the basic assumptions used to develop the AS

IS versus TO BE plans. Once the basic plans and assumptions were approved, quantification was relatively simple. A key component was the sensitivity analysis used to test the critical assumptions, to see what impact they had on the financial results.

Once plant management was in agreement with the bundle and satisfied that it fit into the entire plant PWAF vision, their findings were presented to a corporate approval committee. Each of the 77 bundles was approved by this committee to assure that it fit with the entire corporate PWAF strategy.

## THE BUNDLE MONITORING

After the bundles were approved and the investments made, monitoring the progress of the planned results became necessary. A bundle monitor Characteristic Summary Sheet was used to report progress to plants and corporate management on key financial and non-financial measures of the bundle's performance.

The key measurements included:

1. **Total Capital Spent** - the amount of capital approved for the bundle was listed along with the trend of the amount spent. An indication of whether the bundle will be overspent is readily evident from this analysis.
2. **Manpower** - a major portion of the bundle benefits was identified in all manpower areas, direct hourly, indirect hourly, and salaried. This provided an indication of whether the current plans would continue to produce the original employment reduction benefits.
3. **Return on Investment** - plants were required to indicate if the original ROI bundle (Caterpillar terminology for IRR) was on track, ahead of schedule or behind.
4. **Average Throughput** - this was a very important measure of the bundle's flow, indicating the average number of days it took a product to get from gate-to-gate in the old AS IS environment, the planned TO BE environment and the latest forecast.

**Exhibit 10-6**

## CHARACTERISTIC SUMMARY SHEET

| Characteristic | AS IS | TO BE | 12/89 | 12/90 | 12/91 |
|---|---|---|---|---|---|
| Total Capital Spent (MM) | | $20.5 | $12.6 | $15.1 | $20.5 |
| Manpower | | | | | |
|     Direct Hourly | 266 | 137 | 204 | 169 | 144 |
|     Indirect Hourly | 92 | 62 | 67 | 66 | 59 |
|     Salaried | 50 | 26 | 30 | 27 | 25 |
|     Total | 408 | 225 | 301 | 266 | 228 |
| Return on Investment | 0% | 30% | on track | | |
| Operating Shifts | 3 | 3 | 3 | 3 | 3 |
| Average Throughput (days) | 40 | 5 | 30 | 15 | 5 |
| In-process Inventory (days) | 40 | 5 | 30 | 15 | 5 |
| In-process Inventory (MM) | $5.8 | $0.7 | $4.4 | $2.2 | $0.7 |
| Scheduling | forecast | demand | forecast | demand | demand |
| Quality Control | Q. Gates | SPC | SPC | SPC | SPC |
| Floor Space (000 square ft) | 303 | 194 | 248 | 194 | 194 |
| Product Cost Reduction | | | | | |
|     Material | 0% | 1% | 1% | 1% | 1% |
|     Value Added | 0% | 25% | 14% | 20% | 25% |
|     Total Plant | 0% | 20% | 12% | 16% | 20% |

5. **In-process Inventory** - the in-process inventory reductions related directly to reduction in throughput and was also measured.
6. **Product Cost Reduction** - when the original bundle was approved, a percent product cost reduction was required to assure competitiveness. The element was monitored against target.

A characteristic summary sheet was required for all 77 bundles and the results were consolidated into a corporate summary for the five key areas of ROI, Capital, Cost Reduction, Employment, and Inventory. These results continue to be reported twice annually to the Executive Office, to measure the progress on the overall program.

## CONCLUSION

Caterpillar has made substantial gains in cost reduction by implementing the PWAF principles of simplification, consolidation, automation and integration. The investment analysis process used by Caterpillar management accountants plays a significant role in the approval and monitoring of this program. Management accountants are required to assist top level management through the entire process. Accountants are an integral part of the team, as both the Operational Models and Financial Models used to justify the Macro and the 77 bundles are developed.

It is Caterpillar's opinion that traditional discounted cash flow analysis is an appropriate method for justifying investment, including investment in new technology. The key resides in first recognizing that a modernization program of such scope and breadth cannot be evaluated on a machine-by-machine basis. The majority of expenditures are interrelated and the investment in any piece of equipment cannot realistically be justified without considering its impact and contribution to the entire plan. The bundle methodology which isolates an entire piece of the factory with all necessary support, has been found by Caterpillar to be the best approach to account for all direct and indirect costs of the investment evaluation process.

Second, a complete understanding and analysis of all relevant production components is mandatory if accurate projections are to be made. Many of the components found in today's manufacturing environment differ from traditional measurements.

Finally, a comprehensive cost audit performance measurement plan is essential if projected benefits are to be realized. Investments of such magnitude demand stringent post-audit evaluations. Careful consideration of the above can lead to successful investments in new technology.

# Chapter Eleven

# COSTING QUALITY AT HUGHES AIRCRAFT

**Glen Neidermann**
**Division Controller, Ground Systems Group**

This case deals with implementing a Cost of Quality program in the Printed Circuit Board department at Hughes Aircraft's Ground Systems Group. Quality is defined as "fit for customer use," and is defined in terms of the person, product or service provided. What is it that determines customer satisfaction? What tells you that the product or service has been successfully provided? In implementing this project, the actual cost of the quality going into the deliverance of the product was examined with Activity based Costing concepts.

## PROJECT PLANNING

The project team consisted of an Activity based Costing theorist; a manufacturing engineer; a Printed Circuit Board production manager; a defense contract agency auditor; a finance manager and an information systems analyst. The Hughes Ground Systems Group has an evaluation criteria for every project team, one that follows a very natural sequence of events: start-up; work performed by the team; and accomplishments. Many organizations have developed goals. Sometimes these are company goals. More typically they are divisional goals that are expected to be implemented at the departmental level. Project teams use organizational goals and make them a part of the deliverable product or service. The ability to show a strong relationship to stated goals helps ensure that the efforts of the team are synchronous. The goals in place at the time of this study were: satisfy our customer; expand our business; establish broad-based individualized training; support General Motors; and increase shareholder value.

A team well versed in quality and continuously measurable improvement techniques would implement a system with a better chance of success. Thus, reading the latest methods and using relevant expertise was considered essential. Some of the techniques used included team problem solving, quality function development, numerous statistical analyses, actual experimentation, and cycle time management. Customer survey results and testimonials were also used. Objective data was gathered in order to verify improvements.

A determination was made to understand the significance of the data and to show cause and effect relationships for specific cases. Were there unique and innovative results associated with the project? Innovation should bring a significant leap in performance, did that occur? The project team should also be able to present the pros and cons of various alternatives and the rationale of method choice. Was the improvement or development systematically derived? Did it include accounting for alternatives and could it withstand an audit?

The project had to demonstrate quantitative results, especially those that could be traced to the customer. The same held true for large scale product or service improvement. Did improvements lay a foundation for future developments or were they simply one shot accomplishments? Were there spin-off improvements? How did the pilot study team fare?

## PROJECT IMPLEMENTATION

The Cost of Quality project goals were to:

1. improve the effectiveness and competitiveness of the division through Continuous Measurable Improvement techniques.

2. develop technologies, tools and resources for the "90s that maintain Hughes at the forefront of design, development and manufacturing.

3. create an environment that fosters teamwork, open communications and participation in training, and encourages individual responsibility for effectiveness of our operation.

4. develop and expand our customer base for division products and services that best utilize available resources.

5. participate in the development of team relationships with our suppliers to enhance their abilities to satisfy our needs.

In planning for improvement, we embraced Total Quality Management principles (Table 11-1).

## QUALITY COSTS

We chose to break quality costs into four functional areas:

1. Prevention Costs
2. Appraisal Costs
3. Internal Failure Costs
4. External Failure Costs

Prevention costs include training personnel and having technology, systems or equipment to eliminate defects before they affect the product. This area will eventually be the largest consumer of costs for the firm.

**Table 11-1**

---

TOTAL QUALITY MANAGEMENT

| Principles | Action Plans |
|---|---|
| o  Participative management | - cross-functional team<br>- the voice of the customer |
| o  Continuous & timely training | - weekly meetings<br>- frequent presentations |
| o  Defined responsibilities | - unique functional expertise<br>- specific assignments |
| o  The use of CMI/TQM tools | - "what/how"<br>- cost model<br>- driver evaluation/robustness<br>- strategic analysis<br>- cost trends/estimation |
| o  Individual responsibility<br>   on fitness for-use | - does it work? |
| o  Strong feed-forward and<br>   feed-back communication | - presentations and reviews at<br>  all levels of the organization<br>- training manual |

---

Appraisal costs include monitoring to see how well the product progresses through the production process. A good appraisal program should point out where defects are occurring. Emphasis will eventually shift from appraisal to prevention as defects in products are reduced and reworking of product minimized.

Internal failure costs are correction costs of defects and disposal of scrap and waste. External failure costs are warranty claims, product returned for rework and repair, and costs of determining why defective product was delivered.

An additional area that has not yet been addressed is the growing cost of Environmental Quality. Usually these costs are borne by the parent corporation or facility site, and include costs of environmental monitoring, disposal of hazardous wastes and equipment protection and training programs.

Unfortunately, the necessary cost of quality information was neither easily obtainable or reliable. Cost allocations were based on production labor and were not based on cost centers readily attributable to the above generic categories. To overcome this limitation, an activity analysis was performed of all components of prevention, appraisal, internal and external failure costs.

Both activity costs and cost drivers were studied. This required careful consideration of the production process, the work cells affected and the definition off what constituted a responsibility center. Cost drivers had to focus on the practical aspects of cost

**Figure 11-1**

## COST ACCUMULATION SYSTEMS

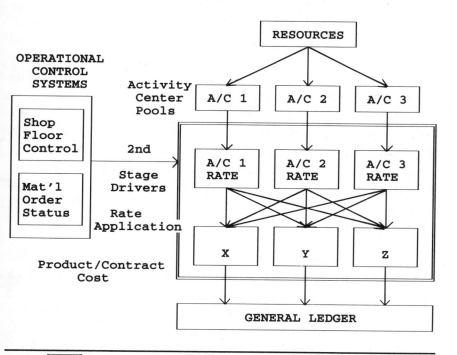

area is ABC MODULE

221

of data retrieval, accuracy and data limitations. The process is shown diagrammatically in Figure 11-1. The number of activities relevant to prevention, appraisal, internal and external failure in the Printed Circuit Board department had to be carefully studied.

This was accomplished through lengthy interviews and detailed flowcharts of the process. Major cost of quality activity centers with common cost drivers were identified, so as to make the cost allocations manageable. The cross-functional nature of the project team, as described earlier, led to innovative approaches, for example in trading off simplicity and accuracy, and in integrating cost of quality allocations into the existing control system.

Table 11-2 shows the activity analysis done by the project team for the Printed Circuit Board department in attempting to analyze the cost of quality.

## PREVENTION ACTIVITIES

Prevention costs comprised 14% of the time of quality and included incoming production checks, training employees, quality paperwork, the total quality system, and producibility. **Incoming production check** was the work of production personnel in validating the quality and quantity of production materials, parts and assemblies received from vendors. It included product testing. **Training employees** included all effort and expense involved with administering, staffing and conducting training of production and quality employees. It included the cost and time of those in training, as well as those in an administrative, supervisory or instructional role.

**Quality paperwork** was measured to develop, update and review Quality Method Sheets (QMSs), quality check sheets,Workmanship Criteria Manuals (WCMs), and contract summary sheets. It included review and approval of production related paperwork, including Process Engineering Instructions (PEIs), planning packages for routing, and Purchase Orders (POs). Process Engineering paperwork was also measured for review of Process Engineering Instructions (PEIs), Program Operating

**Table 11-2**

### COST OF QUALITY MATRIX ANALYSIS

|  |  | % of time |
|---|---|---|
| **PREVENTION** | Incoming production check | 0.1 |
|  | Train employees | 3.2 |
|  | Quality paperwork | 1.0 |
|  | Total Quality System | 9.1 |
|  | Producibility | 0.7 |
|  |  | 14.1 |
| **APPRAISAL** | Vendor Liaison/Problem solving | 1.1 |
|  | Source Surveillance | 1.3 |
|  | Production check and FACT test | 20.9 |
|  | Production surveillance | 9.3 |
|  | Production trouble shooting | 10.7 |
|  | Quality Inspection | 16.9 |
|  | Laboratory Chemical Analysis | 3.9 |
|  | Laboratory Physical Analysis | 3.9 |
|  |  | 68.0 |
| **INTERNAL FAILURES** | Production Corrective Action | 2.6 |
|  | Production Rework | 9.9 |
|  | Scrap and Spoilage | 3.0 |
|  | Obsolescence | 0.1 |
|  |  | 15.6 |
| **EXTERNAL FAILURES** | Quality Audit | 2.3 |

Procedures (POPs), and physical configuration of items. Finally, Test Engineering Paperwork was analyzed in developing, updating and reviewing test procedures, methods and programs.

**Total Quality Systems**, Statistical Quality Control, Demming, Cost Improvement Program (CIP), quality circles, and Continuous Measurable Improvement (CMI) teams all added to a significant portion of the prevention costs. **Producibility** was the work required to verify that the drawings and artwork met MILSTD 275, MILP 55110, C1 Standard for Producibility Manual and contract requirements. This included design engineering interface support and preparation of Operational Maintenance Reports (OMRs).

## APPRAISAL ACTIVITIES

Appraisal costs, amounting to 68% of total quality time, represented the overwhelming amount of where the Printed Circuit Board department spent its time and effort. These activities included the following. **Vendor Liaison/Problem Solving** was the travel time and effort expended in analyzing and resolving quality, delivery or other problems with vendors and suppliers. This included surveys, vendor tracking, and Supplier Material Report disposition. **Source Surveillance** was the travel time and effort involved with conducting source (vendor) surveillance, including hardware audits, process audits, vendor interface, certification and Product Quality Improvement implementation.

**Production Check and Fact Test** was a major activity. This was the effort involved in logging in, inspecting and testing parts, components and finished assemblies by production personnel. It included incoming kit-check and associated document check. **Production Surveillance** included the effort and expense required to monitor and maintain the proper factory processes and work flow. **Production Troubleshooting** involved searching for deficiencies, analyzing fabrication and assembly problems, assessing impacts, and answering manufacturing and quality problems. It included the running of tests to verify and solve problems.

**Quality Inspection** was the effort involved with logging in, inspecting and documenting discrepancies of parts, components and finished assemblies in conformance with the quality plan. It included incoming, in-process and final inspection. **Laboratory Chemical Analysis** included the work of providing laboratory chemical analysis support for qualification and inspection requirements. It included electrolysis copper analysis, atomic absorption, infra-red and emission spectroscopy, and gas chromatography. **Laboratory Physical Analysis** was the work of providing laboratory physical analysis support for qualification and inspection requirements. It included tank qualification, micro-sections, X-ray fluorescence, pull test, micro and macro photos, recertification of shelf life items, copper clad certification and thermo analysis.

## INTERNAL FAILURE ACTIVITIES

Internal failures accounted for 15% of quality time and effort costs. Internal failures included Production Corrective Action, Production Rework, Scrap, Spoilage and Obsolescence. **Production Corrective Action** involved the effort associated with processing Reports For Investigation and Corrective Action (RFICA), Inspection Deficiency Reports (IDRs), Non Conforming Material Reports (NCMRs), Standard Repair Reports (SRRs), Quality Deficiency Reports (QDRs), and Material Review Board actions (MRBs). **Production Rework** represented the effort associated with the rework of both internal and purchased components and finished products to correct manufacturing or specification problems. It also included rework modification planning activities. **Scrap and Spoilage** included all material which could not be used as planned in the production process, as well as the labor involved in handling, accounting for, and disposing of it. **Obsolescence** was the effort involved in handling, accounting for, and disposing of materials, components and finished products which were no longer used in the production process, or sold in the marketplace. This activity included all material costs.

## EXTERNAL FAILURE ACTIVITIES

External failures accounted for only 2% of the effort as very few items were returned from customers for warranty or rework. There was an on-going quality audit process that ensured that the system worked and therefore a quality product was delivered to the customer. **Quality Audits** were performed to verify compliance with contractual requirements as defined in the Product Assurance Program plans, engineering documents, and military specifications.

This included audits of product test activities and test procedures, including participation in first article tests.

## ENVIRONMENTAL QUALITY ACTIVITIES

In addition, quality surveys and audits for Health and Safety and Waste Management were performed. **Health & Safety** included training and checking for compliance with health and safety rules and regulations, and natural disaster preparation. Waste Management involved hazardous material management, waste treatment plant interface, and Environmental Protection Agency (EPA) and Air Quality Management District (AQMD) compliance.

## FINDINGS

The implementation process needs to consider three factors for integration into the existing Information Systems: alignment of costs to activity centers; relieving these costs; and quantifying the results in terms of time and dollars. Aligning activities into Prevention, Appraisal, Internal and External activity centers and then assigning the personnel that work in these activities is invaluable. Developing drivers to relieve costs to the cost objective can be based on items such as labor hours, number of defects, work orders or units.

As can be seen in Table 11-3, Hughes spends a significant amount of total product cost on quality, in the neighborhood of 30%. The most significant portion of this is appraisal cost. In contrast, Boeing's cost of quality mix is more focused on internal failure costs. This data suggests two future courses of action. The first is a move towards greater expenditures on prevention cost. If quality can be built into the product, then subsequent internal and external failure costs can be reduced. The second course of action is a reduction in the overall cost of quality through time. As prevention costs more than pay for themselves through reduced internal and external failure cost reduction, overall cost of quality

**Table 11-3**

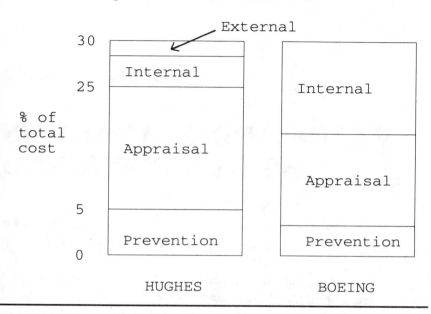

QUALITY COST/TOTAL COST

should decline relative to total product cost.

In focusing on individual activities that made up the total cost of quality, activity based costing proved very helpful. It allowed cost visibility heretofore not available. Previously, cost of quality information was neither easily understood or intuitive to operations personnel. Cost reports were not always timely, making it difficult to target cost reductions. The new cost system breaks down production activities that are easily understood and intuitive to production personnel.

The new system is also integrated into the traditional financial accounting systems, providing useful and timely information. The Federal Government, through its project team participation, became very involved in the project. The Defense Contract Audit Agency (DCAA) has encouraged Hughes to continue its new cost management experimentation. In the long run both Hughes and its customers will benefit by these quality improvements.

# Chapter Twelve

# VALUE ADDED ANALYSIS AT ALLIED-SIGNAL

**Brian Ahlborn**
**Deloitte & Touche**

Allied-Signal's Automotive sector is one of the world's largest independent suppliers to the automotive industry, with annual revenues exceeding $4 billion. The cost management strategy which the Automotive Sector has adopted is based on Activity Based Costing techniques. Deloitte & Touche worked with the sector in the implementation of this strategy and assisted in the introduction of ABC methodology to a pilot business unit. During the course of the pilot, Allied-Signal management came to appreciate Non-Value Added activities, their cost drivers and associated "downstream" costs. This understanding helped to more effectively manage the business.

* It highlighted Non-Value Added activities which were most costly, identifying where the business should focus its continuous improvement.
* It highlighted superior practices found between products, among plants, and vis-a-vis competition.
* It introduced a consistent and easily calculated definition of the Cost of Quality.
* It provided a more accurate means of evaluating capital investment alternatives.

# NON-VALUE ADDED ANALYSIS

The analysis was completed at a component division which had several manufacturing facilities and a separate headquarters location. Its product cost structure, as shown in Exhibit 12-1, indicates that direct material and direct labor together accounted for little more than a third of the actual product cost. Allied's existing cost accounting system provided limited insight into these costs which comprised the remaining 65% of product cost. Furthermore, it was not known what percentage of these non-direct costs were Value Added.

A team of Allied-Signal representatives and Deloitte & Touche consultants worked together to determine exactly what activities were performed, the cost of these activities, and whether or not the activities were Value Added. Departmental expense reports were obtained and an analysis was performed to relate expenses to activities. This was achieved through interviews with department leaders in which costs were related on a line item basis to activities performed by identifying cost drivers. The interviews and analysis were conducted over a four week period. Interviewees prepared for their interviews by:

1) Identifying activities performed in their department.
2) Determining the best cost driver for each activity.
3) Using the identified cost driver to determine what percentage of the department's expenses were incurred in order to perform each activity.

In the short term, Value Added activities can be defined as the minimum direct labor, material cost and associated overhead to get the product out the door. Over the long term, this definition can be extended to include activities that improve product quality and reduce its cost, such as product improvement and more efficient production methods.

Conversely, Non-Value Added activities in the short term are overhead items that do not add essential customer product value. These include items such as engineering changes, scrap and

**Exhibit 12-1**

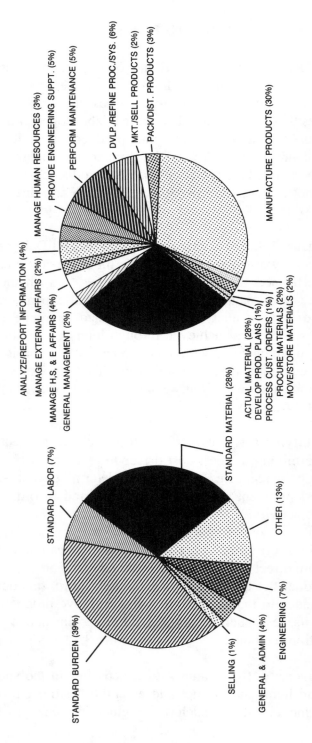

PRODUCT COST COMPOSITION

ANALYZE/REPORT INFORMATION (4%)
MANAGE EXTERNAL AFFAIRS (2%)
MANAGE H,S, & E AFFAIRS (4%)
GENERAL MANAGEMENT (2%)
MANAGE HUMAN RESOURCES (3%)
PROVIDE ENGINEERING SUPPT. (5%)
PERFORM MAINTENANCE (5%)
DVLP./REFINE PROC./SYS. (6%)
MKT./SELL PRODUCTS (2%)
PACK/DIST. PRODUCTS (3%)
MANUFACTURE PRODUCTS (30%)
ACTUAL MATERIAL (28%)
DEVELOP PROD. PLANS (1%)
PROCESS CUST. ORDERS (1%)
PROCURE MATERIALS (2%)
MOVE/STORE MATERIALS (2%)

ACTIVITY COST COMPOSITION

STANDARD LABOR (7%)
STANDARD MATERIAL (28%)
STANDARD BURDEN (39%)
OTHER (13%)
SELLING (1%)
GENERAL & ADMIN (4%)
ENGINEERING (7%)

CURRENT COST (P&L) COMPOSITION

230

material handling. In the long run, any "slack" in the production system can be viewed as a Non-Value Added activity. Inventory management, internal and external product failures and logistics costs are examples of long term Non-Value Added activities.

Exhibit 12-2 indicates where the dollars were being spent at Allied. Ten activities accounted for one half of the product cost found in overhead, which as mentioned earlier, represented two-thirds of product cost. Of these ten activities, five could be considered Non-Value Added: unscheduled maintenance, defective parts, area maintenance, parts inspection and excessive material removed from parts. These Non-Value Added activities represented close to 30% of overhead costs!

This information surprised management. Management did not realize for example that unscheduled maintenance was such a large percentage of total activity costs, almost 10%. Although plant management understood quite clearly that many resources were being used for unscheduled maintenance, it was not aware of the magnitude, nearly $2.5 million. The Value added analysis focused management on the fact that reducing the cost of unscheduled maintenance had to become a high priority in its cost management efforts.

Also highlighted by this analysis was the economic effect of a process which had fallen out of control. A particular manufacturing process was incapable of producing product within specifications which had recently been tightened by a customer. As a result, an additional activity was introduced in the production process to trim the excess material from parts produced for that customer. The Non-Value Added analysis showed this activity cost to be nearly $1 million per year. Again, although the problem was well understood, the magnitude of the issue had been previously unknown.

The activity analysis enabled identification of best practices within an individual plant, among plants, and against competition. Within each plant, the analysis showed division and plant management areas where similar activities were performed at

**Exhibit 12-2**

### HIGHEST COST ACTIVITIES

| Activity | Name of Activity | Amount | Percent | Accum. Pct. |
|---|---|---|---|---|
| 9.2.1 | Unscheduled maintenance | $2,304,589 | 9.8% | 9.8% |
| 5.7.2 | Machine parts | $1,705,692 | 7.2% | 17.0% |
| 5.11.2 | Scrap defective parts | $1,482,770 | 6.3% | 23.2% |
| 5.8.2 | Perform subassembly | $1,332,984 | 5.6% | 28.9% |
| 9.3.1 | Perform area maintenance | $1,174,866 | 5.0% | 33.9% |
| 10.2.2 | Develop & test prototype parts | $1,038,543 | 4.4% | 38.3% |
| 5.6.3 | Process parts | $ 982,756 | 4.2% | 42.4% |
| 5.11.1 | Inspect and test parts | $ 965,106 | 4.1% | 46.5% |
| 5.9.3 | Perform final assembly | $ 869,324 | 3.7% | 50.2% |
| 5.11.3 | Trim excess materials from parts | $ 840,188 | 3.6% | 53.7% |
| 8.1.1 | Design and develop new products | $840,161 | 3.6% | 53.7% |
| 5.1.0 | Set-up/start-up equipment | $798,448 | 3.4% | 60.7% |
| 6.2.1 | Package parts | $750,825 | 3.2% | 63.8% |
| 5.5.0 | Drill parts | $702,796 | 3.0% | 66.8% |
| 4.1.2 | Manual material handling | $632,904 | 2.7% | 69.5% |
| 14.2.1 | Building operating costs | $583,302 | 2.5% | 72.0% |
| 12.4.2 | Maintain part file data | $520,857 | 2.2% | 74.2% |
| 6.3.2 | Expedited outbound freight | $487,643 | 2.1% | 76.2% |
| 9.2.2 | Preventive maintenance | $448,173 | 1.9% | 78.1% |
| 7.4.0 | Communicate with customers | $401,174 | 1.7% | 79.8% |
| 11.3.0 | Manage employee relations | $348,911 | 1.5% | 81.3% |
| 11.4.1 | Employee technical training | $318,726 | 1.3% | 82.6% |

different levels of efficiency. This facilitated setting goals for improvement. For example, at one plant two similar products A and B were manufactured for different customers in the Automotive OEM market. The products were produced in separate areas within the plant, but with relatively similar volumes. Product A was an OEM part manufactured in an area featuring processing operations and equipment dedicated solely to that product. Product B was an OEM part manufactured in an area that was used to produce many different products for both OEM and aftermarket customers.

The processing efficiencies realized through dedicated equipment were demonstrated by quantifying a classic Non-Value Added activity - material handling. Material handling for product B was shown to be 2.5 times greater per unit than for product A. Although one could leap to the conclusion that dedicated manufacturing was less expensive than shared, the numbers had to be carefully analyzed. Was the cost differential a result of the production layout or was it because of other intangibles, such as better supervision and product design?

In this case, supervision was the same, quality standards were all exacting, and products required similar manufacturing processes. The higher material handling costs for Product B were simply the result of a manufacturing process which required more material moves over a greater distance than the process for Product A. The business therefore used this information when considering further investment in dedicated manufacturing.

For division management, the identification of best practices among plants was also of great interest. Manufacturing innovations occur regularly at each plant. Management was eager to highlight areas where such innovation had truly made a "bottom line" impact in order to establish successful procedures throughout the division. Activities involved with "Finishing Parts" was an example of a largely Non-Value Added group of activities which were performed differently at all three plants (Exhibit 12-3).

**Exhibit 12-3**

## DIVISION COST ANALYSIS OF FINISHING PARTS

| Location | Percentage of Total Costs |
|----------|---------------------------|
| Plant 1 | 9.3% |
| Plant 2 | 13.3% |
| Plant 3 | 8.7% |

Plant 3's operations were sufficiently different to render comparison of finishing costs between plant 3 and the other plants inappropriate. The comparison between plant 1 and plant 2, however, showed a significantly higher finishing cost at plant 2. Further analysis showed that the practices in the Finishing Area had been recently improved at plant 1. The quantification of the resultant cost differences between the plants identified for plant 2's management a clear opportunity for improvement.

Procurement of materials was shown to be performed much less efficiently at one of the plants. The less efficient plant did not have preferred suppliers and spent much more time identifying and evaluating vendors than did the other two plants. Because expenditures on non-productive materials were approximately equal, the extra procurement activity was shown to be Non-Value Added. Value Added identification of best practices can clearly be extended to include other business units within the corporation, as well as competitors who perform similar activities.

## COST OF QUALITY ANALYSIS

Allied-Signal devoted considerable resources to quality improvement. Improvements still needed to be made as customer requirements grew even more stringent. There was much internal discussion as to whether the cost of achieving higher quality would be adequately rewarded by the market. The debate was particularly frustrating because a consistent understanding of the business' cost of quality did not exist. Each plant used different measurement criteria and, within a plant, they often changed with each ad hoc study.

The Value Added Activity analysis provided a consistent format which divided the Cost of Quality into four types: Prevention, Appraisal, Internal and External Failure. The report did not address the distinction between Value Added and Non-Value Added activities, although one could argue that only some of the prevention activities could be considered Value Added. Exhibit 12-4 shows the division's Cost of Quality Report for one quarter.

The report shows that the division is currently experiencing external failure quality problems that reach the customer. The division's number one goal is to reduce these costs to zero. Additionally, the report shows that the division currently avoids external customer issues by spending a great deal of money on identifying failures internally. Large expenditures on quality inspectors and scrap indicate that the manufacturing process is still unable to regularly meet quality standards. More emphasis on Prevention activities is necessary to minimize the overall Cost of Quality.

This report, along with the Non-Value Added Activity Report, Exhibit 12-2, generated the greatest interest at nearly all levels of management within the sector. Previously, calculation of Cost of Quality had simply been the cost of scrap plus the cost of the quality department. The actual Cost of Quality was much higher than management had expected.

## CAPITAL INVESTMENT

Clearly understanding the cost of Non-Value Added activities and which plants and product lines are responsible for these costs provides a business with better tools to evaluate capital investment alternatives. The excessive amounts spent on Unscheduled Maintenance, Scrap, Inspection, and Trimming Excess Material were identified as areas which would provide the greatest return.

**Exhibit 12-4**  COST OF QUALITY REPORT

| Activity | Name of Activity | Prevention | Appraisal | Internal | External |
|---|---|---|---|---|---|
| | | | | Failure | |
| 3.6.1 | Develop/certify new suppliers | $13,229 | | | |
| 3.6.2 | Inspect/test/audit purchased material | | $58,244 | | |
| 3.6.4 | Transport inbound material (expedited) | | | $5,321 | |
| 4.3.1 | Locate misplaced material | | | $11,018 | |
| 4.3.2 | Scrap/write-off damaged/lost material | | | $41,048 | |
| 5.4.1 | Process/reclaim materials | | | $21,522 | |
| 5.10.7 | Inspect parts | | $166,766 | | |
| 5.11.1 | Inspect/test parts | | $414,090 | | |
| 5.11.2 | Process/sort/rework/customer claims/returns | | | | $152,875 |
| 5.11.3 | Inspect/rework defective parts | | | $167,945 | |
| 5.11.4 | Scrap defective parts | | | $598,696 | |
| 5.11.5 | Adjust equipment | | | $82,467 | |
| 5.12.1 | Manufacturing delays/problems | | | $61,741 | |
| 6.7.1 | Transport outbound products (expedited) | | | $115,398 | |
| 6.7.2 | Re-package products | | | | $235 |
| 6.7.3 | Scrap packaging | | | $781 | |
| 7.2.3 | Address quality/delivery issues with customer | | | | $44,780 |
| 8.2.1 | Design, develop, test & evaluate - quality improvements | $136,303 | | | |
| 8.2.2 | Acquire, install and implement - quality improvements | $48,796 | | | |
| 8.2.3 | Rearrange, remove and rebuild - quality improvements | $22,202 | | | |
| 10.3.1 | Evaluate/revise product design (quality improvements) | $54,373 | | | |
| 10.3.2 | Implement design changes (quality improvements) | $6,576 | | | |
| 12.3.1 | Internal quality information | | $48,020 | | |
| 12.3.2 | Audit/report supplier performance | | $12,742 | | |
| **Cost of Quality for the Division:** | | $281,479 12.32% | $699,872 30.63% | $1,105,935 48.40% | $197,891 8.66% |

Total Cost of Quality   $2,285,177
Total Activity Cost   $13,183,060
Cost of Quality As % of Total   17.33%

236

Plant management had been trying for some time to justify capital necessary to introduce a Preventative Maintenance (PM) program featuring regularly scheduled maintenance and the replacement of problematic machinery. This analysis demonstrated to division management the attractive economic benefits that a well focused PM investment could bring. It also pointed out the immediacy of that need.

Engineering and Manufacturing management could better quantify the benefit of increased integration of Product and Process Engineering and Manufacturing in order to eliminate problems. Subsequent to this analysis, one plant introduced several U-cells in order to reduce Non-Value Added activities such as material handling.

## SUMMARY

The Value Added analysis performed at Allied Signal was effective because it made intuitive sense to managers. The following responses were voiced:

* "I've always suspected that to be the case. I just didn't know how to get upper management to believe me. Now I have some quantitative support for my argument."

* "I just didn't understand how I was supposed to manage costs like 'Indirect Hourly' and 'Sundry Supplies.' Finally, I can understand what the accounting people have been trying to tell me."

* "When I'm told to cut costs I'm never certain whether I am really attacking the **cause** of our problems. Now I am."

Because Value Added analysis is consistent with the way line managers **think** about their business, they feel a kinship with its findings and understand how they can capitalize on identified strengths and rectify costly weaknesses.

# Chapter Thirteen

# ACTIVITY-BASED COSTING SOFTWARE AT PARK-MED LABS

**Ian D. McKillop**
**Howard M. Armitage**

**School of Accountancy**
**University of Waterloo**

Dr. Goodman, Director of Operations at Park-Med Laboratories Ltd., was reflecting on the advantage that his laboratory now had over its competition. "Who would have thought that a cost accounting system could be a source of competitive advantage", he mused. Unlike other firms in the industry, Park-Med not only knew aggregate costs, but also costs of individual laboratory tests. Armed with this information, Dr. Goodman was able to make decisions based on facts rather than instinct. These decisions were paying off with an ever increasing bottom line. Thinking back, he realized how fortuitous it was that he came to learn about activity based costing, a new way of thinking about product costs that allowed Park-Med to determine its costs on a per test basis.

## PARK-MED LABORATORIES

Park-Med was a medical laboratory that provided testing and

diagnostic services to physicians. Human specimens such as blood and urine were analyzed for a variety of conditions that included hepatitis, bacterial infections and vitamin levels. The lab made extensive use of technology. Although some tests required human intervention, such as microbiological culture preparation, most tests were performed by computerized analyzers that directly interfaced with computers for the recording of test results. Park-Med had been a leader in this field. Some of the first direct "computer to lab analyzer" interfaces in North America were installed in its laboratories.

From its headquarters in Toronto, Ontario, Park-Med serviced South-Western and South-Central Ontario, one of the most populated regions of Canada. Although there were a number of other medical laboratories servicing this same area, Park-Med's attention to service had allowed it to succeed in a very competitive market environment. During the past few years, Park-Med enjoyed phenomenal growth and in 1990 employed close to 300 people.

Service was the key to Park-Med's success. With its own fleet of courier vehicles and a highly automated testing laboratory, Park-Med was able to promise less than 24 hour turnaround. For example, if blood samples were taken from a patient on Monday afternoon, Park-Med would have the results on the physician's desk by Tuesday morning. In the health care field, speed and accuracy were hallmarks that endeared a firm with physicians. Park-Med's ability to deliver on both accounts helped contribute to the firm's overall success in the marketplace.

## THE BUSINESS OF MEDICAL LABORATORIES

The Ontario Ministry of Health operated a comprehensive medicare program for residents of Ontario called OHIP (Ontario Health Insurance Program). Hospitals, physicians, medical labs, and other health care providers were compensated by OHIP for their services according to a prescribed set of fees. For medical labs, these fees were determined by OHIP using a schedule that equated each test with a certain number of fee paying units, called

LMS units (an LMS is a Laboratory Medical Standard unit). A medical lab could determine the "selling price" of any of its testing services by multiplying the current value of an LMS by the number of LMS units that the government allowed for the test.

An interesting feature of the LMS payment system involved retesting and rework. A medical lab received a certain number of LMS units each time a test was **requested** by a physician, regardless of the number of times that the lab actually **performed** the test to get an accurate result. These numbers could differ because certain tests had to be repeated at the lab's expense if a positive result was obtained. Similarly, tests had to be repeated if either equipment calibration problems or an error in the testing methodology occurred. Much like rework in a conventional factory environment, these repeats of previously completed work added to the laboratory's costs. Minimizing this expense was a key success factor in the medical laboratory business.

To operate in Ontario, a medical laboratory required a licence for each category of test that it wished to offer. The Ontario Ministry of Health restricted the number of licences in circulation to minimize both over and under-capacity in the system. No new licences were expected to be issued in the near future, which placed a premium on the value of licences currently held by medical laboratories. Park-Med's licences permitted them to perform 150 different tests, which allowed the firm to offer a wide and comprehensive range of testing services.

Medical labs obtained business from two sources. Some labs, including Park-Med, operated walk-in specimen collection centres. Patients presented themselves at these centres with a "Laboratory Services Requisition" form completed by their physician. Patients referred to free-standing specimen collection centres were free to select the testing laboratory of their choice and were often influenced by the convenience of the centre's location. The results of tests originating through specimen collection centres were sent directly to the originating physician. In cases where the physician was not already a subscriber to the lab's services, the prompt delivery of an accurate report could be an excellent sales tool to encourage additional business.

Medical labs also obtained business directly from physicians. Physicians were encouraged to place all of their testing business with one lab, in return for which they received prompt and consistent service. In Park-Med's case, this comprehensive service included daily pickup of specimens by a dedicated courier fleet and daily delivery of test results.

Although labs such as Park-Med were licensed to perform a wide variety of tests, occasions arose when a physician ordered a test that the laboratory was not licensed to perform. To shield doctors from having to determine which lab could perform which test, the laboratories established arrangements with each other that permitted them to quickly and efficiently trade tests to ensure that the test was performed by a laboratory holding the appropriate license. The lab that originally received the specimen managed the paperwork and was responsible for reporting the results to the originating physician. To remain licensed to perform a specific type of test, labs were required to perform the test a set number of times each year. There were some tests, however, for which the number of LMS units allowed was not sufficient to cover the cost of performing the test. Although labs deemed the test to be unprofitable, they had to perform at least the minimum number of tests required to retain their licence. Thus, it was common for labs to perform tests that they believed to be unprofitable.

Although a test might be unprofitable for one lab, it might be profitable for another even though both labs would receive the same number of LMS units for the test. This situation could arise if one lab had more sophisticated equipment, or if it performed a sufficient volume of tests to purchase reagents and other specialized supplies at a lower price. Consequently, it was common for labs to strike deals amongst themselves in which Lab #1 offered to give all of its Test X to Lab #2 in return for Lab #2 sending all of its Test Y to Lab #1. Even when opting to trade away a complete test category to another lab, a lab would still want to perform at least a minimum number of tests to retain its licence, despite the fact that these tests would be performed at a loss.

Thus, when making trading arrangements, it was important for labs to know both what they were trading away, and the **profitability** of what they were receiving in return. Because of the unsophisticated nature of cost management systems in medical laboratories, these decisions were generally made on instinct. The costs and benefits of the tradeoffs were seldom, if ever, known with precision.

Park-Med had enjoyed five years of significant growth. Anxious to continue as a major player in the medical lab field, it was searching for ways to increase both its market share and profit. As Toby Hatch, Park-Med's Department Head of Software Development explained,

*"Because we didn't have a really good way of getting a handle on the cost per test, we were going on volume - trying to keep the number of tests up and the number of people down".*

This strategy had worked well for Park-Med, and was responsible for their growth in profit. To become a large lab, however, it was important to attract more doctors and to gain a better understanding of the testing process. Not knowing what it cost to perform a test procedure was increasingly viewed as a liability in a period when the lab was actively seeking new business. With more accurate information, the lab would know the types of business to solicit and which categories of tests would be best left for other labs to handle.

Like many people with years of experience in a particular industry, Dr. Goodman had a general feeling for which tests made money for the lab and which were probable "money losers". For example, if a test used expensive reagents, required manual intervention and had a low LMS unit factor, it would be assumed to be a less profitable test than a fully automated procedure that used few reagents but paid the same number of LMS units. It was on heuristics such as this that the lab relied when it sought trading arrangements with other labs. All of this was to change, however, in 1987 when Park-Med became aware of activity based costing.

# EXTANT INFORMATION SYSTEM

Park-Med used an IBM System/36 to support its administrative and accounting functions. The system generated a variety of reports, including schedules of supplies purchased, courier costs, and summaries of tests ordered by different doctors. The system also generated quarterly reports that compared amounts billed to the provincial health plan with payments received from the plan. As John Craig, Park-Med's Assistant Director of Operations explained,

*"We could look at the total cost of supplies and other inputs and we knew our total revenue. The difference was profit... but what [tests] generated those profits we couldn't tell."*

John Craig went on to explain other limitations of the old information system. These included obtaining historical information on reagent purchases, labor statistics, and equipment utilization rates. Making the right decisions in these areas was important to the success of the laboratory. For example, historical information on reagent purchases was valuable when deciding how much of a chemical to order. Some reagents were very expensive, and most had a limited useful life. If extra was ordered to qualify for a volume discount, the chemical might spoil before it could be used. Conversely, if too little was ordered, the lab risked running out and would be unable to perform certain tests. Management knew the information it wanted to have for decision making. Unfortunately it couldn't be generated by the existing information system.

Like John Craig, Dr. Goodman knew that the information problem was larger than not being able to quickly aggregate data on items such as historical purchases. It was the **true** cost of performing a test that he needed to know to make informed management decisions. Unfortunately, Park-Med's conventional cost accounting techniques employed arbitrary methods of allocating indirect costs to individual tests that prohibited a true test cost from being generated. He knew that if Park-Med was to continue growing, the firm needed to obtain an improved picture of its underlying cost structure. As Dr. Goodman explained,

*"If an LMS unit was worth 50¢ and the cost of performing one LMS was thought to be 30¢, then the procedure seemed profitable, BUT the stepped fixed costs threw a wrench into the planning. At what point do we need to rent more space, hire another technician, get new machinery, buy a new computer? I've got twelve years experience in this business and sometimes I just can't get a handle on these questions."*

It was with these concerns in mind that Park-Med began searching for a possible solution to their costing dilemma. If corporate growth was to be sustained, a better understanding of Park-Med's cost structure was required.

## ACTIVITY-BASED COSTING SOFTWARE

Although the existing information system did an excellent job of preparing reports that outlined profit from a financial accounting standpoint, it was internally oriented financial data that both John Craig and Dr. Goodman were seeking. By chance, an acquaintance of Mr. Craig's was associated with a software company that had developed a modeling package that, while not originally designed for cost accounting problems, seemed ideally suited for solving the problem that Mr. Craig had described. It allowed each test to be modeled in terms of the activities that were required to perform the test. A share of resource costs, such as the cost of the machinery, or the labor required to operate the equipment, could be associated with each test based on the demand that each test placed on these resources. This represented a dramatic departure from existing accounting practice that assumed that the tests were the cause of costs.

The model recognized that activities, not tests, caused costs and that tests created the demand for the activities. For example,

244

performing a hepatitis test was an activity that required resources such as salaries, reagents and specialized machinery. Receiving a batch of samples to be tested initiated the work involved in the hepatitis testing activity. The individual tests themselves were the cost objects that drove activity. The more tests conducted, the more the hepatitis testing activities would need to be performed and the more cost would be incurred. Mr. Craig could see that this approach would make a difference to product costing because, under the activity based costing procedure, costs were first assigned to the activities, as opposed to departments or cost centres in the existing system, and then allocated to the tests on the basis of activity drivers that related more closely to the consumption of the activity. Mr. Craig felt that this method of attributing costs to tests was more accurate than the existing system which distributed overhead costs to tests on an arbitrary basis.

John Craig invited the software vendors, Sapling Corporation of Toronto to demonstrate its product to the management team at Park-Med. Convinced of its potential merit, Park-Med agreed to enter into a test phase during which the vendor would demonstrate the software's utility by modeling the medical laboratory process. If the results of the test were positive, Park-Med would purchase a copy of the software and proceed to use it elsewhere in their organization.

Sapling had developed a powerful but simple diagramming convention that allowed Park-Med to model the interaction between the various resources, such as supplies, assets, etc., that were used during the testing process. Figure 13-1 shows a small component of the model that Park-Med prepared using this diagramming notation. The figure portrays a part of the process required to perform a hepatitis test. It illustrates most of the constructs used to prepare the schematic version of the activity based costing model.

Circles were used to represent **demand**, such as the number of hepatitis tests to be performed, and to denote a **variable supply**, such as the use of reagent during a test. Demand and supply circles were distinguished from each other by whether the line that

**Figure 13-1**

ACTIVITY FLOWCHART: Single Product

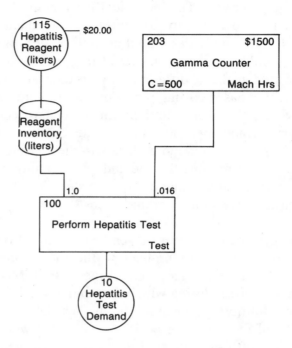

linked the circle to the rest of the diagram entered from above (a demand circle) or left through the bottom (a supply circle). The rectangle was used to denote **activities**, such as performing a hepatitis test. Rectangles were also used to indicate **fixed costs,** such as the capital cost of an analyser machine.

The schematic model was a powerful visual tool. A rich variety of information was conveyed to the reader via the diagram. Boxes were numbered to aid in their identification within the model and the unit of measure for each activity was indicated. Where appropriate, capacity information was also given and variable and fixed cost amounts were shown.

In Figure 13-1, Box #203 represented the fixed cost of owning the Gamma Counter machine. The fixed cost of this machine was

$1500.00 per month, as shown in the upper right corner of the box. The unit of measure for this asset was "Machine Hours," shown in the lower right corner of the box, and this machine had a capacity of 500 machine hours during the period that was being modeled, shown in the lower left corner of the box).[1]

Two other constructs were required to complete the functionality of the model. The first was the diamond which indicated a choice in the **route** that demand for a test could follow.[2] The model also allowed **inventory** levels to be maintained if desired. This might be required in the case of a supply of a reagent. Although the reagent is consumed on a per test basis and would be treated as a variable cost, it might be necessary to have a certain number of liters in stock at all times. Thus, the inventory construct would be used to simulate this constraint. The existence of inventory was shown by drawing a "barrel" shape in the schematic diagram.

The relationship between the various components of the model was explained using "factors." A factor explained **how many** units of the preceding activity that the next activity required. For example, a factor of .016 explained the relationship between the **activity** of performing a hepatitis test and the unit of measure of the Gamma Counter. This meant that for each **test,** the unit of measure of the "Perform Hepatitis Test" box, .016 **machine hours** of Gamma Counter time would be required.

Based on demands, the software used factors to determine if the necessary capacity to perform an activity was available, and if this was found to be true, to pull the resulting costs "down" from the

---

[1] Capacity and cost information was not shown directly on the schematic models prepared by Park-Med Laboratories. This information was captured on separate reports which allowed cost and capacity numbers to be changed without having to redraw the schematics. Numbers have been included directly on the diagrams in this discussion to aid in the presentation of the activity based costing concept.

[2] The route box was not used in the simplified example presented in Figure 13-1. For an example of the application of the route box, see Figure 13-2 where it is used to select between using Pro-Quantum Analyser #1 or Pro-Quantum Analyser #2 when performing a hepatitis test.

higher level resource costs to the activity. This pulling of costs from above was based on the demand that the lower activity placed on the activity above it in the model. Testing to first see if the necessary capacity existed to perform an activity was a powerful feature of the computerized version of the model. It ensured that costs were never generated for an activity that was not feasible to be performed at the desired level.

It may be useful to pause at this point to demonstrate how the model functioned using the simplified activity shown in Figure 13-1. Assume that in a one month period, Park-Med estimated that it would perform 1000 hepatitis tests and wanted to know the "per test" cost of these tests. The software would calculate the cost as follows:

Step 1:     Determine if there is sufficient capacity to perform 1000 tests in a month.

i)    To perform 1000 tests would require 1000 x .016 machine hours of Gamma Counter time, which equals 16 hours. The machine has 500 hours available, and is dedicated to hepatitis testing, so this constraint would not pose a problem.

ii)   The supply of hepatitis testing reagents is infinite, conveyed to the reader by a lack of a capacity note attached to box 115.

Conclusion:   It is feasible to perform 1000 hepatitis test in a one month period.

Step 2:     Calculate the per test opportunity cost by "pulling" the appropriate cost amounts into "Box 100 - Perform Hepatitis Test".

i)    Gamma Machine cost:
$1,500/1000 tests = $ 1.50/test
or
$1,500/16 hours = $ 93.75 per machine hour

ii) Reagent cost per test (totally variable)

$20.00 per liter x .10 liters per test = $2.00/test

Conclusion: There is a $ 3.50 full opportunity cost to perform a hepatitis test.

This is a simplified example of the intricate relationships that existed between an activity an its associated resource costs. This example ignores the shared use of analysers by different testing activities and makes no allowance for overhead allocations. To see how these factors would impact on the development of an activity based cost model, the next section explores a richer version of the activity based cost models developed at Park-Med.

## PREPARING THE MODEL

### Phase I

The first phase in the test process was the preparation of a schematic model that captured details of the resources, processes and outputs of the laboratory testing procedures at Park-Med. As Toby Hatch explained, key executives, area supervisors and laboratory staff all participated in interviews that helped determine "what goes where and when." At the conclusion of these interviews, a model of the activities at Park-Med was prepared for review by area supervisors. The purpose of this review was to have area supervisors validate the diagram that had been prepared, modeling the flow of tests through their area. Figure 13-2 shows a part of the model drawn of the RIA Department at the conclusion of Phase I.

The process of creating the schematic diagrams required Park-Med to closely examine the interaction between the various functional areas of the laboratory. Although the purpose of creating the schematic model was to support the implementation of a computerized model, an interesting side benefit arose. The schematics provided a useful tool for identifying bottlenecks in the testing process. Area supervisors were able to visualize the

**Figure 13-2**

# ACTIVITY FLOW CHART: Multiple Products

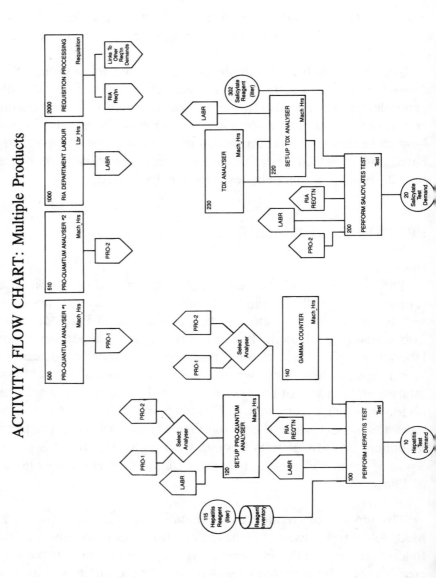

implications of a bottleneck in one area on the activities of another, and could work together to help eliminate the problem. Prior to these schematics, areas did not know the impact their actions had on other testing areas. A number of significant and beneficial changes in the handling and routing of specimens were made as a result of reviewing the information available in the schematics generated in Phase I of the modeling process. The consultants stressed the importance of the initial phases of the modeling process - particularly the preparation of an accurate schematic representation of product flows. The experience at Park-Med bore this out. The preparation of the schematic model was found to be such a powerful tool for gaining an understanding of the underlying operations of the laboratory that it led John Craig to comment,

*"if you can model the laboratory, ...then you understand the lab."*

## Phase II

With the model validated to confirm the accuracy of the flow patterns of specimens through the laboratory, the second phase of preparing the schematics began. This involved adding cost and operational data. Park-Med used two broad categories of costs. The first of these were **test** costs - costs that were directly related to the activity of analyzing a specimen. These included such costs as reagents, equipment lease or depreciation charges, and labor. The second cost category was **requisition** costs. These were costs associated with documenting the test such as collecting demographic information on the patient and reporting results to the patient's physician.

Many of the costs could be determined by searching through historical financial records. However, Park-Med's information system had not been designed to track specific test and requisition costs and consequently, the process was quite time consuming.

The nature of the cost determined where in the model the cost would be incorporated. For example, marketing costs were considered to be a function of the number of requisitions processed. It made sense that the more effective the marketing effort, the more requisitions for services would be received from physicians.[3] Costs such as reagents or lease charges were directly associated with their related testing machines.

In addition to cost data, it was important to gather data on the time that it took to process specimens through the various testing activities. As with many efforts aimed at capturing accurate "in process" times, Park-Med met with only moderate success when time studies were used to gather this information. Although employees knew that the time information was being gathered to assist with the preparation of a financial planning model (and not to evaluate their individual job performance), they were uncomfortable about being carefully observed. In the end, it was decided to ask the area supervisors to provide time information for the various activities based on their experience with the testing process. Park-Med did not believe that this secondary source of data would corrupt the project, a fact that was later proven correct during the validation of the computerized model.

Once cost and time data were collected for the various activities within the laboratory, it was necessary to convert the data into machine readable form. Cost and time information was converted to **factors** within the model in order to properly explain the relationship between the various boxes. Factor calculations were often quite complex. This could be caused by situations such as an analyser that operated using batches of various sizes but required the same amount of reagent irrespective of the number of vials being tested. Even with such complications, the model seemed capable of capturing even the most intricate cost and demand factor relationships. Figure 13-3 portrays the RIA Department's activities seen earlier with cost, capacity and factor information added.

---

[3] Overhead associated with the activity of processing a requisition for tests was collected by Box #2000 in the schematics of the RIA Department. In order to simplify the examples used in the case, the activities and cost pools that fed into the requisition processing activity have not been explicitly shown. For illustrative purposes, it is assumed that the cost of processing one requisition was $10.00.

# FACTOR ENHANCED ACTIVITY FLOWCHART

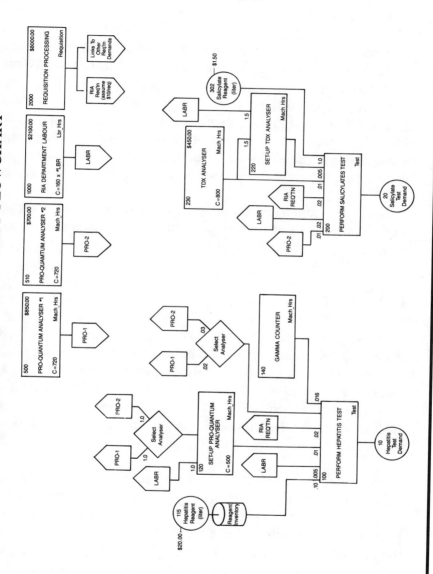

With the schematic model completed, diagram data was incorporated into the modeling software. It was important at this stage to once again validate the accuracy of the simulated model of the laboratory that had now been prepared.

Scenarios were run using known historical information for each department, such as the number and type of tests actually run by a department in the previous months. The resulting reports showing projected resource consumption and costs were then compared with the known resource consumption and costs that had been incurred in those months. When the projected figures generated by the software matched those known from actual experience, the model was considered to be functioning correctly.

With the computerized model prepared and now operational, Park-Med was ready to begin using the software to assist in making management decisions.

## PRINTOUT

This section demonstrates how activity based costs were generated for a portion of the testing activities within the RIA Department. It makes use of the data presented in Figure 13-3 and assumes a demand of 4,540 hepatitis tests and 5 salicylates tests in a one month period. The utilization rate and cost information calculated by the NetProphet software for this level of activity is presented in Exhibits 13-1, 13-2, and 13-3.

For example, Exhibit 13-1 shows that 95.40 machine hours of Pro-Quantum Analyser #2 time would be required during the month to perform 4,540 hepatitis tests and 5 salicylates tests. This represents a utilization rate of 13.25%, given that the machine has the capacity to operate for 720 machine hours per month. Utilization rates were provided for the other flows in the model as well.

Exhibit 13-2 provides costing information specific to the demand for hepatitis tests. Tracing the Pro-Quantum Analyser #2 on this report (see category #202) shows that 95.34 machine hours

# Exhibit 13-1

Preliminary Results

DETAILED FLOWS RESULTS REPORT

MODEL ID    : LAB
MODEL TITLE : PARK-MED CASE

SCENARIO # - 1    1st_Out    Period # - 1    1_Month

---

BOX #: 140    TYPE: PROCESS    NAME: Gamma Counter
             CAPACITY:    600.00    Mach_hrs    UTILIZATION: 12.71%    OUTPUT FLOW:    76.27 Mach_hrs
             ENTRY LINK BOXES
             9999 SUPPLY    Dummy                                      INPUT FLOW:     76.27 Mach_hrs

---

BOX #: 230    TYPE: PROCESS    NAME:    Tax Analyzer
             CAPACITY:    800.00    Mach_hrs    UTILIZATION: .01031%    OUTPUT FLOW:    0.88250 Mach_hrs
             ENTRY LINK BOXES
             9999 SUPPLY    Dummy                                      INPUT FLOW:     0.08250 Mach_hrs

---

BOX #: 508    TYPE: PROCESS    NAME:    Pro-Quantum Analyzer 1
             CAPACITY:    720.00    Mach_hrs    UTILIZATION: 9.93%     OUTPUT FLOW:    71.51 Mach_hrs
             ENTRY LINK BOXES
             9999 SUPPLY    Dummy                                      INPUT FLOW:     71.51 Mach_hrs

---

BOX #: 510    TYPE: PROCESS    NAME:    Pro-Quantum Analyzer 2
             CAPACITY:    720.00    Mach-hrs    UTILIZATION: 13.25%    OUTPUT FLOW:    95.40 Mach-hrs
             ENTRY LINK BOXES
             9999 SUPPLY    Dummy                                      INPUT FLOW:     95.40 Mach-hrs

---

BOX #: 1000   TYPE: PROCESS    NAME:    RIA Dept Labour
             CAPACITY:    160.00    Lbr_hrs    UTILIZATION: 44.78%     OUTPUT FLOW:    71.64 Lbr_hrs
             ENTRY LINK BOXES
             9999 SUPPLY    Dummy                                      INPUT FLOW:     71.64 Mach_hrs

---

BOX #: 2000   TYPE: PROCESS    NAME:    Requisition Processing
                                                                      OUTPUT FLOW:    900.00 Req's
             ENTRY LINK BOXES
             9999 SUPPLY    Dummy                                      INPUT FLOW:     900.00 Mach-hrs

---

255

# Exhibit 13-2

Preliminiary Results

DETAILED REVENUE\COSTS RESULTS REPORT

Net Prophet   Version : 01.01.09
Date : Jun 28, 1991
Page : 1

MODEL ID   : LAB
MODEL TITLE : PARK-MED CASE   SCENARIO #  1   1st_Out   Period #  1  1 Month

Box #  10  Hepatitis Test Demand    OUTPUT FLOW  4540.00  Tests

| Category # Name | Qty | UNITS | Fixed $ | Qty | UNITS | VARIABLE $ | TOTAL $ |
|---|---|---|---|---|---|---|---|
| 101 Labour Cost | 71.51 | Lbr_hrs | 2155.85 | 0.00 | | 0.00 | 2155.85 |
| 201 Pro-Quantum Analyzer 1 Lease | 71.51 | Mach_hrs | 850.00 | 0.00 | | 0.00 | 850.00 |
| 202 Pro-Quantum Analyzer 2 Lease | 95.34 | Mach_hrs | 699.60 | 0.00 | | 0.00 | 699.60 |
| 203 Gamma Counter Lease | 76.27 | Mach_hrs | 1500.00 | 0.00 | | 0.00 | 1500.00 |
| 301 Hepititis Reagent | 0.00 | | 0.00 | 476.70 | Litres | 9534.00 | 9534.00 |
| 401 Requisition Processing Cost | 95.34 | Req's | 953.40 | 0.00 | | 0.00 | 953.40 |
| TOTAL COSTS | | | 6158.85 | | | 9534.00 | 15692.85 |

| SUMMARY | FIXED | VARIABLE | TOTAL |
|---|---|---|---|
| TOTAL COST | 6158.85 | 9534.00 | 15692.85 |
| UNIT COST | 1.36 | 2.10 | 3.46 |

256

# Exhibit 13-3

DETAILED REVENUE\COSTS RESULTS REPORT

MODEL ID    : LAB
MODEL TITLE : PARK-MED CASE

SCENARIO # 1     1st_Out          Period # 1    1 Month

Box # 20  Salicylate Test Demand                OUTPUT FLOW    5.00000  Tests

| Category # Name | Qty | UNITS | Fixed $ | Qty | UNITS | VARIABLE $ | TOTAL $ |
|---|---|---|---|---|---|---|---|
| 101 Labour Cost | 0.14 | Lbr_hrs | 4.15 | 0.00 | | 0.00 | 4.15 |
| 202 Pro-Quantum Analyzer 2 Lease | 0.0550 | Mach_hrs | 0.40 | 0.00 | | 0.00 | 0.40 |
| 204 TDX Analyzer Lease | 0.08250 | Mach_hrs | 450.00 | 0.00 | | 0.00 | 450.00 |
| 302 Salicylate Reagent | 0.00 | | | 5.50 | Litres | 8.25 | 8.25 |
| 401 Requisition Processing Cost | 0.11 | Req's | 1.10 | 0.00 | | 0.00 | 1.10 |
| | | | ======== | | | ======== | ======== |
| TOTAL COSTS | | | 455.65 | | | 8.25 | 463.90 |
| | | | ======== | | | ======== | ======== |

SUMMARY

| | FIXED | VARIABLE | TOTAL |
|---|---|---|---|
| | ------- | -------- | ------- |
| TOTAL COST | 455.65 | 8.25 | 463.90 |
| UNIT COST | 91.13 | 1.65 | 92.78 |

257

of the analyser was required for hepatitis testing which caused $699.60 of the fixed cost of leasing the analyser ($700.00/month) to be associated with hepatitis testing. The remaining $0.40 was attributed to the salicylates testing process. Salicylate testing used this machine for 0.0550 hours to perform 5 tests - see Exhibit 13-3, category #202. The unit cost of performing hepatitis and salicylate tests was calculated as $3.46 and $92.78 respectively. (See the last line on Exhibits 13-2 and 13-3.)

## USES OF NETPROPHET BY PARK-MED

The computer simulation of the laboratory on the NetProphet software was used for a variety of tasks. These have included disaster planning, purchase planning and evaluating potential co-operative arrangements with a competitor.

In the disaster planning scenario, Park-Med was curious about the effect of losing a particular major trading partner would have on its business. Park-Med was responsible for testing a large number of reference tests for which the partner did not hold a licence. The results of the simulation showed the firm how reliant on the trading partner it had become and that it would experience difficulties if the arrangement was to end abruptly. As fate would have it, the other lab was subsequently bought out by new owners and the trading arrangement did come to a halt. Fortunately, Park-Med had already begun to protect itself by seeking alternate arrangements because of the intelligence information that they had generated using the activity based costing model.

Purchase planning became a common scenario for the activity based costing software to explore. The laboratory was routinely offered deals to buy expensive reagents at various discounts based on volume. Similarly, opportunities to upgrade analysers and other equipment were regularly offered by vendors. Changing analysers usually also meant having to purchase a new type of chemical. The model allowed the lab to explore the impact of the various purchase options on their bottom line prior to actually committing to the purchase.

One of the most valuable uses of the revised costing system was Park-Med's ability to critically evaluate the trading opportunities offered by other laboratories. Some ten to thirty such opportunities arose each year. A laboratory would contact Park-Med and offer to send over all of its Test A in return for receiving all of Park-Med's Test B volume. The amounts involved could be significant, often around $35,000 per month in potential extra revenue.

Using its ABC software, Park-Med was able to determine the cost of performing tests that they were being offered. This could be accomplished even if the new tests required the purchase of additional equipment, hiring extra staff or renting additional space. Additional costs such as these were easily added to the computerized model of the laboratory. The simulated cost of performing the new tests generated by the system was compared with the LMS revenue that would be received, and a decision as to how "profitable" the additional business would be was made. With the new costing system it was possible to avoid the situation where Park-Med would inadvertently trade away a very profitable test and receive in return a test that was only marginally profitable, or worse still, would actually lose money performing the test.

Park-Med exploited this advantage after learning the costs of a thyroid stimulating hormone test. It appeared to be a highly profitable test, and Park-Med was interested in acquiring additional tests in this category. At the same time, the firm became aware that parasitology tests, while numerous, were not very profitable; in fact, some of them, according to the model, were unprofitable. The company was able to arrange a trade with another laboratory in which they offered the other lab a significant volume of parasitology tests in return for a nominal volume of the other lab's thyroid tests. The other lab eagerly entered this trading partnership, excited about the significant extra volume that they would now be acquiring.

The software was also capable of noting situations where the lab would be unable to handle additional volume. For example, the software would identify that an analyser required to complete the new tests would be overloaded if the new volume was acquired.

The routings and testing procedures were sufficiently complex that identifying this capacity constraint would have been difficult to accomplish manually. Department heads could now be told how much of a particular supply they were using, or how much analyser time they were consuming. This latter information was particularly useful in the case of shared analysers.

If one department was not at capacity and sought to attract additional tests, bottlenecks would develop if the analyser required to perform the test was shared with another department that was already running at capacity. If the first department was successful at getting more business, the only way that these tests could be performed would be if the second department cut back on its business. The activity based approach to examining flows and costs allowed rational decisions to be made about scarce resource allocations, such as the analyser. Prior to the model, analyser time in a situation like this would have been allocated on a first-come, first-served basis.

It was in evaluating analyser purchases that activity based costing helped to clearly identify some of the shortcomings in the traditional approach to cost allocations. The Chemistry Department had been using a Beckman analyser. It was a slow machine, used cheap reagents, didn't cost much to run, was eight years old and therefore almost fully depreciated. The chemist running this department was quite resistant about buying a new analyser because she believed the capital cost charges, combined with the new expensive reagents it required, would have an adverse impact on her department's financial performance.[4] When the Chemistry Department was modeled and activity costs were assigned to tests that would be performed on the new machine, it was discovered that her department would profit from the acquisition. John Craig commented that "profit would actually go through the roof" if the new machine was purchased instead of continuing to use the

---

[4] Analysers were expensive, specialized pieces of equipment often costing in excess of $500,000 each. A department such as chemistry would make use of a number of different such analysers.

Beckman analyser. His overall observation was that these "what if" scenarios seemed to be particularly useful when dealing with old, reliable machines because people were very hesitant to put in the new technology unless they could be convinced that it would be cheaper.

The implementation of activity based costing has had the effect of creating a more information technology oriented focus within the laboratory. In the past, problems such as a bottleneck would be solved by "throwing more people at it". After management had become familiar with activity based costing, they noticed that they would begin to explore options such as switching testing methods or buying newer equipment. Three years ago, most activities within the laboratory were performed manually. The new focus on technological solutions saw the growth of micro-computing in all departments, the development of lab-wide databases for collecting test information, and a new emphasis on using information technology to improve the overall operations of the laboratory.

When asked about the downside to using a computer simulated model of the laboratory to generate costing information, Dr Goodman commented that from a manager's standpoint,

*"The danger is that I don't fully understand the model. If the machine says that I'm going to make 39¢ profit, how do I know that? What if there is something missing in the model? You can make a ten year plan based on the model and two years later be wondering 'where is all the money'? You have to have a great deal of trust in whoever did the model"*

This comment echoes the advice given to potential users of the activity based costing concept by the company's consultants - that it is important to place significant emphasis on the development of a true and accurate schematic model of the operation prior to implementing the software. Activity based costing requires such a large investment in time and resources to prepare a schematic model that the process is used as much as a planning tool as it is a method of product costing.

On the control side, one of the structural changes to the model that Park-Med hopes to implement is to collect costs on a per department basis. The existing model had been designed to focus specifically on a "per test cost." With some tests requiring involvement from more than one department, it is difficult to extract departmental information from the software's output.

Park-Med was able to make a number of strategic planning decisions based on information generated by the computerized model. Capital budgeting decisions involving expensive analyser purchases and negotiating trading opportunities were two such strategic decisions that were often mentioned by the staff. Implementing ABC software is not necessarily motivated by the finance/accounting department. Engineering, manufacturing and others may be the functional areas interested in generating a more reliable indicator of product or service costs. This was true at Park-Med, where the team charged with developing the model came from the operations side of the firm and not from the accounting department, although the latter's input was sought for historical information to use in the model.

The computerized model that was prepared functioned independently of the financial reporting system, and other than during the validation stages, no effort was made to reconcile the output of the two systems. Park-Med's financial reporting structure has remained unchanged by the adoption of activity based costing. This does not mean, however, that the laboratory's accounting department was unaware of the efforts being made to generate costs on a per test basis using activity based costing. Naseem Somani, the firm's comptroller saw a future for the model in the accounting department to run scenarios to reflect recent changes in the laboratory and to allow the accounting staff to ensure the system's integrity. She felt that the accounting department would also provide the historical information that was required to develop new model components.

Overall, Park-Med's experience with activity based costing seems consistent with other firms that have explored this new cost accounting method. What makes its experience somewhat unique is the dedicated software package that was able not only to model cost data but also to determine the demands that would be placed on the firm's resources at various levels of activity.   Using this innovative approach to product costing, the laboratory has made a number of strategic decisions that will position the firm for growth in the upcoming years.

# Chapter Fourteen

# ABC COST ANALYSIS AT AUTOMOTIVE COMPONENTS CORPORATION

**Frank Gonsalves, Senior Manager**
**Ashish Pradhan, Manager**

**Price Waterhouse, Cleveland**

This case study portrays a company for whom an activity cost analysis engagement was conducted using an activity based-product methodology employing Price Waterhouse's proprietary ACTIVA software. The software played a vital role by assisting in the identification, documentation, and analysis of activity generated costs. The name of the client, products, product structures, operations, and plant locations have been modified to protect the privacy of the client. The operations have also been consolidated in order to facilitate exposition.

## COMPETITIVE ENVIRONMENT

Automotive Components Corporation (ACC), headquartered in the Michigan area, is a manufacturer of instrumentation panel and car radio electrical wiring harnesses for cars, trucks, and other light duty vehicles. The wiring harness is the major product line and is assembled from several components that include the wiring rubber sheath, connectors and the wires itself. The dimensions and characteristics of the wiring harness are custom designed to meet the engineering and quality specifications of the original equipment manufacturers (OEMs).

The first step in the introduction of a new wiring harness model requires the development of a prototype. After appropriate engineering testing and design and draft revisions are completed, a final version of the product is released for production. The production process includes a number of diverse operations including: rubber extrusions for wiring sheaths; wire cutting to precision measurements, plugging the connectors; and small parts assembly. The rubber extruder and wire cutting equipment are automated, and the plant machining and assembly equipment are configured for long production runs.

In 1990 ACC's revenues were approximately $200 million of which 75% came from supply contracts that were negotiated with automobile and heavy equipment manufacturers. Big original equipment manufacturers (OEMs) constitute the company's major product market segment. The remaining 25% of revenues are derived from the replacement parts after-market for car radio connections, speedometer and fuel gauge connections, and radio housings, which are supplied to large discount automobile service chains. ACC faces intense price competition in both market segments.

**OEM Market Developments:** In the 1970s ACC had experienced substantial and uninterrupted growth. The business relationship with the big OEMs began to erode in the early 1980s primarily due to two reasons: a) the inflationary period in the latter half of the decade, which resulted in severe cost increases in energy and raw materials, including rubber; and b) the influx of high quality and low cost automobiles from Japan, and, later Korea. This forced the OEMs to improve quality while simultaneously reducing cost, resulting in severe price pressure on OEM suppliers. The transplant automobile manufacturers would typically out-source their parts to two suppliers and reserve the flexibility of controlling their relative production volumes as a means of enforcing quality and delivery schedules.

The initial success of the Japanese automobile led to a slight decline in the volume of business being conducted with the OEMs, and sales to the automotive after-market actually increased. The profit margins of the suppliers were still perceived to be comfortable and the market position of their industry secure. This situation continued in the early eighties. In the mid-eighties, everything changed with the introduction of transplanted automobile assembly factories for foreign car makers.

The indigenous manufacturing of foreign automobiles was initially restricted to assembly and minor fabrication operations with the bulk of the value added manufacturing of components remaining within the jurisdiction of the foreign automobile suppliers. Over time, the foreign automobile companies induced their first and second tier suppliers to set up operations in the United States, elevating the overall level of direct competition for OEM business within the supplier industry. The perception that foreign automobiles were of higher quality translated to an improved image for their suppliers. At the same time OEMs were emphasizing quality, thus giving the transplant suppliers additional leverage in the OEM market.

**After-Market Developments:** The after market for replacement parts was less influenced by the arrival of the transplant automobile suppliers since they were not configured to mass produce low cost generic replacement parts for the vast American automobile market. The after-market customers did not impose stringent quality control requirements. The added burden from high engineering, prototyping, and testing costs required by the OEMs was largely alleviated.

The ability of American automobile suppliers to mass produce low cost replacement parts of reasonable quality seemed to be the primary basis for success. The supply contracts with the discount automobile service chains were typically negotiated for large volumes with slim unit profit margins. The overall profitability of such contracts in the past was lucrative. However, newly imposed quality requirements resulted in higher costs and lower sales volumes, since the replacement parts lasted longer.

The move to Just-in-Time (JIT) techniques in the 1970s and 1980s caused several automotive component manufacturers to locate plants close to JIT assembly and sub-assembly OEM plants. In 1981, ACC decided to locate a new JIT manufacturing plant in Juarez, Mexico, under the auspices of the Mexican government's Maquiladora program. Establishing this plant would permit ACC to attain full time JIT supplier relationship to the major OEM customer and other automobile manufacturers. The products would be supplied to a nearby OEM automobile plant.

With the building of this new plant, ACC had the opportunity to rectify a number of existing problems:

* ensure a continuation of the strong relationship with the OEM by becoming a preferred JIT supplier
* automate the manufacturing and assembly process
* take advantage of lower cost labor in Mexico
* utilize the customs duty retraction granted to manufacturers in the Maquiladora zone that would be normally imposed on the additional value added manufacturing

Maintaining the plant in Juarez, Mexico involved participating in additional operations and procedures in contrast to ACC's plant in Michigan. Maintenance problems, lack of training, and inadequate transportation infrastructure, together prevented the manufacturing process from attaining a state of synchronized work flow. Meeting a tight delivery schedule was of utmost importance in order to remain a JIT supplier for the major OEM. Most production was scheduled as small work orders to meet the frequent shipment consignments. Routine expediting of orders caused confusion with the daily dispatch schedules and the material and resource requirement plans. Air freighting raw materials and parts from the US resulted in exorbitant premium freight.

As costs increased, ACC was forced to consider raising prices in order to remain profitable. Over time, the price markups became unacceptable to both OEMs and discount chain auto maintenance stores. In fact, for a two year period in the late eighties, ACC was not granted any price increase by its major

OEM customer, who accounted for some 40% of sales revenues in 1990.

Faced with potentially high losses and declining market share, in early 1990, ACC decided to negotiate price increases with its major OEM customer. It was reasoned that successfully targeting this particular OEM could relieve substantial pressure on profit margins since the OEM was one of its larger customers and had historically provided 45% of pre-tax profits.

ACC attempted, without success, to make the case that frequent engineering design changes, re-engineering, and extensive prototype testing, (initiated by the stringent quality control requirements of this OEM) added significantly to overhead costs. ACC also made the case that the OEM required many short production runs, resulting in higher costs through disruptions in its scheduling, inventory and labor crewing processes. Once again the overhead cost detail could not support ACC's position and was rejected by the OEM.

Since most of ACC's wiring harness sales to the OEMs and replacement parts to the automobile service discount chains were priced with negotiated agreements, it was imperative that the cost system serve as a support tool for achieving fair pricing. This was not the first time that their sales personnel were unable to pass on ACC's cost increases to their customers.

## ACC'S BUSINESS ACTIVITY REVIEW

The customer negotiation process caused ACC to focus on developing more meaningful cost information. This led to an activity-based costing pilot focusing on one product -- WH-57, accounting for $17,332,100 in revenue, and contributing roughly $1,953,000 to the bottom line. WH-57 was part of the instrumentation panel harness product line, and was chosen for its significant sales volume, medium complexity and dual manufacturing locations (in the U.S. and Mexico). An ABC team, comprising an ACC industrial engineer, an ACC cost accountant, and two Price Waterhouse consultants began by profiling all business processes associated with WH-57. These processes were decomposed into specific activities needed to design, produce, and distribute the product.

To ensure widespread understanding and a basis for comparison, prior year costs were used to develop activity cost pools. The process of developing activity cost pools covered six weeks. Each General Ledger department, comprising between fourteen and forty four line items, was mapped to activity pools, by conducting interviews, observing business and manufacturing processes and through team experience. The activity pool mapping process was facilitated through the use of product costing software which mapped general ledger departmental information into specific activities. In all, fifty-three cost pools were analyzed and constructed. In this case study, to facilitate easy comprehension we provide explanations of consolidated activities.

## PURCHASED MATERIAL

Requisitions for production raw materials and miscellaneous supplies were individually authorized by plant managers and transmitted by modem to corporate offices in Michigan. Centralized purchasing consolidated all of ACC's plant and corporate requisitions and prepared procurement orders for purchased supplies used in production. Material was received directly at the plant loading docks where it was inspected and stacked in a central staging area.

ACC maintained its purchased material costs and wiring harness bills of material on a PC based spreadsheet system. The WH-57 harness required twelve connectors, costing 50 cents each, to connect wires to the instrumentation panel. Standard-sized roll wire was purchased in bulk at an average price of $0.05 per foot. Fourteen two foot leads were required for fabricating a single intermediate wiring stem assembly for the WH-57 Wiring Harness. Rubber for the wiring sheath was purchased in 400 feet long coils wrapped around drums. The purchased cost of each drum was

$200. Approximately five feet of rubber coil had to be extruded to make a single wiring sheath.

Connecting parts for the wiring harness assembly such as screws, plastic links, and binding tape were purchased from a number of small suppliers through a centralized purchasing department. The parts were organized into packets enabling easy access during assembly. The average aggregate parts cost $0.75 per assembly packet. Three such packets were required for the final assembly of the wiring rubber sheath with the intermediate wiring harness bundle assembly.

A summary of the material costs for the WH-47 Wiring Harness is presented in Exhibit 14-1 below:

**Exhibit 14-1**

MATERIAL COSTS

| | | |
|---|---|---|
| Connectors | = 12 x $0.55 | = $6.60 |
| Purchased Aggregate Parts | = 3 x $0.75 | = $2.25 |
| Insulated Leads | = 14 x 2 x $0.05 | = $1.40 |
| Rubber Coils | = 5ft x $200/400 ft | = $2.50 |
| Total Material Cost | | = $12.75 |

## PRODUCT ACTIVITY FLOWS

The activity analysis was conducted based on annual production of 1,000,000 WH-57 harnesses. The activities span product reconfiguration through distribution. Corporate support departments and field support for all plant operations were also included in the analysis. Once activity pools were identified and constructed, the corollary process of determining cost drivers and output measures was undertaken.

For example, the major driver identified for material handling was plant layout. This was not easily translated into an output measure that could be used to assign cost. A process improvement initiative was identified for the long term by earmarking a work in

process staging area (covering 30% of Michigan plant space) for re-configuring the wire cutting, and plugging connector and harness assembly lines. The surrogate output measure for product cost development purposes, pounds of finished products shipped, was chosen due to ease of access and widespread acceptance.

Hereafter the case study will examine that part of an ABC analysis that deals with cost assignment for product costing and pricing purposes. Therefore cost reduction and process improvement opportunities have not been discussed.

**Product Reconfiguration and Tool Design:** Engineering studies for product reconfiguration on the shop floor was performed by the industrial engineering group and was required for validation of the engineering modifications incorporated by design engineers. This activity pool included process changes precipitated by internally-generated engineering change notices (ECNs). Customer generated ECNs are discussed in the section "Customer Level Costs."

Each manufactured component in the WH-57 Wiring Harness Model must be tested for manufacturing process validity. Therefore the output measure selected to assign Product Reconfiguration and Tool Design cost was "Number of Part Nos in the BOM." The WH-57 BOM contained 3 such final and intermediate assembly part numbers. WH-57 was assigned 3/78 of activity pool dollars of $677,520. Specifically, WH-57 accounted for 3 BOM part numbers, and other reconfigured ACC products, instrument as well as other wiring harnesses, accounted for the other 75 BOM reconfigured part numbers.

**Reconfigured Product Field Support:** All new or reconfigured products required initial engineering field support at the customer's site. At ACC, this process required similar efforts for most product offerings, except for specialty engine harnesses, which were direct charged. Activity pool costs were equally assigned to all new and reconfigured instrument panel harnesses. In this case, $234,400 (including free samples) was equally distributed to 21 reconfigured products.

**Purchasing and Receiving:** The purchasing department conducted the selection, buying, and receiving of several million dollars of material supplies annually, with an administrative budget of $1,468,500. Raw material components such as connectors, binding tape, and other fasteners were purchased with blanket purchase orders.

The analysis revealed that non-value adding (NVA) activity in purchasing and receiving was caused by the following drivers:

* antiquated systems
* inexperienced buyers
* excessive paperwork

The systems department was in the process of reviewing packaged software options for an integrated manufacturing MRP II system, including purchasing and receiving dock modules. The purchasing department was also in the process of writing a document covering required policies, practices and procedures, with a view to training new staff. Internal audit agreed to review control procedures to eliminate some of the matching and audit trail requirements in receiving.

Theoretically, the preferred output measure to assign Purchasing and Receiving cost was number of purchase order line items by ordered part. The team concluded, properly, that this measure needed a practical surrogate since existing systems could not easily access data to support the theoretical best driver. A compromise measure was selected-number of active purchased items within the BOM. Therefore, WH-57 was assigned 2/157 of Purchasing and Receiving cost.

**Plant Scheduling:** Weekly production planning sessions were conducted in the Juarez plant for the final assembly of the WH-57 wiring harness, the measurement and cutting of the wiring stem, and the extrusion of the wiring rubber sheath. The production planning meetings at the Juarez plant were particularly difficult, due to the shortage of skilled labor and the required detailed contingency planning of alternate routings.

Alternate operations were specified in the dispatch lists, since the shop floor supervisors had not mastered the ability to mix and match the various assembly fixtures into a streamlined process flow. Consequently, the planning effort escalated with an increase in the type of manufactured assemblies. The Michigan plant scheduling pool dollars of $76,800 were uniformly assigned to 61 manufactured parts, and Juarez plant scheduling dollars of $763,400 were assigned to 46 manufactured parts.

**Set up:** The set up process for wire cutting machines required the adjustment of the machine for eleven different lengths of leads that were required for bundling the fourteen leads in the WH-57 stem. Each lead adjustment required careful manipulation of the different tension adjustment dials, and the calibration of the cutting blade sliding lever.

The rubber extrusion machine also required significant set up. The set up process is initiated with a journeyman helper selecting an extrusion die from the tool room. After installing the die in the rubber extrusion machine, and making the necessary calibration adjustments, a trial production run was started. A number of sheaths had to be extruded and measured for accuracy and tensile strength before normal production could commence for the day.

The team calculated set up pool dollars for WH-57 based on wire-cutting set ups and rubber extrusion set ups respectively. Based on the analysis conducted by the project team, wire-cutting set up pool dollars for WH-57 totaled $323,000 at the Juarez plant and $115,000 at the Michigan plant. Set up pool dollars for rubber extrusion were $458,000 (Juarez) and $293,000 (Michigan).

Set ups affected production cycle time considerably. Juarez set up costs were high due to inexperienced workers, and maintenance problems. Set up and production scheduling were identified as primary areas to analyze and implement process improvements. A detailed implementation plan was separately developed to address these issues.

**Production Operations:** (Consolidated for Exposition) Final assembly and testing of the harness was performed at the Mexico plant. The three operations and engineered standards for each of the major components are listed in Exhibit 14-2. There was no differentiation between crew grade levels. Support pit clean-out and local material handling staff costs were included in the labor rate. The direct labor rates for these operations represented the estimated labor cost rates to ACC for current year operations.

## Exhibit 14-2

### OPERATION STANDARDS

Plant Operations Labor and Machine Costs

| Juarez Operations (based on 400,000 harnesses) | Hours | Rate |
|---|---|---|
| Wire Stem Bundling and Assembly | 12,000 | $5/hr |
| Measurement and Wire Cutting | 45,000 | $5/hr |
| Wire Sheath Rubber Extrusion | 6,800 | $7/hr |

| Michigan Operations (based on 600,000 harnesses) | Hours | Rate |
|---|---|---|
| Wire Stem Bundling and Assembly | 8,000 | $17/hr |
| Measurement and Wire Cutting | 40,000 | $18/hr |
| Wire Sheath Rubber Extrusion | 4,200 | $22/hr |

Operation costs were computed after noting that a machine operator was assigned full time to tend to each machine. The machine operators were instructed to report their hours on the time tickets against a direct labor charge code.

**Other Indirect Product Costs:** As part of the study, several other costs, both direct and indirect were evaluated and assigned at Michigan and Juarez. Exhibit 14-3 provides a list of these costs, output measures selected to assign cost to products, and the cost for each line item at Juarez and Michigan.

**Exhibit 14-3**

### PRODUCT LEVEL WH-57 WIRING HARNESS COSTS

| WH-57 Activities | Output Measure | Michigan Cost | Juarez Cost |
|---|---|---|---|
| Material Handling | Qty Finished Goods Shipped | $320,000 | $223,000 |
| Inventory Control and Stocking | Number of Part Numbers | 12,000 | 18,000 |
| Packaging and Quality Assuarance | Qty Parts Produced | 75,000 | 164,000 |
| Accounts Payable | $ Purchased Parts and Raw Material | 41,000 | 27,000 |
| Shipping, Handling, Data Entry | Qty Finished Goods Shipped | 35,000 | 28,000 |
| Tooling, Testing, Process Engineering | No. New/Reconfigured Products | 18,000 | 115,000 |
| Industrial/Process Engineering | Qty Parts Produced | 60,000 | 230,000 |
| Utilities | Qty Parts Produced | 530,000 | 375,000 |

# HIGHER LEVEL ACTIVITIES

An underlying assumption in activity-based-costing is that factors causing cost (cost drivers) if managed properly will affect cost-behavior patterns, leading to increases or decreases in cost. For example, in ACC, the product redesign process was found to be an area of high cost. The ABC study focused on eliminating these non-value added costs from the process. For example, the major cost drivers identified for product redesign were:

* multiple change requests from customers
* lack of coordination between design engineering and manufacturing operations in the plants
* inaccessibility of engineering drawings for similar products produced in the part

The first, i.e. multiple change requests from customers, were affected by customer related characteristics, and needed to be assigned to those customers who initiated specific change requests. The second and third drivers relates to plant specific problems, and as such should be managed at the plant level where they are caused. If specific plant costs are traceable to a product produced in that plant, they will be assigned to specific products -- as is the case for different labor and machine rates in the Production Operation sections.

To ensure proper visibility for reporting and management control, ACC decided against arbitrary allocation of cost to products, using the logic that "the chairman's corporate jet should be managed at the business level rather than at the product level." Specifically, the four cost assignment levels were:

* product
* plant
* business
* customer

Product costs which have been described in previous sections include the "buildup" of cost from parts to sub-assemblies and to

276

the final product.

**Plant Costs:** Several costs at the plant level, if attached to the product, would have been arbitrary allocations at best. For example, the decision to locate a new plant in Mexico was motivated by the savings gained from lower labor rates, and the customs duty retraction granted to manufacturers in the Maquiladora zone.

To document the effect of producing WH-57 in Mexico, the project team calculated costs for running each of the plants. These costs were traced from general ledger details. All plant level costs were assigned to products on the basis of direct and indirect conversion costs at the plant. That is, the costs to transform raw materials and purchased parts to finished harnesses were used as the ratio to assign plant level costs to products. On this basis, Exhibit 14-4 indicates WH-57 costs at each plant.

**Business Costs:** Business level costs represent a major portion of the total cost profile. Any assignment of these costs to product would be arbitrary at best. The team concluded that the best method to assign business costs to product lines would be to

**Exhibit 14-4**

PLANT COSTS FOR WH-57

| Plant Activities | Michigan | Juarez |
|---|---|---|
| Personnel | $4,500 | $8,100 |
| Maintenance and Repair Orders | 2,200 | 4,000 |
| Administration | 9,000 | 16,300 |
| Plant Support and Facility Maintenance | 7,500 | 13,600 |
| Environmental Control | 1,800 | 3,200 |
| Labor Management | 2,100 | 3,800 |
| Trouble Shooting / Expenditures | 6,000 | 11,000 |
| Import Duties and Import / Export Doc | 0 | 8,200 |
| Corporate Allocation | 600 | 1,000 |
| TOTAL | $33,700 | $69,200 |

## Exhibit 14-5

### BUSINESS COSTS

| Corporate Activities | Costs |
| --- | --- |
| Corporate Administration | $34,600 |
| Manufacturing Administration | 10,200 |
| Engineering Corporate Administration | 1,900 |
| Accounting and Payroll | 7,600 |
| Systems Development and Computer Operations | 13,400 |
| Human Resources | 1,100 |
| Marketing Sales and Customer Service | 21,000 |
| No Plant Depreciation | 3,800 |
| TOTAL | $93,700 |

estimate the approximate time spent by various functions either on specific customers, plants, or products. Based on these estimates WH-57 was assigned costs outlined in Exhibit 14-5.

**Customer Level Costs:** ACC's major OEM customer imposed several requirements on the company ranging from special testing requirements to participation in its own Design for Manufacturability teams.

A list of these costs was prepared and presented to ACC management (Exhibit 14-6). Highlighting these costs indicated the expense of dealing with individual customers. After constructing its revised cost report using ABC analysis, ACC management felt that it had sufficient evidence to approach its customer and attempt to negotiate a price increase. This customer had always indicated that it had wanted its suppliers to make a "decent return" on products sold to that customer.

In the case of ACC, several factors will affect future operations. Its ability to negotiate price increases with its major clients may be possible in the long run, after current contracts expire. In the shorter run, it will need to concentrate on cost reductions and process improvements in those non-value adding activities identified by the ABC analysis as causing waste and delay.

# Exhibit 14-6

## CUSTOMER LEVEL COSTS

| Customer Driven Activities | Activity Costs |
|---|---|
| Product Reconfiguration (customer driven) | $15,200 |
| Tool Design | 10,800 |
| Prototype Approval Process | 7,500 |
| Special Requests of Sample Orders | 4,600 |
| External and Internal Testing of Products and Parts | 15,800 |
| OEM Customer Relations | 5,200 |
| OEM Customer Service | 20,000 |
| Premium Freight | 30,400 |
| Corporate Allocation | 21,000 |
| TOTAL | $130,500 |

# INDEX

282